AN INTRODUCTION
TO THE STUDY OF
COMPARATIVE EDUCATION

Teaching a Modern Language
None can be called Deformed :
Problems of the Crippled Adolescent
Power and Politics in Belgian Education
Modern Belgian Literature (1830–1960)
Belgium

An Introduction to the Study of
Comparative Education

BY

VERNON MALLINSON

PROFESSOR OF COMPARATIVE EDUCATION
UNIVERSITY OF READING

FOURTH EDITION

HEINEMANN

LONDON

Heinemann Educational Books Ltd

LONDON EDINBURGH MELBOURNE AUCKLAND
SINGAPORE HONG KONG KUALA LUMPUR
IBADAN NAIROBI JOHANNESBURG
NEW DELHI LUSAKA

ISBN 0 435 80573 8

FIRST PUBLISHED 1957
SECOND EDITION 1960
REPRINTED 1961, 1964
THIRD EDITION 1966
FOURTH EDITION 1975

PUBLISHED BY
HEINEMANN EDUCATIONAL BOOKS LTD
48 CHARLES STREET, LONDON W1X 8AH
PRINTED IN GREAT BRITAIN BY
WILLIAM CLOWES & SONS, LIMITED
LONDON, BECCLES AND COLCHESTER

For
Emeritus Professor
H. C. BARNARD
in gratitude and
affection

Contents

Preface to Fourth Edition

THE need for a new edition of this work has fortunately coincided with the implementation of plans for the reform of education (often debated over many years) in most of the countries with which we deal. In earlier editions we could speak only of possibilities for the future. Now we can discuss the reforms in some detail and see the way ahead for at least a decade. In consequence of this we have been able to extend the number of diagrams (Appendix II) depicting educational structures, elaborate them, in some measure standardize them, and so provide for the first time adequate material for seminar discussions on chosen topics—e.g. different interpretations of the meaning of the word " comprehensive ", education for ability groups, mobility within the given framework, the relative importance given to technical and vocational studies. From various scraps of paper resulting from such discussions with my own students my colleague, Mr. S. J. D. Charters, has (with much ingenuity and painstaking effort) produced the final versions and I am much indebted to him.

It has, of course, been necessary to re-write and expand much of the text from the third edition. This has afforded the opportunity to add two further chapters. The one on *Pre-School Education* became necessary because of increasing importance attached everywhere to such provision. The one entitled *In Search of an Identity* was urged on me by seminar students who eagerly debated it (and supplied the diagram). It proved more convenient to print it as Appendix I rather than upset the structure of earlier chapters on national character. A proposed additional chapter on university education was finally abandoned because (a) matters at the tertiary level of education are still too much in a state of flux and, more importantly, (b) A. R. Hearnden has just published *Paths to University*. I strongly recommend this text as a sound interim assessment of present difficulties and perplexities.

University of Reading,   VERNON MALLINSON
June, 1974.

Preface

MY purpose in writing this book has been to provide a conspectus of the contemporary scene in matters of educational policy and practice in Western Europe and to try to trace, on a comparative basis, how and why problems common to all Western European countries are being tackled in different ways and with what results. Inevitably, of course, America and Russia had also to be considered for they have made their own peculiar impact which cannot be ignored. With the exception of Russia all the information offered is based on immediate observation of current practice. In the case of Russia I have had to rely on reports furnished by friends who have had the good fortune to spend some considerable time there, and who have been most meticulous in answering as fully and as carefully as possible the many questions I put to them. The responsibility for the correct interpretation of the data received is, however, entirely mine.

It is hoped that the book will appeal not only to students in training to become teachers but also to practising teachers and to the general public. The study of comparative education is still in its infancy, and though we are in the midst of a critical phase of one of the most momentous expansions of educational effort in the world's history, too few people recognize the relevance and importance—I might almost add the vital necessity —of such a study. In order therefore to introduce the subject I have attempted to be as simple and as direct as possible, and I have not hesitated to sacrifice elaboration which would be tedious without being rewarding in favour of a simplification which I hope might prove illuminating, if nothing else. Ideally, the reader should feel compelled to push his studies much further in one particular direction that interests him. The success or failure of this approach will ultimately be determined by such interests as it is capable of rousing.

CHAPTER ONE

The Purpose of Education

THE various attempts that have been made to define the purpose and scope of a study of comparative education since the pioneering days of Matthew Arnold and Sir Michael Sadler have made it increasingly clear that no satisfactory definition can be obtained until the whole purpose of education as a social force has been closely examined. Thus, Sir Michael Sadler himself reminds us that " in studying foreign systems of education we should not forget that the things outside the schools matter even more than the things inside the schools, and govern and interpret the things inside "; that " a national system of education is a living thing, the outcome of forgotten struggles and difficulties and ' of battles long ago.' It has in it some of the secret workings of national life. It reflects, whilst seeking to remedy, the failings of national character." [1] Dr. Hans, in an illuminating account of the work of "English Pioneers of Comparative Education," and in his own book on the subject, has claimed that the purpose of Comparative Education " is not only to compare existing systems but to envisage reform best suited to new social and economic conditions. . . . Comparative Education quite resolutely looks into the future with a firm intent of reform. . . . Thus, our subject has a dynamic character with a utilitarian purpose." [2] He then goes on to argue that " as their national past was formed by factors often common to many nations and as their ideals of the future are the outcome of universal movements, the problems of education in different countries are similar and the principles which guide their solution may be compared and even identified. The analytical study of these factors from a historical perspective and the comparison of

[1] *How Far Can We Learn Anything of Practical Value from the Study of Foreign Systems of Education ?* Guildford, 1900.
[2] *Brit. J. Ed. Stud.*, Vol. I, No. 1, pp. 56-9.

attempted solutions of resultant problems are the main purpose of Comparative Education." [1] For Professor Kandel, the study of Comparative Education becomes " a comparison of variant philosophies of education based not on theories but on the actual practices which prevail. . . . The study of foreign systems of education means a critical approach and a challenge to one's own philosophy and, therefore, a clearer analysis of the background and basis underlying the educational system of one's own nation." [2] Harold Nicolson in his book on *Good Behaviour* reminds us pertinently that " every society invents for itself a type, a model . . . of what the perfect member of that society ought to be. These heroes are myths which repeat the legend of the past and enhance the dreams of the future.   They are much more than the product of existing social and economic conditions." [3]

Education, then, is a social force in the sense that any educational system must reflect closely the ethos of the people it is called upon to serve. To know what we want from education we must know what we want in general, and in this sense our theories of education must derive from our philosophy of life. Thus, the first task of the student of Comparative Education must be that of getting quite clear in his own mind what exactly are the purposes of education, using the expression in the broadest possible sense to cover the way of life of any social group from the most primitive to the most complex.

Dr. Joad—who had a flair amounting almost to genius for clarifying the most complicated philosophical argument to make it both intelligible and attractive to the layman—was himself in no doubt on this score and has listed three such purposes :

    (*a*) to enable a boy or girl to make his or her living;

    (*b*) to equip him to play his part as a citizen of democracy;

    (*c*) to enable him to develop all the latent powers and faculties of his nature and so enjoy a good life. [4]

More profoundly, Professor Jeffreys implicitly admits all this, stresses as a prime function of education " the nurture of personal growth," [5] and insists (with Harold Nicolson) on the social function of education which makes of it " an instrument for conserving,

1 *Comparative Education*, N. Hans. Kegan Paul, 1949, p. 10.
2 *Studies in Comparative Education*, I. L. Kandel. Harrap, 1939, p. xx.
3 *Good Behaviour*, Harold Nicolson. Constable, 1955, p. 1.
4 *About Education*, C. E. M. Joad. Faber and Faber, 1945, p. 23.
5 *Glaucon*, M. V. C. Jeffreys. Pitman, 1950.

transmitting and renewing culture." [1] In this latter sense he may be said to distinguish between what can be called the conservative function of education—that of handing on tradition—and the creative function, which can be simply defined as that of producing critical and creative individuals capable and willing to initiate social change. Thus, for both Joad and Jeffreys, education's concern is with the double role of the individual, firstly as a person and secondly as an active member of a duly constituted society. They both envisage the educative process as being one partly of adaptation to society as it is, partly of preparation for the society we want it to become. And at a severely practical level they both mean, as we all mean, some specific training of both mind and body.

But what kind of training? No one would quibble with the first strictly utilitarian aim of Joad—that of enabling the boy or girl to make his or her own living. But what about the second? What exactly does he mean by the phrase " a citizen of democracy "? Presumably, since he is writing in England in our time he means the kind of democracy we both enjoy and encourage in England in our time. Ask, however, any American, any Frenchman, any German, any Russian, if he believes that a prime function of education is to prepare a boy or girl to play his or her part as " a citizen of democracy " and each of them will return a most emphatic " yes " in answer to the question. Ask them now in turn to define exactly what they mean by democracy! *Quot homines tot sententiae* . . . Similarly with " the nurture of personal growth." The nurture of personal growth towards exactly what end?

We are in still deeper waters when we try to define " the good life." All religious implications apart, if by this phrase we mean (as we must mean) the kind of life society considers good, then once again we must ask ourselves the question : " Which society? The Frenchman's, the American's, the German's, or the Russian's? " And if we insist—as we must insist—that it must be the good life as defined by the kind of society which gave us our infant birth and nurture, then we are irrevocably committed to a programme of educational adaptation to environment, that is to say to the particular routine kind of democracy to which, by the accident of birth, we " belong."

Thus, we must conclude that every definition of the purpose of education has implicit or concealed in it some philosophy that

[1] *Ibid.*

aims at producing, not the " natural man " so dear to Rousseau, but rather the kind of man that a particular society at a given period in its history wishes him to be. Every effort will be made through education to secure a community of purpose and experience, to foster a common identity of interests through the development of a common identity of ideas, desires and ambitions so that all are united, consciously or unconsciously, in one common aim : the preservation of the existing culture pattern, which implies the gradual discarding of outmoded ideas and their replacement, cautiously but surely, by newer ones in strict accord with the inevitability of human change and progress. For all of this a disciplined approach is necessary. It is the function of education to foster in the minds of men that necessary discipline. In one of his addresses on *Education and the Moral Basis of Citizenship*, Lord James has repeatedly stressed this very point. " The first duty of moral education," he writes, " is to implant in the child a code of behaviour which is recognized by the community as good. . . . The aim of the highest social education is thus to encourage the individual to exercise his own moral judgment in a rational and disciplined way." [1]

This common identity of ideas, desires and ambitions is achieved through the development of what we can best describe as " a national character "—through the building up over the centuries of a kind of fixed mental constitution that guarantees a common purpose and a common effort from the whole group. It is a kind of large-scale sentiment and is the result of the qualities needed by the whole group, as a group, for the attainment of the group ideal. Obviously, the development of a set of relatively permanent attitudes that build themselves up into a sentiment spreads very slowly from the home to the village to the province to the whole geographical unit,[2] repeatedly calling for review as a given civilization moves gradually from primitive beginnings to a more complex and involved system. When that civilization reaches its peak of attainment, then the " national character " becomes the essential stabilizing force, allowing for further development and maturation only along fixed and clearly defined paths. Thus, it is the character of a people and not its intelligence that determines

---

[1] *Op. cit.*, Heinemann, 1955, pp. 4 and 20.
[2] This can go well beyond the geographical unit and also ignore racial, linguistic and religious barriers.

its future. And it is from a people's character, and not from its intelligence, that stem its political constitution, its ideals and aspirations, its social and cultural outlook. The growth and development of the U.S.A. as a nation is a striking example of how this comes about, as we shall later see.

We shall also have more to say about national character in later chapters. Here, we are primarily concerned with national character as a disciplinary force; with showing that any apparently revolutionary change that takes place in a people's outlook and way of life is really the outcome of slow cumulative effort in strict keeping, in reality, with national characteristics; and with proving that if men of ideas ahead of their times try to force and accelerate the pattern of change then there will be, sooner or later, a reversion to type.

There are two obvious examples to make this last point clear : France at the time of the French Revolution, and Russia from 1918 onwards. Because the rulers of these two countries had allowed the culture pattern to remain too static and were in consequence educating for a type of social existence that no longer bore any resemblance to other patterns elsewhere in Europe, the thinkers —the men who should have been usefully employed within the existing culture pattern to effect *slowly* the desired changes— broke loose, preached a new era that should rapidly dawn and plunged their fellow-countrymen into a hysteria from which only slowly they were to emerge to return in all fundamental respects to something in the nature of a *status quo ante*.

In France, the revolutionaries attempted a complete break with the past, set up in Paris excellent *Ecoles Centrales* in a serious and enlightened attempt to bring a new kind of education to the people —and yet fifteen years later most of the traditional institutions had been restored, there was a highly centralized system of control and direction, and the Napoleonic *lycée* was an established fact and destined to become a living memorial to the efficacy of the former Jesuit *collège*. Those in power in Russia in the post-1918 period undertook to sweep away all superstitious beliefs and deplored the veneration of ikons and the awe in which the Holy Father was held; entirely recast the educational system of the huge continent in an attempt to eradicate all this; set themselves the gigantic task of educating hundreds of thousands of people to the Marxist way of life. Yet to-day impartial observers speak of the *superstitious* veneration of the memory of Lenin (and until recently of Stalin); note that the earlier widespread educational reformers are returning to a more traditional pattern—the secondary school system even to the point of retaining the familiar school uniform of pre-revolutionary days; conclude that fundamentally, despite the thorough and large-scale indoctrination of the people, the national *character* remains much as it was before : the old idols have gone, but new ones have taken their place; the former system of loyalties, uncritically championed with a kind of oriental fatalism and in a spirit of resignation, is replaced by a new system equally resignedly and fatalistically accepted. One form of dictatorship is replaced by another that the national character can equally well accept.

On the other hand, one revolution that was successful was the 1830 revolution which gained for the Belgian people their independence from Dutch rule and resulted in the establishment of a strongly bourgeois but highly individualistic democratic government. This revolution was successful—as the others could not be—because the tide of events was smoothly following the pattern of change. The time was more than ripe for revolution. Men's minds had been slowly prepared for it over centuries of attempted absorption of the Walloon and Flemish communities into the structural whole of some greater European power. A " fixed " mental attitude had been developed—the national character had been formed —which gave rise not so much to a positive kind of patriotism based on a national ideal as to a definite insistence on each and every Belgian's right as an individual to protect his own liberty, his property, his religious beliefs, customs, traditions, folk-lore— all, in fact, that his education as a Belgian meant and stood for.

Thus, when on the fatal night of August 25th, 1830, the solid bourgeois classes packed the Théâtre de la Monnaie to enjoy themselves and conscientiously to applaud the patriotic sentiments in the fourth act of a rather mediocre operetta, *La Muette de Portici*; when the dandies in the audience and the young bloods in particular were out for a lark; when the crowds outside the theatre were hopeful at the most of some amusing diversion, because they scented mischief; when the populace, carried along on a wave of mass hysteria, rushed to proclaim liberty at last and to burn and pillage and loot—it was the bourgeoisie who, appalled at the pillaging and looting, and sensing where all this might lead, took counsel together overnight, succeeded in restoring law and order as the Dutch stood impotently by, and found themselves (in some amazement) asserting their right to set up an independent separatist state.

So we may draw the threads of our argument closer together by concluding that the purpose of education as a social force and seen on the national scale is that of assuring cultural continuity mainly through fostering the growth and development of national characteristics that will act as a stabilizing force. " Surely the aim and consummation of all education," said Socrates, " is the love of loveliness." Plato argued that education should teach a man to fight against the ugly and the false and to strive constantly for the good and the beautiful. Idealists, they were none the less stressing the importance of permanence of aim and objective. In a more practical vein Aristotle informs us that " nobody could possibly doubt that the chief concern of the lawgiver must be the education of the young." Neither was Napoleon in any doubt about this, for, as he succinctly puts it, " there will be no fixed political state if there is no teaching body with fixed principles." Equally frank is the Hadow Report of 1926 which gives as the general aim of education in England that of offering " the fullest scope to individuality whilst keeping steadily in view the claims of society." The problems of education can never be isolated from those of society as a whole. And those problems will differ from society to society in space and in time. We shall have much more to say on this point later. In the meantime, let us remind ourselves of the greater significance of meaning that can now be attached to the dual definition of the purpose of education as enunciated by Professor Jeffreys : " the nurture of personal growth " and " the conserving, transmitting and renewal of culture." Culture we will here briefly define as those capabilities acquired by man to make of him an acceptable member of the society to which he belongs.[1] If the prime aim of education is to assure cultural continuity, it is only through individual persons that the values which cultures should perpetuate and enrich can be realized. Hence again the importance of " the nurture of personal growth."

All of which means—as the researches of the sociologists have amply proved—that there can be no society of human beings,

[1] The culture of a society is the total way of life of that society, and, as it " comprehends all that is inherited or transmitted through society, it follows that its individual elements are proportionately diverse." *Race and Culture*, Michael Leiris. Unesco, 1951, pp. 20-1.

however primitive, without some kind of educational system.[1] It is through the education of the immature that each society strives to protect and perpetuate its traditions and its aspirations. And each educational system, when closely studied and analysed, reveals quite clearly the culture concept and pattern or way of life of each and every society. To put it still another way, the national characteristics of any given nation will find their expression in the nation's schools, and those schools are being constantly used to strengthen and perpetuate the national characteristics and outlook. A child is taught to fight against the ugly and the false and to strive for the good and the beautiful as interpreted by that society into which he is born or in which he receives his infant nurture.

Conversely, of course, there can be no system of education without a clearly defined group of people living together as a society. That society needs its young and needs to assimilate them as closely as possible into the culture pattern in order to renew itself, to strengthen itself, and to progress. For if a society is not to stagnate or to perish it must be constantly invigorated by a properly disciplined succession of new members, carefully prepared to fit into the existing culture pattern and so to maintain the dominant ideals and aspirations, equally carefully prepared to be capable of initiating, at the right and opportune moments, all desirable changes. If the discipline is too strict there is lack of initiative on the part of the younger members and decay is inevitable, however slowly it may come. If discipline is not strict enough, or is seriously weakened, then licence, selfishness, egoism and *libertinage* will abound and disintegration will speedily follow.

Indeed—as the French sociologist Gustave Le Bon has repeatedly stressed—a point is eventually reached when a civilization seems to reach its peak of power and complexity, when its ideals as a result are weakened, when all its religious, political and social beliefs are challenged, and when what was once a thriving and disciplined community rapidly degenerates :

Avec la perte définitive de l'idéal ancien, la race finit par perdre aussi son âme. Elle n'est plus qu'une poussière d'individus isolés et redevient ce qu'elle était à son point de départ : une foule. Elle en représente tous les caractères transitoires sans consistance et sans lendemain. La civilisation n'a plus aucune fixité et tombe à la merci de tous les hasards. La plèbe est reine et les barbares

---

[1] Consult, for example, Margaret Mead's *Growing Up in New Guinea*.

avancent. La civilisation peut sembler brillante encore parce qu'elle conserve la façade extérieure créée par un long passé, mais c'est en réalité un édifice vermoulu que rien ne soutient plus et qui s'effondera au premier orage.

Passer de la barbarie à la civilisation en poursuivant un rêve, puis décliner et mourir dès que ce rêve a perdu sa force, tel est le cycle de la vie d'un peuple.[1]

In a word, a people can become too civilized; discipline is weakened; initiative and will-power are sapped; and what was once the co-operative person has become the competing individual. The things which make life worth living (to use here T. S. Eliot's simple definition of culture) are seriously challenged, attacked or derided. Ancient Greece and Rome are the obvious examples to which to point. Yet not a few people wonder to-day if our much-vaunted democratic Western civilization is not slowly moving in the same grim direction. Are we " the hollow men " :

> Shape without form, shade without colour,
> Paralysed force, gesture without motion; ?[2]

As Lord James has again reminded us, democracy as we know and enjoy it to-day is extremely vulnerable because of its " reverence for majorities, particularly at a time when the moral authority of religious faith is declining." [3]

Be that as it may, we cannot escape the conclusion that the real power for survival of any given social group with its attendant culture pattern is the discipline with which its individual members set about the job of corporate living and the intelligence they bring to bear on the solution of immediate problems. The impulsive, the ill-disciplined, will seek quick or apparently ready-made solutions, or fall a prey to grandiose but unpractical schemes; the balanced members of the group will see well ahead and will cautiously feel their way. It is again a main purpose of education to secure a majority of such balanced members, and this is done through the building up of a solid but slowly changing body of traditions. To quote again from Gustave Le Bon :

Aussi les deux grandes préoccupations de l'homme depuis qu'il

---

[1] *Psychologie des Foules*, Gustave Le Bon. Presses Universitaires de France, 1947 ed., p. 135.
[2] *The Hollow Men*, T. S. Eliot, 1925.
[3] *Education and the Moral Basis of Citizenship*, Lord James. Heinemann, 1955, p. 14.

existe ont-elles été de créer un réseau de traditions, puis de les détruire lorsque leurs effets bienfaisants sont usés. Sans traditions stables, pas de civilisation; sans la lente élimination de ces traditions, pas de progrès. La difficulté est de trouver un juste équilibre entre la stabilité et la variabilité. Cette difficulté est immense. Quand un peuple laisse ses coutumes se fixer trop solidement pendant de nombreuses générations, il ne peut plus évoluer et devient, comme la Chine, incapable de perfectionnements. . . . Aussi la tâche fondamentale d'un peuple doit-elle être de garder les institutions du passé, en les modifiant peu à peu.[1]

It follows most obviously from all of this that a nation possesses a sure key to its future only if it understands the purposes and the reasons for the slow evolution of its own particular culture pattern. Education, used intelligently, is a means to obtaining that key. But as the late Lord Eustace Percy pointed out:

If the common features of British education at home and overseas are to be intelligently observed, it is also necessary to study British education against the background of the educational systems of other nations. There is an educational tradition common to the whole of Western Europe and America, and the student must beware of attributing to British education qualities or defects which the British Empire shares with all countries whose cultural origins lie in the Roman Empire, in Roman Christianity and in the Renaissance.[2]

Thus, in considering in some detail the main purposes of education we are led to the real purpose behind the study of Comparative Education. By the expression " comparative study of education " we mean a systematic examination of other cultures and other systems of education deriving from those cultures in order to discover resemblances and differences, the causes behind resemblances and differences, and why variant solutions have been attempted (and with what result) to problems that are often common to all. To identify the problems of education thus becomes the most important preliminary task of the research worker in the subject. To become familiar with what is being done in some other countries than their own, and why it is done, is a necessary part of the training of all serious students of educational issues of the day. Only in that way will they be properly fitted to study and understand their own systems and to plan intelligently

[1] *Op. cit.*, p. 58.
[2] *Year Book of Education*, 1932. Evans Bros., pp. xiv-xv.

for the future which, given the basic cultural changes that have taken place with such astonishing rapidity throughout the nineteenth and twentieth centuries, is going to be one where we are thrown into ever closer contact with other peoples and other cultures.

CHAPTER TWO

Education and National Character

WE have already claimed that the main purpose of education is that of assuring cultural continuity, and that each group of people—in order to achieve this continuity—sets itself the deliberate task of fostering among its members a common identity of interests that make for a common purpose and a common effort from the whole group, geared towards the group ideal. That common identity of interests, that common purpose, leads over the centuries to the establishment of a kind of fixed mental constitution that we have so far defined as the national character of the group. The field of education, therefore, covers not only the social relations of individuals with one another, but also their concept of citizenship which has implicit in it a definite allegiance to some form of political entity. It covers the accumulated knowledge of a people about its past—the virtues which have constituted its strength throughout history, its religious beliefs and practices, its ethical and moral values, its present possibilities and the use to which they can be most effectively put. It is now time to analyse more closely the workings of this " fixed mental constitution," and to clarify the meaning of the term *national* character.

Firstly, then, what is a nation? Let us rid ourselves immediately of the idea that national consciousness springs from a common racial origin, an idea (it will be remembered) strongly fostered by the National Socialists in Germany. True, a primitive tribe's main unifying force is its sense of common ancestry, but as soon as movement takes place then there comes very quickly a mingling of the races. To-day, therefore, most nations cannot be said to be of the same racial group. The population of the British Isles, for example, includes elements of the three great races of Western Europe : namely Celtic, Nordic and Alpine. Nor can it be maintained that the possession of a common language is the criterion of a nation.

Switzerland has four official languages, Belgium has three, and great moves are being made in Eire (as in Wales) to foster the development of ONE national language. Again, one of the first moves made in the U.S.S.R. when the revolution was an established fact was to revive the languages, folklore and culture of the several provinces of the Union (strongly discouraged under the Tsarist regime) in an attempt to bring about a greater feeling of national solidarity—strictly interpreted, of course, from the Marxist point of view. Finally, it is no longer true to-day to say that nations necessarily live in clearly marked geographical regions, however true that might have been in the early days following the cessation of large racial movements throughout Europe. Geographical regions like the Danube Basin or the North European Plain are divided politically with no relation at all to physical features. The national outlook to-day is a common tradition and culture, this entailing a common history and cultural ideal, the latter often being based on a religion introduced at some period in the history of that nation—though it must again be remembered that in the Christian Church to-day there are a great number of sects and denominations and that it is now possible for many divergent religious beliefs to form part of the general ethos of a given nation. As Hartshorne succinctly puts it, a nation is " a group of people occupying a particular piece of territory who feel held together in common acceptance of particular values of prime importance to them, organized into a distinct state where these values may be preserved."

Roughly speaking, there can be said to be two types of nations : those which have developed around a region of characterization, round some focal point from which authority has spread; those where there is little or no physical unity, the nation developing through a series of historical " accidents." An example of the first type is France. This country grew up around the Paris Basin, and there seems always to have been a tendency for centralization on Paris. Belgium illustrates the second type of nation—a group without any geographical focus, yet held together in common acceptance of prime values, despite clearly marked and often antagonistic racial, linguistic and religious differences. The south of Belgium was Romanized whilst the north was overrun by Germanic peoples. Yet there is a pronounced feeling of national unity of purpose that springs from centuries of resistance to oppressive measures adopted by a series of foreign rulers. It has also been claimed with some truth that the purpose of a state is to establish itself and then develop a national consciousness, and this certainly holds for the U.S.A., as we shall later see.

Thus, it is clear that there are generally within a nation certain prime values which the majority accept. There will, however, always be some minorities. The duty of the State is to foster unity in these prime values and so develop the national consciousness, and the nation's schools are a vital and necessary aid to this. At the same time, in a true democracy the minority viewpoint will be allowed expression and will be considered an important element in the tricky business of " renewing culture." As to national *character*, it can now be attributed to the existence of a number of relatively permanent attitudes—to these prime values—common to a nation. These attitudes are what the psychologists would term " sentiments "—fixed notions grouped about an idea which are formed largely by suggestion in the growing child. And the hierarchy of values respected by any given nation both causes and is caused by the education given by the nation to its individual members. National character can finally best be described as meaning " the totality of dispositions to thought, feeling and behaviour peculiar to and widespread in a certain people, and manifested with greater or less continuity in a succession of generations." [1] We had now best leave full discussion of the forces that shape and determine national character to our next chapter and concentrate here, in very broad outline, on how the national character determines educational policy and affects the structure of the educational machine.

Belgium. The marked characteristics of the Belgian are stolidity, good humour even in the face of repeated adversities, individualism, tenacity of purpose, and a quick temper to defend his own private rights and liberties allied to a shrewd realism and an eventual readiness to compromise. There is in him, as one Belgian writer puts it, " un mélange de mysticisme et de sensualité, de catholicisme et d'un goût presque païen de la vie." Possessed of a tireless energy, he indulges himself on the one hand in the fullest use of all the material comforts and blessings civilization can bestow, and on the other cares seriously about the wide variety of cultural interests in

[1] *Sociology*, Morris Ginsberg. O.U.P., 1949 ed., p. 76.

which he excels, and also about the benefits that can accrue from a traditional type of education offered throughout the country. To "get on" in life is the great thing. And a firmly established bourgeoisie that has repeatedly carried the country safely through wars and crises is most willing to open its ranks to all who give proof of ability and zeal. With all this the Belgian is deeply conscious and proud of his Belgian nationality, and Flemings and Walloons, Catholics and Liberals, have again and again—despite marked racial and religious differences of opinion—rallied whenever a crisis on a national level threatened their joint safety.

It was because William of Holland *imposed* on the Belgian people an educational system they would not have that the revolution of 1830 came about; it was because they laid such tremendous store on individual freedom that all Belgians united to make the revolution a reality and to issue the famous declaration that education must be free and a matter for individual conscience and concern. It is because of this concept of individual freedom that education in Belgium to-day is still one of the freest and most democratic in the whole of Europe, and it is also because of it that educational issues even to-day are closely bound up with all forms of political life. The successful politician must negotiate shrewdly and in a spirit of realistic compromise, bearing in mind always the individualistic temper of the people. Thus, the structure of the whole educational machine is one of shrewd compromise. There *is* central control—but the provinces and local authorities have their own peculiar influence in determining actual policy. Further, anyone may open his own school or educate his own children as he best thinks fit, subject only to the usual safety and health precautions. Finally, in matters of educational reform the Belgian is loth to exchange substance for the shadow. As one Belgian educationalist recently put it : " In matters of reform you have to begin with the people as they are and not as you want them to be."

Holland. The love of liberty that characterizes the Belgian is no less strong in Holland, a country that with silent yet methodical stubbornness repeatedly resisted the Spanish and Austrian yoke and built up for itself a commercial prosperity of which it has every right to be proud. The result has been a constantly forward-looking enlightened policy in education with a high degree of decentralization that arises from the wish to give as much scope as possible to the energy displayed by the different sections of the community. Thus, if certain sections of the community are not satisfied with the kind of education provided in the official State schools, and wish to establish their own schools side by side with the official schools, then they are at perfect liberty to do so, and the State is bound by law to assist the development of such schools provided guarantees are given that the instruction in them is in quality equivalent to (though not necessarily identical with) that which is provided by the State. Again, historical factors having led to the settlement of a strong Catholic minority (roughly between 35 to 40 per cent.) mainly in the south of the country, careful administrative and financial arrangements have been made to give to each and every religious denomination the opportunity to provide for its children the kind of education it thinks best.

Scandinavia and Switzerland. The democratic way of life holding in these countries, so clearly and admirably reflected in their school systems, is indeed in Sir Michael Sadler's words the result of "battles long ago." The emergence of the Swiss Republic as an independent political unit was an achievement of the late Middle Ages, and its geographical configuration as well as its position led to the country becoming a *pays de passage* as well as one in which a system of decentralization on a basis of *cantonal* autonomy was imperative. Thus the democratic ideal holding in Switzerland that makes each and every citizen personally responsible for good government inevitably leads to a most diversified school system with the emphasis on real intellectual and technical ability. The final acceptance of the Lutheran reforms by all three Scandinavian countries became one of the most important factors in their national life. As early as 1620 Gustavus Adolphus was advocating compulsory universal education, and in Norway and in Denmark in particular the people's schools speedily established themselves as the expression of the aspirations of a people who were not under any feudal obligations but whose rulers had heard and heeded the message that State, Church, family and community were in the eyes of God of equal importance, being all both natural and divinely ordained forms of life.

France. The usually noted outstanding qualities of the French are clarity and intelligence. Intelligence and clear, precise and logical reasoning, based on a sound humanistic culture, have been the pride and strength of the French as a nation for centuries, and the avowed aim of the schools for centuries has been to turn out an intelligent, logical, rational and unsentimental bourgeois type. It is fashionable to attribute much of this to the prolonged influence of Jesuit teaching. It would be more accurate, in my view, to maintain that the pattern the Jesuits undoubtedly have imposed on the French educational system was seen to be the most desirable one to be used to work towards the attainment of the group ideal. That is why it perpetuated itself and flourished even when the Jesuit order was eclipsed and discredited. In other words, alter but one word in the Jesuit motto: " Ad maiorem Dei gloriam," changing it to " Ad maiorem Francorum gloriam," and you have the fullest expression of the aspirations of the French that reached a zenith of unparalleled brilliance in the reign of Louis XIV and in the years prior to the French Revolution, to be resurrected triumphantly by Napoleon—one of whose first tasks, it will be remembered, was to create the modern *lycée* and once again strongly to centralize all forms of administrative endeavour. To-day as yester day the Frenchman believes profoundly in the inestimable value of his own culture which he seeks (with some justifiable pride) to spread far afield.

Less stolid and phlegmatic than the Belgian, and much more mercurial and lively, the Frenchman is none the less equally cautious and realistic when fundamental questions of reform are in the air. Thus the ambitious projects for educational reforms— brooded over during the dark days of German occupation during the last world war and published as challenging manifestos in 1944 and 1945 by the Algiers and Langevin Commissions respectively— have been carefully pruned of what in terms of the national character can only be regarded as extravagances. There has, of course, been much sensible post-war planning, many desirable changes have been effected, many innovations imposed. Yet it all adds up to the same thing : to a reaffirmation, healthy and progressive, of the Frenchman's belief in the value of his traditional heritage and culture; to a desire, in meeting the demands of modern times and in reacting against arid traditionalism, not to rush to extremes; to a recognition of the fact that, as the organization of present-day society does not yet confer upon us the task of preparing the child for an ideal existence, we must go slowly. The well-bred man of the twentieth century ought to acquire a culture corresponding to the age in which he lives, yes, but he must at all times keep a sense of proportion. The lack of this sense of proportion was to the Greeks " barbarous." So it is to the Frenchman of to-day.

So far so good. But so far we have been considering only those countries of Europe with age-old traditions. When we turn to the U.S.A. and remember that we have already mentioned it as a country in which a deliberate and planned attempt has been made through education to develop a national consciousness, the temptation is strong to ask the question : "But cannot education itself become a major instrument in bringing about desirable cultural changes—desirable, of course, from the point of view of the self-interest of the people concerned?" With justifiable pride the American will point to the splendid uses to which education has been put to weld together into one whole and into one American nation the many peoples from various countries who, for a variety of reasons, have flocked to the shores of the New World and in the name of democracy claimed admittance. He will argue that the whole history of the American people is the fascinating story of how, through education, this welding process has been achieved. He will stress rightly that this formation of an American nation has been more rapid and more concentrated than any other example the history of civilization can afford, and it has been deliberate.

Again, opponents of totalitarianism in any form will point to Germany, or Italy, or the U.S.S.R., and produce persuasive evidence to show how the schools have been geared, deliberately, to change the whole character and outlook of the people. " Nazis, bring up tough guys!" cried Goebbels—and the school system obliged. " The whole function of all education is to create a Nazi. The State must throw the whole weight of its educational machinery, not into pumping children full of ideas, but into producing absolutely healthy bodies. The development of mental capacity is only of secondary importance. . . . It is characteristic of the German never to be satisfied with what he has achieved, and to criticize himself. We have not the Englishman's silly pride in old fussy customs, nor the American's childish boasts of records. We only want to forge ahead, and we know no rest." [1]

In a minor key, and without the German fanatical belief in their chosen leader as a divinely-appointed Saviour, the Fascists

[1] Extracts from monitored reports of Goebbels' broadcast speeches to the German people in the early days of the last war.

in Italy also trumpeted their reforms that were to instil a fresh and courageous heart into their easy-going fellow-countrymen.

Methodically and ruthlessly (by Western European standards) the Communists in Russia set about the rejection of their entire Christian cultural heritage, replacing it by enforced adherence to the utilitarian principles involved in the kind of Marxism they preached. " Russia is what it is to-day," writes Professor Northrop, " not because there was any necessity for it to be that way, but largely because . . . the leaders of the Russian revolution took the speculative philosophical theory of Marx, and by persuasive and forceful means brought others to its acceptance, and built political action and cultural institutions in terms of it." [1]

All this is undoubtedly true to a point, but—as Professor Northrop is careful to note later in his argument—it is by no means the whole story. We have already seen how—despite deliberate and calculated Marxist indoctrination in the schools, factories and workshops over the last fifty years or more—the Soviets have been powerless to eradicate the superstitious element in the people's make-up: they have merely diverted it to a veneration of the memories of chosen leaders. Similarly, rites, festivals and ceremonial occasions of all kinds are still craved after and in-dulged in. " In our Socialist society," claims the Soviet Ministry of Culture, " the fir tree has been liberated from its religious trimmings, but we keep it as part of a merry old custom which adds colour to our life."

Again, the opening of a new school year has often been made a merry occasion and the young boys and girls entering school for the first time at the age of 6 or 7 have been almost sacrificially offered up to the care of the teachers and older pupils. In the more remote rural areas, and under the old system before boarding schools became popular, the few pupils who had given promise of good intellectual ability at the completion of the then seven-year schooling had to be sent away as boarders to the nearest town in which a ten-year school existed. At first, the peasant farmers were reluctant to see themselves deprived of valuable youthful manual labour and were suspicious of this continued education scheme. They were won over by the simple

---

[1] *The Meeting of East and West,* F. S. C. Northrop. Macmillan, New York, 1946, p. 246.

expedient of making the departure of the bright children not a subject for lamentation, but rather one of jollity and ritual celebrations: the corn had ripened; the intellectual harvest was to be gathered in; and with pomp and ceremony, drinking, dancing and laughter, the youngsters departed—fêted and " prayed over " (in the Marxist sense) to acquit themselves well and to return intellectually triumphant.

> The Russians are a very old people who existed long before the advent of Marx and Lenin . . . (and are) absorbed in the intuitive and mystical religion of the Greek Orthodox Church. No amount of dictatorship by the proletariat will ever succeed in removing completely from the nature of the Russian people all these aesthetic and religious influences and sentiments.[1]

It would appear that despite the most complete Marxist indoctrination, and despite a general present-day acceptance of all that this involves, the Russian people—as a people—still retain their marked national characteristics. It is evident also that in the Russian satellite countries the kind of communism practised varies in many respects from the Russian model, often to the discomfiture of the Russian leaders. Similarly, conversations with English, French or Belgian members of their respective countries' Communist parties reveal pertinent differences in outlook that can only be attributed once again to national character. Is there not here a key to the reason why, though Mussolini ended his career ignominiously as a corpse dangling in a public square, Hitler should disappear in a grand Wagnerian manner? It will repay us at this stage to look more closely and in some detail at the history of the German and Italian peoples.

Germany. In Germany, throughout the centuries, there has been a constant conflict between the opposing ideas of force and freedom—a conflict culminating in 1870 in the complete Prussianization of the country, against which the ineffectual Weimar Republic battled in vain. Already, the " blood and iron " policy of Bismarck was part of the feeling tone of the people.

In the eighteenth century, German patriotism had meant love of the individual *Land* in which one lived. Nineteenth-century German nationalism emerged as a very necessary attempt to maintain political independence and freedom from French domination

---

[1] *Ibid.*, p. 260.

of German cultural traditions and outlook. The University of Berlin was founded in 1806, and the philosopher Fichte, in his inspiring address to the German people—first published from Berlin in 1808—made articulate to them their own aspirations. Moral regeneration, he argued, could only come about through the establishment of a new system of education that was German and embraced all Germans without exception. A close admirer of the earlier philosopher Kant, he stressed the virtues of duty, sacrifice, self-abnegation, and argued that to exclude from man everything that is not reason is to rob the soul of its greatest impulses. Man is only man as he has his definite part to play in the world; and he plays his part, not through passively observing what goes on, but by actively intervening. All our thought is founded on our impulses; as a man's affections are, so is his knowledge. Will, reason and emotion have together an equal right, and together form a unity :

> Schmerzt dich in tiefster Brust
> das harte Wort : Du musst,
> so macht Dich eins nur still
> das stolze Wort : Ich will! [1]

This peculiarly emotional concept of duty that, through the educational system, was to embrace all Germans—so different from the British, French or American democratic ideal that stemmed from the liberal thought of Hume, Locke and Descartes —was taken a stage still further by Hegel who stressed again and again the oneness of mind and spirit. For Hegel, mind is the all-embracing reality; it is identical with behaviour and experience. And since all experiences have their source and become unified in the individual, then the main purpose of education must be that of producing well-rounded and harmoniously developed personalities, actively seeking perfection, actively striving towards the perfect German State. Thus Hegel led the German people to conclude that man makes history and that the ideal must be what is made factually real. The progression from Fichte through Hegel to pan-Germanism and to the Hitlerian cult is thus inevitable, once the concept of the superman has been formulated. And it was to Nietzsche that the task of advocating such a superman fell. In 1872 (a historically significant date) Nietzsche published his

[1] Lines from a popular poem learned by countless German children under the Hitlerian regime. Compare the one-time popularity of Kipling's *If* in this country.

The Future of our Educational Institutions, and claimed that true education can never be utilitarian. Knowledge can never be a substitute for culture. True culture is only possible through the full development of the personality. " Every conquest, every step forward in knowledge, is the outcome of courage, of hardness, of cleanliness towards oneself." The weak in spirit, therefore, must be annihilated. The superman must triumph. We do not want cultural philistines, nor a superficial culture of the masses. The few must dominate, and it is on the few that we must concentrate :

Nazis, bring up tough guys !

The transition through Nietzsche to Goebbels and Hitler is complete—tragically so in that the Germans, attempting to make the factual real, willed a puppet to be the longed-for superman. And even to-day, in conversation with men who have every reason to curse the follies of the Hitlerian regime, one repeatedly hears the nostalgic wish for a strong man, a personality who can make the people enthuse, at the head of state affairs.

Italy. In the final months and weeks of catastrophe, Hitler raged bitterly against those who had served him best, against those who had blindly and with unquestioning loyalty to the superman ideal maintained him for so long on his pedestal. Mussolini, throughout his long and in many respects brilliant career, was many times moved to complain of the lack of real fighting spirit in his Italian compatriots, of their lack of a determined will to do. And therein lies the essential difference between the Fascist and the Hitlerian regimes. Italy's story is one of repeated betrayal of sound liberal principles; Germany's is that of a definite rebuttal of such principles. And the Italian people, steeped in a humanism that dates from the prosperity of the various city states—that is to say from the fifteenth century—have found themselves constantly and as a matter of expediency paying lip-service to a succession of ruling masters without themselves holding any deep convictions at any particular time. Yet the country has never ceased to throw up sound and courageous thinkers who, though they have been discouraged or ignored, though their writings have been twisted to suit political or religious machinations, have still managed to preach their message of enlightened liberal principles, of toleration, and of real democracy within a framework of conscious national endeavour.

Italian humanism, as we may call it, is characterized by three important trends : the tradition of the strong state which reaches back to the Renaissance, to Dante, to Machiavelli; a movement for national union first sponsored by Napoleon; an idealistic conception of the state which is, in reality, a peculiarly Italian reinterpretation of the Hegelian ideal. In short, the Italian is both a realist and an idealist, and will accept a *fait accompli* (as the Mussolini *coup d'état* and subsequent regime) for the stability and economic security it immediately offers, though he resents as irksome the bonds that hold him and will seek to cast them off as the opportune moment arises.

Mazzini, with the founding of his Young Italy Movement in 1831, his Young Europe Movement in 1834, his Working Men's Association in 1840, first made articulate the aspirations of the Italian people at a national level, and linked the idea of national independence to that of liberal, social and political progress. The Casati Law of 1859 laid the haphazard foundation of the national school system that more or less still holds : compulsory elementary education to be followed by various types of secondary instruction in vocational and technical schools and in the classical *ginnasi-licei*, and leading to the universities and teacher-training establishments. In 1861 the kingdom of Italy was proclaimed from Sardinia, and in 1871 the rest of Italy was brought in with Rome as the capital city. From that point onwards a constant effort has been made to make the Italian conscious of his heritage, and liberal idealists have been ceaseless in their attempts to shape the whole pattern of instruction in the schools towards that end. Foremost amongst these must be reckoned Benedetto Croce (1866–1952).

Croce—with whom Gentile (Mussolini's minister for Public Instruction in the 1922 cabinet) must be associated—whilst retaining the Hegelian view that mind is fundamental to the universe, concentrated above all on the immediacy of changing individual experience. Life for him is a persistent moral struggle, an endless effort to create good out of evil and passion. Reality is to be found only in the progressive revelation of history, and history must be thought of not as just past, but here and now and endlessly becoming. The reasons for his quarrel with Gentile, the proved opportunist, remain shrouded in mystery, but it occurred well before the Fascist regime swept over Italy and used for its own ends the influential teaching of such men as Croce. Thus, whilst Gentile was moving his educational reforms in 1923 on the basis of a development of a moral personality, the stressing of popular literature and folklore traditions, the deintellectualizing of the curriculum, and the urgent need for moral regeneration that could only come through the practice of the Catholic religion (this in accordance with Mussolini's concordat with the Pope), Croce—an opponent of Catholicism and of positivism and direction in any form—was not afraid to attack. Fascism, he wrote, was " an incoherent and bizarre mixture of appeals to authority and demagogy, of professions of reverence for the laws, ultra-modern concepts and moth-eaten bric-à-brac, absolutism and Bolshevism, unbelief and toadying to the Catholic Church, flight from culture and sterile reachings towards a culture without a basis, mystical languors and cynicism." [1] To put the State first and the individuals comprising the State a long way second, as Fascism set out to do, was for Croce the absolute denial of the principles attaching to a liberal democracy that had been the goal of all thinking Italians since Italy had become a kingdom. His manifesto against Fascism, in reply to Gentile's *Manifesto of the Fascist Intellectuals*, appeared in 1925. Yet Croce went unmolested, his books were still printed and sold, and his famous literary review, *La Critica*, was able to enjoy uninterrupted publication from the date of its foundation in 1902 right down to 1943. Could this have happened anywhere but in Italy?

Now, in this second half of the century, liberal thought in Italy is striving to see its way through the Communist and Catholic antagonisms, and in matters of educational policy is laying once again great stress on the great liberal thinkers and writers on education neglected during the Fascist regime. It becomes immediately apparent, particularly when the new projects for the reform of Italian education are considered, how little over-all effect the Fascist regime has had in its deliberate attempt to make of education an instrument of social change.

The U.S.A. Here the story is a much more subtle one than in the case of Germany, Italy or the U.S.S.R., if only because the situation is so novel and unique. Why has the American process of using education as a major instrument in bringing about desirable cultural changes succeeded where other attempts have failed except in so far as they closely followed lines determined by the

[1] *Croce*, Cecil Sprigge. Bowes and Bowes, Cambridge, 1952, p. 18.

national character and outlook? Who were the educators? If we take the last question first, we have the key to the answer.

Ultimately, those responsible for the American approach to the problem were the early pioneer colonizers who dared to renounce the warmth of home ties and the safety of established custom because they were firmly wedded to ideals they found impossible of realization in their home surroundings. They were the people who could proclaim proudly : " We hold these truths to be self-evident : that all men are created equal; that they are endowed by their creator with inalienable rights; that amongst these are life, liberty, and the pursuit of happiness." They are also the people who, meeting with constant danger and hardship, learned to solve empirically the real-life situations that faced them, and who developed a flexibility and versatility of outlook and an adaptation to constantly changing circumstances that led them increasingly to distrust traditional or (what proved for them) outmoded ways of life, behaviour, or thought :

> Come forward, wrap us round in words that say :
> Not yesterday, or Europe, but to-day.[1]

They are finally those people who found the fulfilment of their early aspirations in the person of Thomas Jefferson who, with his school plan for the State of Virginia, was the first to implant in their minds the theory of education as a function of government. Believing firmly in the blessings of local self-government, Jefferson sought earnestly to educate the people for the opportunities he sensed were dawning. He believed sincerely that the people were capable of self-government, that they meant well, that they would act well when once they understood, and that the purpose of education was to make them understand. Thomas Jefferson was born in 1743 and died in 1826.[2]

Thus the first requirement of American public education is that it must be democratic. Education must prepare for living in a democracy, and must develop the child's whole personality to fit him adequately to fulfil his role in that democracy. The individual needs of *all* children must be catered for. And the curriculum must experience continual growth and change. In this especial sense education has been and continues to be an instrument for

[1] Robert D. Abrahams, *Saturday Evening Post*, New York, October, 1945.
[2] There is a very full biographical essay on Thomas Jefferson in the *Encyclopaedia Britannica*, q.v.

bringing about desirable cultural changes, and the whole outlook of the American people is one guaranteed easily to absorb the foreigner and make him a loyal American citizen. And that is the point. As Professor D. W. Brogan rightly says : " If these millions of (American) boys and girls are to be judged by their academic accomplishments they will be judged harshly (in comparison with the academic standards of a good English, French or German school). But they are not to be so judged, for their schools are doing far more than instruct them; they are letting them instruct each other in how to live in America." [1] The whole process is a long-term policy extending back over the years and conditioned the whole time by factors deeply rooted in the national past.

So we may conclude that any attempt, no matter how thorough and deliberate, to use education as an *immediate* remedy to change an existing culture pattern is bound to fail. Slow changes through education can be brought about if these are conceived in terms of the national character. And, indeed, as we shall have occasion to note in the next chapter, this is the normal process through which a people seeks to adapt itself to necessary changed circumstances brought about through a changed economy. France furnishes the example of a country which acknowledges the vital necessity for educational reforms but which—in order to make them work— cautiously strips off the proposed reforms extravagances that are not in keeping with national aspirations. Nazism in Germany diabolically succeeded for a time because it so closely followed a pattern that the people had to recognize as familiar. Mussolini pathetically failed because he never really understood his own people. The Communists in Russia and China would appear to be successful because they are initiating (or have initiated) long-term policies—recognized and recognizable as such—that bring hope to the people and which, to be in certain aspects immediately success- ful, build carefully on the various facets of national character. In fact, what the Communists in these countries are doing in terms of their own ideology is in many respects similar to what the Americans have been doing in terms of theirs for more than 150 years. Thus education—though a function of national character —can, over a long-term period, taking people as they are and not as it is ultimately desired they should be, be a definite instrument

The American Character, D. W. Brogan. Knopf, New York, p. 135.

for instituting social change.

It is now time to examine the nature and relative importance of the various factors which have contributed to the creation of that attitude of mind that guarantees a common purpose and a common effort from the whole group, and which we have termed the national character.

CHAPTER THREE

The Determinants of National Character

WHEN we ask ourselves what is the process that goes on to condition men to form that peculiar conception of life and living which makes them singularly alike in their group character, we have to list four principal factors : heredity, their natural environment, their social heritage, and education. The French philosopher Fouillée has put it rather more simply by claiming that the key to the behaviour of different groups lies primarily in a study of their physical surroundings and social conditions. It will pay us best to subdivide these two main divisions into what we will describe as geographical, economic, historical, religious, political and social influences—bearing in mind that in this technological and scientific age there must also be a technological influence cutting right across the whole and affecting especially the economic and social factors.

We must also remember that very slow changes in national character and outlook can be brought about, and these will be found to be due mainly to : (a) competition from more progressive groups—the struggle for survival; (b) scientific progress and discovery; (c) the gradual spreading and acceptance of new beliefs that eventually result in a new outlook—and this, of course, stemming from both competition and scientific progress and discovery; (d) education which in this respect, however, has only an indirect influence in that it acts on the intellectual quality of the group rather than directly on its character.

We should also do well to remember that, if the period of the Renaissance and Reformation marked the rise of a national consciousness in Europe, this present age of invention which makes the world grow smaller and smaller is thereby blurring to some extent national differences in that it creates problems for solution that are becoming increasingly common to all nations. So is the way eased to a steady cross-fertilization of cultures and to a growing transnational outlook. If the League of Nations can be considered as a simple (if abortive) step in this direction, then Unesco and Uno (to mention only two obvious organizations) are an indication of the shape of things to come. Though it may be rash to prophesy, I have a feeling that future historians will see quite clearly our present muddles and discontents at both a national and international level as the " growing pains " inseparable from transnationalism as an inescapable solution to present world problems.

Let us now take in turn the several factors we have listed as shaping and determining national character, bearing in mind the whole time that the national character of a given group is never determined by one factor alone but rather by an intricate combination and interweaving of all the factors, some being dominant in one particular group, recessive in another, and so on.

The geographical and economic factors. It is, of course, a commonplace to assert that people who live crowded together will be amongst themselves sociable whilst those who live isolated from human contacts will tend to be morose or shy. Similarly, city dwellers have little manual dexterity or power of " self " employment in comparison with country folk who are driven by necessity to be handy in all kinds of ways and to band together in various forms of social endeavour for their well-being and amusements.

It is equally axiomatic to state that where there is a subsistence economy—that is, one in which people are just able to make ends meet—then education must be informal, occurring on the job. Such an economy is characteristic of primitive civilizations. And such an economy was that to be endured for some considerable time by the second wave of early colonizers of North America who, land-hungry, swept down the western slopes of the Appalachians to meet deprivation and hardships in plenty, to face real-life situations that had to be solved immediately and empirically. Such an existence, totally unlike that they had known in Europe, soon gave rise to a flexibility and a versatility in outlook and a ready adaptability to constantly changing circumstances that quickly engendered a certain contempt for book-learning and academic training or intellectual pursuits that are at all times a proper pursuit of a people who enjoy a surplus economy.

We will return in some greater detail to the strange story of the growth and development of the U.S.A., towards the end of this chapter. It is important to note here that formal education is only possible where production exceeds consumption, and that this is brought about either through man's tremendous industry, or through favourable natural circumstances (fertility of the soil or the sudden discovery of unknown mineral resources at a time when man's ingenuity can best make use of them), or through improvements in techniques and in man's art and skill, or (obviously) through a combination of all these resulting in man obtaining a greater leisure time to think, to reflect, and so go on improving himself and his conditions of life.

It is as true to-day as it has been throughout history that the poorer classes have tended to content themselves with a minimum of education for their children, just as the richer classes have kept their children longest at school. Similarly, the periodic advance and decline in education throughout history, in no matter what country it is being investigated, can always be traced to coincide with periods of economic prosperity or depression. Thus, down to the nineteenth century there was never enough surplus wealth in any European country (or in the U.S.A.) to allow more than a relatively small percentage of the population leisure to profit from that type of education we have characterized as " formal."

In the Catholic countries of Europe—all of which have a predominantly large peasant population—free, compulsory primary education became attainable only after the impact of the Industrial Revolution had made itself felt, and after it had been made possible through the utilization of the mineral resources a country possessed to build up surpluses sufficient to warrant the step. The more backward industrially a country was—or had to be through paucity of mineral resources or through inability to exploit them properly—the later did compulsory, free primary education become a possibility. Even the Scandinavian Protestant countries—vowed though they were to the principle of a democratic education since the seventeenth century, could make little headway towards the fullest attainment of their ideal until a surplus economy had been achieved. Their real enforcement laws on school attendance came only in 1852 for Sweden and in 1889 for Denmark and Norway. In Spain it was not until 1911 that the principle of compulsory school attendance was accepted, though not enforced. In Italy, even to-day when primary education is in theory compulsory until 14, in the poorer south the children often leave school at 11.

And this situation was equally common in France in the 1930's in the markedly agricultural areas.

Let us now consider the effect of these geographical and economic factors in determining the outlook and shaping the educational pattern in a few selected and representative European countries.

Norway. The climate of Norway is a rigorous one. In the north of the country the sun will not rise in winter until 10 a.m. and the temperature often falls to 20° below zero. The configuration of the land is such as to force people to live (for the most part) in small isolated communities. The soil itself yields but a meagre livelihood to the farmer or smallholder. And though half of the working population is to-day classified as " industrial," industry is widely scattered and compels a large majority of industrial workers to live in rural areas. In fact, industry has had to go to the country to the people—the converse of what happened in England at the time of the Industrial Revolution.

In such climatic and geographical conditions not only is the architectural structure of farmstead, house, school and village affected, but also the whole way of life and thinking of the people. The home becomes the focal point of activity, the family unit is all-important. Because of the rigours of the climate it is considered impossible to send children to school before the age of 7, and because of the closeness of family ties it is equally unthinkable to have boarding schools for children—except for the few who come from the most inaccessible places. The most formative period of the child's life is thus spent at the mother's knee, in the home. And it is in the home that the child is educated, in the school that he receives his instruction. Thus the schools are in a very special sense the people's schools, and they are required to give conscious expression of the people's needs and aspirations. They are happy, friendly places, and no matter what part of the country the visitor is in he cannot fail to be impressed by the warmth of fellow-feeling they manage to engender.

Because families have been driven to be self-supporting there is a high degree of craft culture and a respect for it. Because they have to help one another, neighbourliness, friendliness and toler-ance abound. No feudal system of society such as we have known in England could have been possible in such a country, and in-deed the whole basis of government is originally one of yeoman farmers and free peasants stimulating and encouraging reforms and encouraged by the clergy and State officials to do so. When in the late nineteenth century industrialization did reach the country, the pattern was firmly set and the industrial workers fitted naturally into a democratic society that believed with all its heart in self-government and freedom as the basis for all progressive development. Thus all men take an active part in public life and in local and national government, and are expected to do so.

From all of this it again follows that there must be the closest of links between the culture of the people and the people's schools. The education system grew naturally from peasant life, and its objective is not to produce a type (as in France, or even Belgium) but to fulfil the needs of the child, the family and the community. The schools are democratically controlled by local and municipal boards, and by parents' and teachers' councils. Wide freedom is accorded to local authorities and individual schools, and the teacher ranks high in the community as fulfilling an important role in the community's interests. He also plays an important part in local and national government.

At the same time there has grown up an intellectual approach to the school curriculum, an almost inherent love of encyclopaedic knowledge. " There is no better baggage on a journey than much of knowledge " runs one Scandinavian proverb. We must trace much of this once again to the geographical conditions which compel long winter evenings to be spent around the fire, as we can be thankful to such family fireside gatherings for the wealth of saga and folklore of Scandinavian legend. None the less, we must also remember that this ultimately is in the main tradition of European practice (as opposed to English—excluding Scottish—and American practice), and that the Scandinavian peoples generally have an added compulsion to intellectualize their curricula because they feel in the backwaters of main European affairs. In other words, they feel they have to prove their abilities.

Switzerland. The picture is in some respects not dissimilar for Switzerland. There also the Reformation proved a powerful impulse towards popular democratic education, and the geographical configuration of the country led to its becoming a confederation of twenty-five autonomous states, some purely Protestant, some purely Catholic, some mixed, all jealously safeguarding their autonomy particularly in matters educational. Some of these states are chiefly agricultural, some chiefly industrial, some densely populated, others sparsely populated.

It is traditional for the Swiss peasant to be an educated man and to be afforded the fullest opportunities for ensuring the education of his children to the highest possible level required for the job he wishes them to take up. It is also the proud and justifiable boast of the Swiss that they owe their political stability and their sense of balance and proportion in all things—as well as their drive —to the sound educational background over the centuries that has made each and every Swiss supremely conscious of his own value to the community, no matter what his employment.

The anomalous situation produced in Switzerland by the Industrial Revolution is curious. The playground of Europe had to industrialize itself in order to survive. Having no natural advantages other than its timber and water power, it had to tap effectively its only remaining source, its man-power. Thus it has become a country renowned for high quality precision work that depends on really skilled technicians and craftsmen. The skilled craftsmen of the pre-industrial era were led to take equal pride in their work in the new factories that sprang up and to attach tremendous importance to the dignity of skilled labour. The technical colleges necessary both to form and to inform the skilled labour required were not built haphazardly to meet an *ad hoc* situation (as in England), but from their inception in the late nineteenth century had a definite plan and purpose and became very much an integral part of the life of the town that housed them as well as maintaining the closest possible links with the industrial and commercial interests they were designed to serve. As a result the Swiss workman and artisan enjoys a very advanced form of instruction, is very highly paid, is as conscious of his social importance and value to the community as any other member of it, and—what is more important—is so impressed by the dignity and fitness of his calling as not easily to be led to abandon manual labour to join what becomes in so many countries an embarrassingly growing body of " black-coated " workers.

Belgium. The Belgians may also be said to favour intellectualism in their school curricula, to be democratic and independent in outlook, to consider the schools as *their* schools (to the extent of fighting bitter electoral battles over them), and jealously to safeguard their local autonomy, customs and privileges. Geographical influences.

however, are by no means as directly responsible for all this as in the case of Norway or Switzerland—as we shall later see.

Belgium is not only a temperate country, but is also (in direct contrast to Norway) the most densely populated country in Europe, and one which—whilst its economic development and prosperity have been conditioned by the nature of the land and of the waterways—has had its whole economy even more determined by its position. For Belgium lies at a crossing of the ways : it is the junction between Western Europe and the great plains of Northern Europe; and across it pass the old trade routes between the north and south of the European continent. When Europe is at peace, therefore, its position is ideal, for it also lies in the heart of one of the greatest industrial and commercial regions of Europe. It has developed into a manufacturing country because of the rich deposits of coal and iron in the south-east. Metal products and textiles are the two groups of products the markets of the world most persistently demand. Yet at the same time it has managed to preserve a balance between industry and agriculture, and its narrow, barren, northern coastal strip shelters a very fertile land that is intensively cultivated. As one Belgian writer so aptly puts it : " Belgium, in all its varied aspects of life, is a synthesis of Western Europe, a miniature continent."

The temperate climate of Belgium, its natural resources and its unique position at the crossroads of Western Europe have made the Belgian people energetic, cordial, businesslike and realistic in outlook, given to good living—and perhaps not a little blatant and ostentatious in this direction. The tireless energy required to exploit to the full all the chances offered the Belgian has also given rise to a distinct type of bourgeoisie (quite different from the almost classical French model), to generations of selfmade men who value increasingly both the opportunities they were given and the opportunities they can in turn afford the newer generations. Education, therefore, is a serious matter and much their concern. They are correspondingly traditionalist in outlook and reforms come slowly. Belgium is emphatically not a country in which progressive schools can ever hope to flourish. On the other hand, when they have decided that steps must be taken to implement proved and desirable changes, they spare themselves no expense and trouble.

Holland. We have already mentioned in Chapter Two some of the outstanding characteristics of the Dutch. They are as enterprising and as independent-minded as the Belgians, and equally resourceful and painstaking. The most recent problem for Holland has been one of a rather shattering awakening from a spirit of self-complacency born of the economic and commercial prosperity of the seventeenth and eighteenth centuries, a period which gave to Holland a rich, contented and placid bourgeoisie that was happy to remain aloof from the main current of European affairs, and a people and peasantry who were frugal, austere and hardworking. An enormous increase in population (threefold in the last hundred years) and keen competition in world markets from more industrialized countries made it suddenly imperative to switch in a determined fashion to industrialization as the only means of national survival. It was not in effect until the early 1930's that educationally the importance of committing Holland to a policy of more intensive industrialization was fully realized, and since then great strides have been taken to improve the quality and variety of technical and commercial instruction at all levels, and also to modernize the curriculum of the schools generally.

France. Though France is mainly an agricultural country she is also a land of small peasant proprietors owning farms that can easily be cultivated on a family basis. Pride of ownership is, therefore, widespread, methods of cultivation are by most modern standards outmoded, and in any case the smallness of the average holding makes the use of agricultural machinery on any large scale uneconomical. Industrious, thrifty and hardworking, the French peasant is the real stabilizing force behind French economy, and time and again the French peasantry has saved France from ruin as it has (incidentally) given to France some of its ablest and most patriotic teachers for the primary schools. The idea of *une culture générale* dominates all primary school teaching, and the textbooks used instil into the pupil a real love, knowledge and appreciation of things French.

The major industries have developed around the coalfields in the north of the country, but industrialization has not had the tremendous over-all effect in a country the size of France that one might be led to expect. There is no highly developed and highly organized factory system (such as is known in America or Germany), but rather groupings of family concerns with the families still much in evidence and the workers—conscious of their peasant origins—still highly individualistic and still very much of the soil of France. In other words, the individualist nature of the Frenchman rebels against any depersonalization through a vast machinelike organization. In all of this lies the key to the peculiar paradox whereby France, firmly wedded to a high degree of centralization of government and control—and this, as we shall see, mainly through historical causes—still remains supremely one of the great democracies of Western Europe. To be provocative one could argue that the French are the one nation in the world to put into practical effect the Rousseau doctrine that to retain your liberty you must first surrender it to the State—surrendering it, of course, *ad maiorem Francorum gloriam*, and surrendering it freely because freely believing in the value of the great humanistic traditions of French culture.

With all this background it is not surprising that the dual system of education in France (a primary stream and a secondary stream that never met) should in a large measure persist down to the proposed Langevin Reforms of 1945, and that technical education became only a reality for the mass of the people by the *Loi Astier* of 1919—that is to say when it became obvious after the First World War that highly trained and highly skilled workers were going to be increasingly needed in industry side by side with the skilled technical experts. A study of present post-war reforms will reveal that, whilst increasingly it has become easier to bridge the gap between primary and secondary education, the creation of the technical and commercial *baccalauréat*, and of the *Collège d'Enseignement Secondaire*, is aimed at tapping to the full all available technical and scientific ability from all sources.

Germany. Of all the main Western European countries, the one that does not follow the general pattern of development is Germany. Germany came quite late to feel the effects of the Industrial Revolution as she came late in the rush for the exploitation of acquired colonial possessions. Overnight almost she found herself switching from a predominantly agrarian economy to becoming a highly industrialized state. Overnight values changed. The old, pleasant life centred on church and family, serene and endless (or so it seemed), was suddenly disrupted. With characteristic Teutonic thoroughness the new industrialists threw themselves into catching up on lost time, eagerly built and expanded sprawling and ugly industrial cities, reared their children there and sent them to the classical *gymnasium* (grammar school) to imbibe a culture they felt that they should have, though such a culture bore no resemblance to the changing conditions of life. These industrialists were the *nouveaux riches*, the new aristocracy. Meantime the new workers in industry were being put through an intensive necessary *Grundschule* training to pass on as apprentices into the works. Meantime also, the sons of the industrialists, chafing under (though influenced by) the unrealistic conditions that held in the *gymnasien* and feeling the need for a larger freedom, found a leader in a certain Karl Fischer of Berlin who organized them as the *Wandervögel*, preached a doctrine of back-to-nature, led them to spend as much of their time as possible in the open, trekking in the country, making acquaintance in a nostalgic way (and against the background of their literary studies) with the abandoned peasant way of life, learning the neglected folk songs and folk dances, and dreaming of " the life of yesteryear." It was a new form of romantically dangerous nationalism. The movement spread rapidly. Power, pleasure and wealth were (in theory) scornfully cast aside, as were the trivialities of a mechanized and material grossness of industry. The spiritual freedom of the individual was to be asserted. " We shall turn our back on the ugly conventions and moral inertia of the established order. For this inner freedom we stand in all circumstances," they proclaimed at a gigantic rally held in 1913. Eagerly and fearlessly they fought the 1914-1918 war, convinced of the rightness of the German cause and intoxicated by their mission. " An exclusively German phenomenon," wrote Professor Gooch commenting on the movement. An important phenomenon, though. The *Wandervögel* were the forerunners of National Socialism in Germany.

The historical factor. Matters political and religious are very closely related to the historical development of any country—as of course are its geographical position and economy. All this will have become increasingly obvious in the foregoing section where we have tried, somewhat arbitrarily, to separate the threads. In discussing the influence of historical factors, therefore, we will in this section limit ourselves to two countries, France and Belgium, on the plea that in these countries at least historical facts have had far-reaching results that tend to dominate all other considerations.

Belgium. To be situated at the crossroads of Western Europe is by no means an unmixed blessing as the Belgians, throughout their long and turbulent history, can testify. In time of peace there is genuine prosperity; in times of war, real hardship. For repeated wars between the rival great powers of Europe have for centuries been fought on Belgian soil, and its people have been in turn under Spanish or Austrian rule, under French or German domination, and annexed for a brief period between 1815 and 1830 to the kingdom of Holland. As a nation they realized their entity only in 1830, thanks to British diplomatic manoeuvring. And for centuries before this they had grown accustomed to the domination (not always harsh or intolerable) of this or that overlord, to grouping themselves together to demand their rights, to forming strongly independent *communes* that sent petition after petition to the rulers and directors of their fortunes *pour un redressement des griefs du peuple*. Usually, be it noted, so tenacious and obstinate were they, they managed for the most part to get their own way or at least to arrive at some workable compromise. When tempers ran too high on either side, then clashes inevitably resulted and some hero died a martyr's death for the people's passion for independence, for individual liberty and local autonomy, for the maintenance of a traditional way of life and the preservation of inherited custom and institutions. Thus the marked national characteristics resulting from the historical past of the Belgians are, as Louis Verniers puts them : " A general tendency to recrimination, to be critical and mocking, to insurrection and to lack of discipline . . . to a dislike of all excessive measures and any show of extremism, of sectarianism, together with a proportionate predilection for temporization, for a ' wait and see ' policy, and for choosing— where possible—the middle way out."

All this, as we have already seen in Chapter Two, is fully reflected in the educational pattern of the country. We may further note here that it is axiomatic for any governmental directive on almost any matter to be most critically examined and often challenged on a point of principle; that any project for reform will be most sceptically reviewed and new ideas rigorously pruned of any extravagances. No attempt can be made to restrict the political or philosophical beliefs of the teaching staff of schools—or indeed of anybody. It is also significant that there are two State universities—one in Liège for the French-speaking part of the population and one in Ghent for the Flemings—and two " free " universities : the Catholic university of Louvain and the liberal free-thinking university of Brussels. Both these " free " universities give instruction in both national languages.

France. During the reign of Francis I (1515–47) France glimpsed briefly the blessings that could accrue from the replacement of the old feudal system by an absolute monarchical control based on the growing importance and wealth of the bourgeoisie. The end of the wars of religion left her weary but fortunate in that she had kings in Henry IV, Louis XIII and Louis XIV (the latter being ably directed by the all-powerful cardinals Richelieu and Mazarin) who had growing prestige, power and influence and who were wedded to the ideal of a great and glorious unified France. Louis XIV's reign not only consolidated the position of the monarch as absolute and all-powerful, but it also brought to France unparalleled splendour and glory in all fields of endeavour and made her unsurpassed and envied throughout Europe. The influence of the Church—and particularly of the Jesuits—was paramount in shaping and moulding the thoughts and aspirations of Frenchmen in the direction in which the country was moving and in slowly piecing together the pattern (glimpsed from the Middle Ages onwards but till now not fully realized) of a central unified government. The Church it was that gave to France its ideal type of bourgeois, the type the age felt it needed and the type the France of to-day still feels it needs—the type we have already at some length discussed.

Thus the cry of the eighteenth-century philosophers—*L'enseignement, fonction de l'Etat*—does no more than echo the Frenchman's traditional belief, based on the facts of his history, that a strongly centralized State controlling all spheres of activity is necessary to the glory of France and to its well-being. Equally obviously, once the fevered anxieties of the French Revolution had died down to the point of allowing national consciousness to reassert itself, it was the logical and almost inescapable step for Napoleon to create the strongly centralized and departmentalized system that holds in France to-day and that the Frenchman of to-day would not willingly change for any other system. Contrast this state of affairs with those holding in Belgium: there, for reasons equally historical, such an abrogation of individual responsibility and prestige in favour of the greater glory of the whole nation could never exist.

The religious factor. Martin Luther's challenge to the supreme authority of the Catholic Church in Western Europe, coming as it did close on the Renaissance, was bound to be identified with the growing idea of nationalism and to have tremendous repercussions that were closely linked with the historical, political and social conditions of the people. We have already hinted at the miseries caused in France by the wars of religion before the Protestants were finally defeated and the Catholic Church, with the Jesuits triumphant, reasserted its authority. It was an authority, however, as we have also seen, geared to enhancing the glory and splendour of France and of absolute monarchical rule based on a solid bourgeoisie that received its education from the Church. It was an alliance between Church and State for the greater glory of France. Neither party sought to exterminate the other. And the Jesuits, loyally and most competently, carried out their self-appointed task of establishing an educational pattern. In varying degrees the Catholic Church may be said to have played a similar role of alliance with the State in such predominantly Catholic countries as Belgium, Italy and Southern Germany.

In those parts of Western Europe where Protestantism triumphed, however, it triumphed because Protestant Church and State were in alliance with a different aim in view—to see that the people were educated. Elementary education was a prime concern, and through it the people were to be brought to appreciate and value the blessings of a Christian democracy. Ignorance, claimed Luther, is the real enemy of the true religion. To kill ignorance must be the first duty of the State. " The prosperity of a city," he wrote to the German magistrates and senators, " does not depend only on its natural resources, on the strength of its walls, on the elegance of line of its buildings, on its military equipment; the well-being and strength of a city depends above all on a sound education which provides it with knowledgeable, reasonable and honest citizens."

In the Catholic countries generally, wedded as they were for varying reasons to the education of an élite, the education of the masses received scant attention. When a French priest, Jean Baptiste de La Salle, first attempted in 1684 to provide a systematic primary instruction he was moved to complain that he was persecuted by the very men from whom he had expected help. It was only in 1724 that Pontifical Sanction was granted to his Order of the Christian Brothers. Meantime in the Catholic countries the eighteenth-century philosophers were becoming increasingly occupied with the idea of the necessity for ensuring man's steady progress towards a better life and were urging their faith in man and in his future, and in the perfectibility of human institutions. Naturally they turned to education as being a prime factor in this concept of human progress. And equally naturally they challenged the Church's control of education and evolved their slogan of *L'Enseignement, fonction de l'Etat.*

From this point onwards the working alliance between Church and State snaps, and the struggle begins for control of the education of the people that even to-day is far from being satisfactorily resolved. Inevitably in all Catholic countries it becomes a controversial political issue : the Catholics have tended to form a right-wing party (though since the arrival of socialism there are also strong left-wing Catholic groups) to champion the " free " school system and to argue that it is only just, if the State is determined to care for education, that the " free " schools should receive adequate subsidies to enable them to compete on favourable terms with the State schools; the non-Catholics (usually Liberals, Socialists and free-thinkers) argue the case for State control of education and point out that adequate safeguards are always taken in a truly liberal democracy, within the framework of the State system, to ensure proper and unfettered observance of Catholic (or indeed any other) practice by the faithful.

The political factor. The most interesting feature in the whole problem of Church and State relationships is, of course, the way in which each individual country has sought its own solution. And that solution is dependent on the kind of political way of life towards which the people are moving. Throughout history the kind and amount of education given has depended on the waxing or waning of this or that political outlook and belief. For certain questions are to be asked and clearly answered. What sort of curriculum is it that best fits a man to manage public affairs? Who are to be selected for the kind of education that fits a man to hold power? How long shall the period of formal education last? What shall be its various ramifications? And what sort of education shall be provided for the masses of the people? It will pay us best once again to take certain representative countries in turn and trace in outline what has happened in each.

Scandinavia. As we have already noted, there could be no problem to be solved in the Scandinavian countries, for Church and State were both moving towards the same end : a real people's democracy which increasingly demanded a high standard of general education and—mainly because of geographical factors— the evolution of a sound system of local government. Not that this was achieved overnight. None the less, it is interesting to note that by a decree of 1739 in Norway schools were to be established in every parish and *all* children were to attend. True, genuine compulsory primary education became law only in 1889, but over the intervening 150 years the principle of the State's right and duty to show initiative in the field of education was clearly determined. The State in alliance with the Church, for even to-day the majority of Norwegian schools are under the administration of a body known as " The Ministry of Church and Education."

In Sweden, local self-government dates even from the pre-Christian era. The old State grammar school (known since the time of Gustavus Adolphus as the *gymnasium*) has always been open to boys from *all* social classes and has through the centuries contributed in no small measure to the elimination of class distinctions throughout Sweden. Responsibility for public instruction is divided between the State and the local authorities. Compulsory primary education became law in 1852.

Much the same holds true for Denmark as for Norway, for they were one kingdom for 400 years down to 1814. As one Danish teacher eloquently puts it : " The Danes love the simple, unpretentious and harmonious life as described by their hero Bishop Grundtvig, and are above all desirous to educate their youth for co-operation and common responsibility, to independent thought and action, and to respect for the highest values of life."

France. The pattern set for education in France not only produced a highly intelligent, rational and logically minded bourgeoisie that should be the mainstay of centralized control. It also produced individuals capable of highly critical attitudes : its philosophers like Voltaire; the men who were to make the revolution a practical reality and to show how inadequate for the times was the kind of education the Church generally afforded; the politicians of the Napoleonic and Restoration periods who— though firmly wedded to the idea of a modern, democratic, political and secular education—were what we might call traditionally " Catholic " in outlook because their cultural concepts stemmed directly from it. Thus they applauded the Napoleonic reconstitution of the University, the creation of the *lycée* and the highly centralized secular State control of education that resulted, and were content to leave to the Church the education of the people in the elements of good citizenship. *Les Evêques et les Curés sont les surveillants naturels des écoles destinées au peuple.* It was because of this that Guizot's early attempt (1833) to make primary education a public service open to all proved abortive, and that the country had to wait until 1881 before the institution of free primary State education for all children became a reality. And even then the idea of the distinct cleavage between the two types of education (elementary and secondary) was so much part of the national way of thinking that it was not until after 1945 that it was in any way successfully broken down.

Naturally this principle of centralization of education in the hands of the State did not go unchallenged by the Church which claimed that freedom of instruction included at least the right of maintaining religious instruction in the schools. The controversy reached a peak in the 1880's, with Victor Hugo fulminating against the Church as an opponent of the enlightenment of the people—and once again at the turn of the century when the Catholic Party were completely discredited over the Dreyfus affair, and when the teaching orders of priests were for several years forbidden to run their own schools, let alone teach in the State schools. However, the men of the Third Republic were just as traditional in their outlook as their predecessors and knew that the mass of the people were fundamentally Catholic in outlook, if not deeply and fervently religious. They followed in general the advice of enlightened Catholics like Thiers who maintained that " the teaching of children must be based essentially on truths . . . that have been proved, that are established," excluded from the compulsory education system instruction in any dogma whatsoever, gave prime importance instead to instruction in civics and ethics, and left religion to be taught by the family and the Church, making Thursday a compulsory free school holiday to this end. To-day many Catholic parents have their children in the State primary and secondary schools, and are quite happy about the arrangement. And, of course, the " free " Church primary and secondary schools (and university institutions) flourish to such an extent to be thought by some to constitute still a challenge to the principle of ultimate State responsibility.

Belgium. As might be expected, tempers in Belgium were much

more explosive, not only because of the Belgian's highly individualistic approach to all matters affecting his freedom of thought and
of action, but also because the Belgian brings a heartfelt sincerity
to his cherished beliefs. For him there can be no slick intellectual
approach to the problems: either he is a devout Catholic, often
almost paganly mystical in his worship, or he is uncompromisingly
in the other camp. Again—though we have so far deliberately
avoided discussion of the question of racial differences (mainly
because we believe that the distribution of cultural traits does not
always follow racial lines, and that the psychology of race has
ultimately little to do with the psychology of a group of people
who, for a variety of reasons independent of race, have come to live
together as *one* people)—it is important as regards Belgium to note
the differences between the Flemings and the Walloons.

Ultimately, and in times of real national crisis, Flemings and
Walloons recognize that Belgium is a closely-knit national unit and
must remain so for the well-being and prosperity of all. None the
less, at all other times the country is split into rival political,
religious, racial and linguistic factions.' The Flemings, living
mainly north of a line drawn west to east through Brussels, are
predominantly Catholic in outlook, right-wing in politics, proud
of their Flemish culture, and fiercely oppose any attempts (real or
imagined) on the part of the French-speaking south to deny them
their linguistic and cultural rights. The Walloons speak French,
are a diversified mixture of Catholics, Liberals and Socialists, have
agricultural as well as industrial occupations, and are conscious of
the obvious superiority and importance of the French tongue as a
world language in comparison with the varied forms of Dutch
spoken in the Flemish provinces.

We have to return once again to the winning of Belgian independence to see how closely the linguistic and religious problems
combine to produce differing political attitudes. When Belgium
was united with Holland after the Napoleonic Wars, " Dutch "
William introduced a secular system of education for the whole of
his country and made the Dutch language a medium of instruction. He thus alienated both Flemings and Walloons and drove
them to unite—as he drove Catholics and Liberals to unite—to
oppose him and form a combined front that was effective beyond
their expectations in achieving at long last Belgian independence.
For though the Flemings accepted the Dutch language in their

schools, as fervent Catholics they were bitterly opposed to secularism; and the Walloons, though accepting secularism, objected violently to the relegation of French to the status of a second language. Once Belgium became an independent kingdom an uneasy alliance between Catholics and Liberals led to the Flemings accepting that French should be taught in their schools and to the Liberals admitting the principle of " free " Catholic schools to operate alongside an official State school system. From 1850 onwards, however, when the new kingdom had become stable and was acknowledged by the great powers, a fierce storm on a basis of party politics centred itself on the scholastic and linguistic problems, reached a peak of savage intensity towards the end of the century, and has by no means now completely died away.

The story is too long to be told in all its fascinating detail here. In brief, the Flemings asserted their rights to use Dutch as their first language and as the medium of instruction in their schools, and the Walloons accepted Dutch as their official second language. In practice, of course, every Fleming really learns French; the Walloons—despite the fact that Dutch is an official subject of study—are by now proverbial in their inability to cope in any serious way with Dutch. The official educational system has become strictly neutral in the sense that it recognizes no one fixed moral philosophy. According to the wishes of the parents the children now *may* be given religious instruction during school hours in one of three recognized branches: Catholic, Protestant, or Jewish, and a minister of the appropriate church will be responsible for this. Any parent who does not wish his child to have religious instruction in this way may apply for a dispensation which is readily accorded. In that case the child will be obliged to follow a special course of study during the periods devoted to religious instruction in what is termed " secular moral instruction." As anyone who wishes can open his own school, there are naturally many " free " schools (mainly Catholic) in addition to the two " free " universities at Brussels (neutral) and at Louvain (Catholic).

None the less, education is still very much a major political issue. There is now a strong Christian Socialist party, and when this party came into power in 1950 it rushed to grant subsidies to the " free " Catholic schools on roughly the same basis as to the State schools. The old enmities flared up once again, and it was not until a new Schools' Pact (1959) was made effective that a workable solution was in some measure arrived at. The result is that every teacher, parent, student, pupil is acutely politically conscious in a way that scarcely holds in any other country; aware of the part educational issues have played and will continue to play in his life; determined (individualistic Belgian that he is) to fight for his rights as he sees them and to secure—the old phrase— *un redressement de ses griefs.*

Holland. The Dutch, individualistic as the Belgians and equally devoted to the principle of local autonomy, fared differently from the Belgians in that the Reformation gave Holland a democratic Protestant Church which, once the Spanish yoke was thrown off, energetically set about the business of organizing the schools and educating the people. The idea of neutrality in Dutch education came at the end of the eighteenth century—inspired, of course, by the writings of the eighteenth-century philosophers and the immediate impact made on Continental Europe by the French Revolution. In 1806 a school bill was passed which aimed at a total reorganization of education under State control, and which made for an efficiency of organization the Protestant Church had not been able to attain. When in 1814 William I became king of the Netherlands (including Belgium) he not unnaturally built on these sure foundations for a State system of education, and between 1815 and 1840 gave to his kingdom a school system based on a strongly centralized control that in one generation raised the standard of education everywhere and beyond all expectations. Ironically, the very Belgians who made Belgian independence a possibility were educated in " Dutch " William's schools!

The Dutch were not slow to follow the lead given them by the Belgians, for they also were chafing under the unaccustomed restrictive centralized control. Protestant parents first raised the cry in 1840, and they were soon joined by the strong Catholic minority. The new liberal ideas that were sweeping Europe and claiming that a good society could exist only in so far as man was given freedom to live his own life to the full in accordance with his own nature and inclinations thus became identified in Holland with a parents' move that insisted on the parent's right to educate his children as he wished, and on the Dutchman's right to be governed locally and not centrally. The struggle between State and parents went on throughout the century, the parents first obtaining the concession that they could set up their own " free " schools (i.e. schools not controlled by either State or municipality, but by parents' associations) in competition with the State system. Finally, as these " free " schools grew and prospered to the detriment of the State system, by a school law of 1920 the present-day system came into force. The outstanding feature of all Dutch life to-day is the strength and importance of the " free " primary school system.

From this very brief comparison of these representative countries we can note several important trends resulting from the interplay of religious and political factors—trends which have shaped and will continue to shape the whole future educational policy of the nation concerned. In countries like the Scandinavian countries, where Protestantism has triumphed on a basis of the recognition of the importance of the ordinary man (the peasant farmer and smallholder), then Church and State have worked in complete harmony towards a real democratic way of life. Such States, however, are in a most-favoured position in that they have not felt the full impact of the disrupting influences of industrialization and of technical development on any really big scale.

In countries where Catholicism has remained dominant— France and Belgium—the various alliances and struggles between Church and State have led first to the establishment of a dual system of education : the establishment of primary, higher primary and continuation schools for the people, and of an academic secondary school for the bourgeois élite; secondly, to the formation of a parallel system organized by the " free " Catholic schools; thirdly, to a strongly centralized State control, much weaker in Belgium than in France for historical reasons; fourthly, to the growth of vigorous politico-religious parties and the constant campaigning by non-Catholics for *laïcité de l'école*; fifthly, as industrialization takes hold of the country, to the growth of strong Christian-Socialist parties warring with the non-Christian Socialists and the Communists. Liberal opinion, whilst often still strong enough to be an important deciding factor in coalition governments, is nevertheless steadily decreasing in influence.

In a country like Holland, where Protestantism has become the State religion despite a very strong Catholic (minority) body of opinion and where the Protestants wrested their final freedom from centralized Catholic control, liberty of conscience in all matters and for all religious sects is the watchword. Though the historical background is different, the same is basically true for Switzerland.

The social factor. Obviously the schools must closely reflect the social pattern holding in any particular country as do reforms in education the changing tone and temper of the people. Similarly when reforms are instituted, the force and value of traditionally held beliefs can be tested by the differences to be noted between the theorizing behind the reform—its idealistic conception—and the actual practical application of it. Thus the experiment of the *classes nouvelles* in France was halted. Reasons of economy, the rising birth-rate and governmental financial stringency may have had some part to play in this, but the fact remains that the traditional outlook of the French has led them to view with suspicion an innovation that mingled *instruction* with *éducation* : *éducation* is still looked upon very much as the responsibility of the home and the family, *instruction* as the business for which school-masters are paid. Similarly the English comprehensive school is having a hard fight to prove its worth and to strike out on its own individual line of approach because the lower middle-classes and many of the working class are still wedded to the idea of secondary education as grammar school education—a high tribute indeed to the achievements of the grammar school in particular since the passing of the Balfour Act of 1902.

Again, the various projects for reform in education also indicate quite clearly what have been the basic cultural changes in the life of a people from the nineteenth into the twentieth century. The impetus that came from the Industrial Revolution was, of course. a vital one. Just as the revival of trade and commerce throughout Europe after the Renaissance had given rise to an important third social class—a middle-class of merchants between the upper and lower classes of feudalism—the consequences of the Industrial Revolution were such as (*a*) to switch the emphasis from a middle-class to a lower-class culture; (*b*) to create a capitalist class largely from among the middle-classes, but which also increasingly was to include men who had risen from the most humble positions; (*c*) to lead to the realization on the part of both bosses and workers that education was vital to the extent of no longer remaining a chancy business but of becoming a definite public service; (*d*) to bring about the gradual but sure decline of the leisure-class ideal of education for a " gentleman " that Locke had so persuasively argued in his *Thoughts on Education*, first published in 1693.

The later tremendous impact that scientific research and technological development have made upon all phases of human life has led first of all to a feeling that nothing is beyond the range and grasp of human ingenuity; secondly, to a kind of complicated intellectual revolt against tradition which usually manifests itself by attacks against established institutions, beliefs and social procedures thus far regarded as impregnable; thirdly, to the domination of economic policy by giant monopolies—either capitalist or State-controlled; fourthly, except of course in the undeveloped areas, to a marked and progressive rise in the standard of living in keeping with the continual rise in the level of material satisfaction due to efficient monopolistic control of industry in all its forms. Because of the greater diversity of new skills needed in industry and commerce a new emphasis has been placed on literacy and on a definite extension of the period of compulsory schooling, and a drive is made to increase facilities for technical education and to give facilities for further education to adults and to young people who have already left school. The number of professions open to proved ability has grown larger and with this has come an insistence on the necessity for acquiring the right kind of education at the right level. Thus bridges have had to be built between the elementary (working-class) type of education and the secondary (bourgeois) type, and this has led in all countries to a reshaping of the educational machinery to make for (a) equality of educational opportunity for all; (b) a widening of the school curriculum; (c) increased emphasis on the importance of the right kind of technical education for the new technological age. The old dichotomy between a liberal and a technical education is broken down and social distinctions which existed mainly because of that dichotomy have become blurred.

Social mobility in the pre-industrial era was small, and children tended almost automatically to follow the same calling as their parents. Industrialization has led to a marked increase in mobility, to a restlessness and dissatisfaction, and to a great influx from country areas to the industrial towns. Family life has been disrupted, the church has ceased to be the binding and compelling force it once was for a community, and machine and life have been confounded, resulting in the tendency to stress to the community the importance of technicians rather than craftsmen. Leisure pursuits, increasingly divorcing themselves from church and family, have become increasingly passive in character as television invades the farmhouse, " pop " music the village hall, and as efficient bus and train services—not to mention the ease of possession of mechanically propelled vehicles of all kinds—carry the countryfolk to share the life of the townspeople, a life once again full of disrupting influences and " canned " and passive pleasures.

New political forms of life have emerged (as we have already seen). The trade unions have grown in power and importance. The State itself has been driven into the position of becoming more and more a welfare State and has developed—often at a bewildering rate—its medical and social services, its town and country planning projects, and has evinced a deeper and growing concern for every member of the community, as it must, since a position has been reached when the well-being and prosperity of the State has come to depend most directly on the well-being and efficiency of its individual members. And all this is equally disruptive of family ties, influences and responsibilities. Contemporary systems of government, argues the French Catholic philosopher Gustave Thibon, are the inevitable outcome of this technological age. They make for centralization instead of unification, and they do not pause to reflect on man's nature and his primary needs. The natural law of man's being requires unity in diversity. By destroying the very foundations of family life (which procure this unity) planners have produced systems of government " where you tend to get either unbridled emotional freedom that must result in anarchy, or a strictly ordered and planned society based on tyranny." As examples of what he means—though naturally they are sweeping generalizations and intended to be taken as such—Thibon would cite on the one hand the U.S.A., and on the other the U.S.S.R.

The two countries in which the social pattern has been least disturbed by the upheavals following the Industrial Revolution and accompanying our present scientific age are Belgium and Switzerland. Not only have the blessings of a stable family life been honoured and sung down the centuries—as witness the famous Plantin sonnet of the middle sixteenth century :

> Avoir une maison commode, propre et belle,
> Un jardin tapissé d'espaliers odorants,
> Des fruits, d'excellent vin, peu de train, peu d'enfants,
> Posséder seul sans bruit une femme fidèle ;

N'avoir dette, amour, ni procès, ni querelle,
Ni de partage à faire avec ses parents,
Se contenter de peu, n'espérer rien des grands,
Régler tous ses desseins sur un juste modèle;

Vivre avec franchise et sans ambition,
S'adonner sans scrupules à la dévotion,
Dompter ses passions, les rendre obéissantes,

Conserver l'esprit libre, et le jugement fort,
Dire son chapelet en cultivant ses entes,
C'est attendre chez soi bien doucement la mort.

but both countries also possess clearly defined peasant and industrial populations, both have achieved and maintained a balanced
economy and a high standard of living, opportunities exist in both
countries for those with ability and initiative to join the ranks of the
self-made bourgeois, and both profess that individual patriotism
and strength of family ties that produce the " unity in diversity "
Thibon desires.

There is no doubt that France also possesses many of these attri-
butes that attach to family life, for in France no less than in Belgium
the Catholic religion is a strong binding force. The mother plays
an important role in the life of her children. All family decisions
and problems are centred on her, and the bonds of affection between mother and children are freely admitted and openly conceded. In a word the family in France, as in Belgium and Switzerland, whether industrial or agrarian, is a closely-knit group united
by bonds of both affection and interest. At the same time, life is
harder in France than in Belgium or Switzerland, greater sacrifices
have to be made for the well-being of the family, and all this leads
to a deep seriousness of purpose often masked by a gay conversa-
tional approach. The important things of life, however, are never
approached lightheartedly, and unnecessary luxuries are sacrificed
for things of more permanent value. It is equally true that the
Frenchman can be irritatingly chauvinistic—but he could never
be guilty of pronouncing judgment upon himself as follows :

In a sense, cricket is—us. It stands for what we practice and
preach—concerted action, team play, the discipline of the individual, the recognition of authority, and the subservience of all
to the common end.

The Scandinavian countries generally, and the Protestant countries, break from the Catholic tradition in that the father of the household is the important figure and is vested with a responsibility towards the State for seeing that each member of his family contributes the maximum of which he is capable towards the general pattern of competence of the community. True, the mother plays an important part in the early education of the children, and she must make the " home." Family ties are none the less much looser, and it is only in the regions where the effects of industrialization have been less severely felt that a close-knit family unit still persists. In Holland, for example (except in the predominantly Catholic areas), there is a feeling prevalent that the children must make their own way and that it is the duty of the parents not to frustrate them. Obviously, much of this stems from the changed and changing economy of the country of which we have already spoken.

To conclude this section it would not be unfair to claim that the general result of these changing social conditions everywhere is one which leaves the parents bewildered by circumstances which they must admit have outstripped their ability to cope as effectively as they once did. The State increasingly intervenes with its child guidance clinics, its youth employment bureaux, its aptitude tests, and all the paraphernalia of the modern psychological approach in an attempt to ensure that there shall be (for the greater good of the State) fewer and fewer square pegs in round holes. Let it be noted that this is said in no derogatory sense. Catholic communities themselves, conservative though they are, have slowly but surely realized the value of a " new " education approach to present problems and have conceded that the modern outlook has both importance and significance. Thus, perturbed by the dislocation of community life occasioned by the industrial agglomeration of young workers in large towns, the Catholic Church has organized its own workers' movements—notably the *Jocistes* (Jeunesse Ouvrière Chrétienne)—which render signal service in countering the forces of disintegration. And in all of this the Church's position is made quite clear : newer techniques and approaches must not be allowed to supersede the binding forces of Church and family life.

So much for the general picture. We have already hinted that the U.S.A., a new country and a "synthetic" nation, is a striking example of how all the factors we have been separately discussing combine to determine the national outlook. It is also a country which, for a variety of reasons, has managed to shake off the binding forces of European tradition and to evolve its own pragmatic approach to contemporaneous problems. We cannot do better than end this chapter with a short, detailed analysis of how all this has come about, and with what results.

The U.S.A. The religious factor, of course, was a most important one in the early colonization of America, and in the first of the three distinct periods of growth of the American nation educational practice reflected the religious motives of the dominant class of the European emigrants. In general the Puritans who settled in the New England colonies insisted on the compulsory maintenance of schools, very much based on the English pattern, and they set up a combined religious and civil form of government. In 1642 and in 1647 laws were passed to make education for all compulsory. In an area like Pennsylvania, where no particular religious sect was in a majority, each denomination became responsible for its own church control of education and no general colonial action was called for. In Virginia and the southern colonies, where men came for gain rather than for religious freedom, the prevalent English pattern for the times was followed : the rich had private tutors in their own homes for their children or sent them to small private and select schools; the poor were catered for on an apprenticeship system and through the establishment of pauper schools. In no sense was there any thought of State interference. When by the eighteenth century there came a definite waning of the old religious interests, then did the idea of State institutions begin to take shape. For the North the general tendency was to modify considerably the existing pattern and to make it conform more closely with what was now the American way of life and thought. In the South the marked tendency was to allow all existing forms to fall into disuse.

The first period of colonization—that of expansion and development—was one in which the colonists expected to remain under the sovereign powers of the King of England and within the confines of the English colonial system. The colonists thought of themselves as free only in the direction of setting up a political and religious community in which their own particular religious beliefs would dominate. That they were often tyrannous because of their peculiar sectarian outlook does not here concern us. What does matter, though, is the influence this hardy and enterprising nucleus of colonists had in shaping the future of the whole country. For once they were embarked on the great adventure there was no turning back. The unknown had to be explored, overt and hidden dangers had to be faced, and the frontiers had to be pushed forward in an ever urgent quest for food and security. Though they built inevitably on their past experience, their new environment forced them to adapt themselves to the essential rootlessness of their existence. So the ties of tradition and of institutions and ideas linking them with Europe were gradually broken. And though the pioneer " guarded his school with meticulous care ... and was content to have the children know God ... he trained them by precept and example to labour in the affairs of practical life." [1] The integrity of purpose born of narrow religious ideals won the day and encouraged later generations, slowly at first but in rapidly increasing numbers as colonial expansion became a grim economic necessity in seventeeth-century England, to follow after.

So came the second period of colonial expansion which culminated in the breakaway from English rule and in the first primitive attempts at welding the various States into one. In this, the National Period as we may call it, dangers from Indians and from the French colonists were being successfully met and overcome. There were struggles and privations in plenty, but—as the land-hungry colonists swept down the western slopes of the Appalachians and as small primitive townships were set up—a sense of consolidation and of expansion was felt and ideas of equality and of progress were soon in men's minds. Again, the variety of activities in frontier fighting, the constant drumming drive west, and the real-life situations which had empirically to be solved gave rise to a flexibility and versatility in outlook and to an adaptability to constantly-changing circumstances that soon engendered a contempt for mere book-learning and academic training or intellectual pursuits. Life and experience were discovered as an ongoing process. Everything was in a process of change and growth, and therefore dynamic. Values could not exist in advance. The only theories of importance were those related closely to the immediate wants of Man. Education's job, therefore, was not to disclose the eternal verities but to define procedures whereby the learner might be placed in a position to develop his own values and to secure a better balance of interests through reconstructing his own experiences.

[1] *Culture and Education in America,* Harold Rugg. Harcourt Brace, New York, 1931, p. 55.

So it was that when the American Revolution came American political thought was very clear and definite about the true aims and ideals of the new democracy. Society was based on a contract agreed on by a group in their common interest. " Men being," wrote Locke, " by nature all free, equal and independent, no one can be put out of this estate and subjected to the political power of another without his consent." [1] Given the intransigent attitude of the Crown and the muddle-headed incompetence of the Crown's ministers in London, it is not difficult to understand in the light of this philosophy the hardening of the colonists' position, their refusal to recognize the Westminster Parliament as other than a local assembly, and the final decision taken to fight it out and break for ever the already weakened ties with the prevailing European outlook.

The nineteenth century heralded the third and in many respects the most important period of development for the new American nation. Overnight almost the American awoke bewilderedly to the fact that, after years of incessant toil and dangers spent in winning a meagre livelihood from an often unkindly soil, he was the natural inheritor of enormous mineral riches. Undreamed-of resources were his, and in abundance. The New World was to become a capitalist force on a gigantic scale that had to be reckoned with in all world markets. The mushroom growth of big towns and the vastness of industrial enterprises centred on the towns took the breath of owner, producer and consumer alike. A new buoyant optimism seized the imagination of the people. Surely all things now were possible! All that was needed was to streamline the mighty industrial machine into ever greater efficiency. As industry became more and more centralized, fewer and fewer men came to control the lives of millions of their fellow creatures. The aim of all the Babbitts [2] now being born was to become an industrial boss. The cosy home, family and motor-car became the watchword for the less ambitious. American dollars came to be valued more and more for what they would buy and for the security they could procure—for with industrial prosperity came also economic slumps and uncertainty about future employ-

---

[1] For a detailed account of the impact of Lockean philosophy on American life and culture consult *The Meeting of East and West*, F. S. C. Northrop. Macmillan, New York, 1946, Chapter III.
[2] Consult Sinclair Lewis' novel *Babbitt*.

ment. The American dollar sign became a mystic symbol of tangible success—the ladder by which, step by step, the American might reach for better because more material things. Onward, ever onward. A modernized version of the old pioneering desire to be moving to lands of greater promise.

The impact of all this in the educational field was enormous, though it was the character rather than the accepted structure of the educational machine that was most affected. The end of the American Civil War brought about a complete overthrow of the old social and industrial order and emphasized the imperative need for compulsory education to be considered as a public obligation and therefore to be paid for out of public funds. None the less, there was to be no form of centralization. Each of the separate States (to-day there are fifty) came to have its own Board of Education responsible to the legislative power of the State, and responsible for issuing general directives and programmes of education for the schools within the State, for the training of teachers, and for meeting roughly 30 per cent. of the total cost of education within the State. The rest of the money was to be found by the separate local education authorities of which, for the whole of the U.S.A., there are to-day some 18,000 varying greatly in size, population, wealth and efficiency. It is, therefore, the L.E.A. that determines more particularly the actual programme of studies and decides what salaries are to be paid. Thus—and this is a point to which we shall return in a later chapter—though in theory there is equality of educational opportunity throughout America, in practice there is inequality due to inequalities of educational provision.

Unparalleled progress, however, was made in organization, equipment and curriculum building, and a more essentially practical turn was given to the teaching which in spirit and philosophy came to reflect more and more the ideals of materialism and individualism. The last shreds of European culture for culture's sake vanished, and the economic motive prevailed. In a world of keen competition values could only exist in so far as they favourably or unfavourably affected the progress of the individual towards a given goal. The emphasis in all study, therefore, must be placed on practicality, on self expression, on spontaneity, on personality development. And so—in the opinion of many thoughtful Americans —was the fundamental idea of a liberal culture betrayed. America might have become the great laboratory for experiment in education as a result of its drive towards streamlined efficiency—but at a price.

And there we must leave the story. Our next concern must be to examine the nature and origin of some of the new education techniques that—trumpeted aloud in America and often fervently practised there—have been applied more recently in Western Europe in various ways in a serious attempt to overhaul the existing educational machine to cope with modern demands. There can be no doubt that we have learned a lot from observing the results of their application in America. There is equally no doubt that America can learn much from studying how the various European nations are carefully adjusting the application of the newer educational techniques to dovetail into the existing national cultural pattern.

CHAPTER FOUR

Education for Living

WE have seen how the new industrial demands that came with the nineteenth and twentieth centuries brought about generally a considerable weakening of the traditional disciplines in a given culture pattern, how they proved a challenge to the accepted culture pattern of the nation concerned, and how a new social conscience, arising from the new democratic groupings caused by migration from town to country, led to an increasing demand for popular education and to a broadening of the school curriculum in keeping with the changing economic situation. We have also noted how the U.S.A. stands out as the one country to implement and develop to the full a " new " education programme well in advance of any other programme in operation in any of the Western European countries, and how the pragmatist approach to educational problems at all levels has turned the U.S.A. into a kind of huge laboratory for experiments of all kinds in educational practice and techniques. It would be wrong, however, either to consider the U.S.A. as the forerunner of the many developments that have taken place recently in Western Europe, or to imagine that the " new " (or progressive) education movement as such in Europe dates from the idealism and scientific realism that were so much in evidence towards the end of the last century. True, the nations of Western Europe have studied in great detail the achievements in education in the U.S.A., as they have hailed the pioneer work of Madame Montessori (and several others) as an important step forward in establishing in Europe the newer techniques. But the mainsprings of present-day action, in Europe at any rate, lie far deeper than that, as we shall presently see.

The " new " education principles of good teaching can briefly be summarized as follows : (a) respect for the child as an individual and as a unique person; (b) emphasis on child initiative and child responsibility; (c) experience as the basis of the curriculum; (d) activity methods in the classroom leading to the gearing of the child's creative ability to the learning process; (e) all teaching to be based on a close study of child psychology; (f) friendly and unstrained pupil, teacher and parent relationships. We can sum up the whole aim in the phrase " education for living," a phrase which implies that education must be much more than the communication of a certain body of knowledge and skills. For there are very definite social implications. Education henceforward must not concentrate solely on the perpetuation of the approved culture pattern but must also deliberately prepare children for social responsibility and to meet the challenge of the times by being made constantly and acutely aware of what the challenge is and where it can lead. As John Dewey put it, education becomes the means for assuring the social continuity of life, and " continuity of life means continual readaptation of the environment to the needs of living organisms." Education is not preparation for life, it is life itself.

All this is not new. When Thomas Arnold in England reorganized Rugby School and introduced his prefectorial system he was, in his own way, teaching boys how to live in a community and hoping thereby to educate them later to be good adult members of the larger world of life beyond the school. His views run counter to Dewey's in that he believed that the boy who has learned to be a good schoolboy will become a good citizen; Dewey maintains that the schoolboy is a citizen already and that the school should therefore be democratically organized to allow him to practice good citizenship from within the school. Both are emphatic in their belief that education does not simply consist of book learning. And both, in their own individual ways, insist on what has come to be termed in popular educational jargon " a child-centred approach." Yet again, however, all this goes back—no matter in how primitive and imperfect a form—at least as far as Rabelais and Montaigne.

What we have to remember is that as long as a society of people has a stable and secure economy, then those educational principles and practices which have helped secure and maintain that economy will be perpetuated. A Rabelais or a Montaigne may with a rare vision well ahead of the times urge changes. He will be heeded only when the necessity for change becomes economically imperative. And when the people are ripe for change, they will then draw on the accumulated and often neglected wisdom of the past, extend and develop it, and bring it to full flowering always strictly in keeping with their character.

The early American colonizers drew their inspiration from the writings of Locke and Rousseau, but, having of necessity to throw away all traditional ties with Europe and to develop their own peculiarly empirical approach, they soon struck out on a highly individualistic line of their own which put them well in the vanguard of reform. The English had a stable economy which served them well, and a respect for tradition. They were therefore more cautious and only slowly implemented changes as the ideas of free and compulsory primary education established themselves. The French, still more cautious—for they had a clearly defined and highly centralized system of education which more than adequately met all needs—waited in effect until the late 1930's before they made any significant changes and contemplated others. So too did the Belgians, their programme for reform dating only from 1936 and being implemented only after the last war. It should also be noted that neither in England, France or Belgium is it possible to say that the traditional methods of instruction, as opposed to the methods of the " new " education have been entirely banished.

They have not been banished because it is realized that, whilst modern findings in the field of child psychology must radically alter so much of teaching techniques and methods of approach, the older methods make for a sound discipline and help to a tremendous extent to perpetuate the culture pattern. The culture pattern of America depends on the empirical approach and therefore demands full implementation and even a constant extension of the " new " education ideas [1]; Western Europe still has a marked traditional outlook. Again, it would be wrong to assume that traditional forms ignored child psychology, or that the " new " education has become the handmaid of psychology, or is entirely based on a study of child psychology. The marked difference between the two approaches is that the traditionalists have always tended to think in terms of docility and malleability of the child, whilst the " new " educationists think of the child as a growing individual, a unique personality who must be given every opportunity to de-

1 " When we get down to any sort of description of a progressive school, we find that the school has soon progressed beyond our description. . . . Progressive education has no fixed creed. . . . It is alive and growing." *Schools Aren't What They Were*, Carleton Washburne. Heinemann, 1953, p. 73.

velop all his latent talent towards the greater good of a progressive democratic community. Traditional forms of instruction put a premium on knowledge and thus—from the "new" educationist's point of view—give inadequate consideration to personality problems. The child is expected to be quiet and receptive rather than active and expressive. Education is looked upon mainly as a preparation for adult life and is therefore never as "child-centred" as the new educationists would have it. We must not forget, however, that the traditional approach lays great stress on the development of a moral personality in its pupils, demands exactness and precision of thought, and seeks to develop such valuable habits as effort, industry, tidiness and punctuality.

Of course, the "new" education starts as a revolt against the stupid abuse of the traditional approach and—as we have already observed—finds its early echoes in Rabelais and Montaigne, its first really serious exponent in Comenius, its philosopher in John Locke (though it must be remembered that Locke was thinking all the time in terms of the education of the English gentleman), its romantic idealist in Rousseau, its first doughty champions at the people's level in Condillac (1715–80) and Condorcet (1743–94). The interesting fact is that the first real impetus comes from France, and that the first exponents of the new approach are the products of the traditional Jesuit system of teaching.

"The degree of equality in education that we can reasonably hope to attain," writes Condorcet, "is that which excludes all dependence, either forced or voluntary. . . . We shall prove that, by a suitable choice of syllabus and methods of education, we can teach the citizen... to be able to manage his household, administer his affairs and employ his labours and his faculties in freedom; to know his rights and to be able to exercise them... not to be in a state of blind dependence upon those to whom he must trust his affairs or the exercise of his rights." Similarly Condillac—some sixteen years before the publication of Rousseau's *Emile*—wrote his *Essay on the Origins of the Human Understanding* (1746) in which he sought scientific detachment from mere metaphysical speculation and argued that the mind was an intricate and complicated machine of many interdependent functions.

But it is now time to pull together the threads of the argument. In the development of the ideas of progressive education three distinct trends are to be noted : a romantic-mystical trend typified by Rousseau; a philosophical trend, merging later with the new psychological approach and stemming from Condorcet through to Dewey and Stanley Hall; a scientific trend based on applied psychology and experimental education, originating with Condillac and leading through Binet and Simon to the modern laboratory of psychological testings of all kinds, to child guidance clinics and psycho-medical centres. Naturally, none of these three trends developed independently of the others. In Western Europe, however, they can distinctly be observed as uniting most strongly and together clamouring loudest for reforms in terms of their findings immediately after the 1914–18 war.[1] It is then that the eloquent plea for the *école unique* (a common school) is formulated, that the *Ligue Internationale de l'Education Nouvelle* is founded at Calais (1921), that the work of the Belgian Dr. Decroly and of Madame Montessori takes on a special significance, and that much earlier pioneer work as exemplified in certain progressive schools is justly appraised and publicized.

The romantic-mystical trend. According to Mme. de Stael, Jean-Jacques Rousseau said nothing new but he set everything on fire. And it is to him that we owe the *mystique*, the romantic outpouring of ideas that were to effect in the educational sphere a kind of Copernican revolution anterior to and comparable with that effected by Kant in the domain of philosophy. Rousseau's approach is the intuitive one, and feeling (not reason) is in effect the mainspring for all his arguments, notwithstanding his reiterated statement that "sentiments divide people, reason unites them." Thus the picture he gives us of the ideal man is more than anything else a nostalgic regret for his own wasted opportunities (real or imagined), and it depicts in effect the kind of man he would have liked to be (and would have us become) rather than the kind of man he really was. His educational doctrines are based neither on observed practice nor are they drawn from reminiscences of his own childhood. Nor can it be claimed for him that he was in any sense a psychologist, as was John Locke, for example. He sensed the need for a systematic psychological approach, but he was incapable of formulating even the first principles.

For Rousseau, liberty is the important issue, and there can be no

[1] Many educational changes are at least accelerated if not caused by wars and by the revelation of social conditions made in war. It is no accident that the great developments of English education in 1902, 1918 and 1944 occurred under stress of war.

compromise possible and no renouncement of it in any direction. Indeed, to renounce liberty is to cease to be a man. Betraying his Calvinistic origins (and in a sense foreshadowing the Kantian definition of *a priori* knowledge as having the two important characteristics of universality and necessity), Rousseau goes on to claim that there are definite laws and rules of life that are inherent in man and that must not be betrayed or vitiated by social trappings and conventions if the good life is to be led. He then formulates his doctrine of the Social Contract, produces the paradoxical idea that if man voluntarily gives himself to all then he gives himself to nobody and so preserves intact his freedom, argues that those who are free will *know* what they want and that if we are all living in harmony then what I truly want another will truly want also, and concludes that the man who is rational will only seek ends others seek, and that if all men were natural the world would all be good because all men would be truly rational. " Everything is good as it comes from the hands of the Author of Nature; but everything degenerates in the hands of man."

From the purely pedagogical angle, Rousseau's importance lies first in the fact that he recognized (as did Plato) that any reform of an existing order of things must be based on a reform in educational techniques and procedure; secondly, in that he attacked the prevalent mania for bookish instruction and made an eloquent plea that the child should be educated for life by being made to cope with real life situations at his level—*l'école pour la vie par la vie*, as Dr. Decroly later more tersely phrased it; thirdly, in that he focused attention on the successive stages in the development of the child; fourthly, in that he reduced the role of the teacher to that of inspirer and not of dictator; fifthly, in that he insisted on the necessity for a close study of the child in order properly to guide him; and lastly, in that he laid great stress on the value of a sound moral education to be acquired by practice and not by precept and copybook maxims.

Naturally such bold innovations that threatened the established order of things could not for a moment be heeded in France where the Archbishop of Paris was moved to condemn *Emile* as containing " an abominable doctrine, ready to subvert natural law and to destroy the foundations of the Christian religion, setting up maxims contrary to the morality of the Gospels . . . erroneous, impious, blasphemous and heretical." Nor could the secular philosophers, steeped as they were in Cartesian thought and in highly abstract speculation, really favour this intuitive approach. It was left to educators in Switzerland and Germany—notably to Pestalozzi, Froebel and Basedow—to attempt to work out in actual practice and with varying results the theories Rousseau preached with such convincing ardour.

So, gradually, the principle of self-activity on the part of the child established itself. In Germany, Basedow attached great importance to the place of manual work and of gardening in the school curriculum of his curiously designed *Philanthropinum*. In Switzerland, Pestalozzi and Froebel laid great stress on agricultural and gardening pursuits, on a non-bookish approach, and on the principle of direct observation of natural laws of cause and effect. Pestalozzi claimed that intuition and the intuitive approach were *le fondement absolu de toute connaissance*. Froebel made a lasting reputation for himself by introducing educational play into schools for young children.

The most fervent disciple of Rousseau, however, proved to be the Russian novelist Tolstoy, who brought to the doctrines Rousseau had preached a Slav mysticism that tended to go much further than Rousseau seems to have contemplated. As the French novelist Romain-Rolland remarks, Rousseau and Tolstoy have none the less one important bond in common : they were both representatives of an ultra-refined civilization which led them both to become uncompromising apostles of a return to nature. According to Tolstoy, no one has the right to educate the child : he will educate himself, given the correct surroundings. Unlike Rousseau, Tolstoy did open (in 1858) his model school and attempt to put his ideas into practice. But his school remained simply a house into which were gathered children who knew that teachers were available to help them learn and master what they desired to learn and master as they felt inclined. Enjoying the blessings of total liberty, Tolstoy's children would not learn useless things such as history or geography, but would develop their own latent talents by all kinds of personal activities, and notably by free, creative literary expression. Left to themselves (Tolstoy maintained) children are capable of real appreciation of poetry, music, literature and art. And they will best learn this necessary appreciation by themselves becoming creators. Love and respect for the child and his growing personality, and a firm belief in educating him far from the corrupting influences of town and artificial social life—back to nature, in other words—are the main tenets of the Tolstoy creed. These ideas of Tolstoy find their echo in A. S. Neill's school. It is also interesting to note that the idea of a country life together with an emphasis on agricultural pursuits is predominant in the founding of Cecil Reddie's school at Abbotsholme in Derbyshire in 1889, in the *Landerziehungsheime* of Hermann Lietz in Germany, and in several other progressive schools founded in various parts of Western Europe towards the end of the last century.

The dominant idea of creative self-expression was taken far beyond the vague fumblings of Tolstoy by the Czech, Franz Cizek, in the field of art; by the American, Satis Coleman, for music; by the Swiss, Dalcroze, through his invention of eurhythmics. Cizek created quite a stir in Vienna in 1897 with his school for child art about which he declared modestly that "it is not I but the children who have founded the school." Mrs. Coleman published her *Creative Music for Children* in 1924, argued that music was for all and not for the talented few, and placed constantly the emphasis on the child's growth and self-release through music rather than on a consideration of music as an art.

The Dalcroze method, of course, stems back to Athenian education and calls attention to the interrelationship of music and rhythmic bodily development. Dalcroze believes—along with many modern psychologists—that muscles and nerves are co-ordinated, and that in the balanced person body and mind are harmonized. Only when a child's body, mind and emotions are under control can he grow in an integrated way. The body, argues Dalcroze, is to be likened to a musical instrument which can best be served through rhythmics and their handmaiden, music. "Rhythmics aims at the bodily representation of musical values." It is interesting to note that within the last few decades, in almost every country without exception, there have been radical changes in the approach to the teaching of art and music in schools along lines similar to those suggested by these innovators; that these subjects have been given a more prominent and important position on the school timetable, particularly in countries like France and Belgium; and that even dance and eurhythmics are slowly if grudgingly finding a place.

The philosophical trend. Obviously, the ideas expounded and advanced "intuitively" in these several ways could never have reached their fullness of expression without the concurrence of the philosophical trend which has tried to systematize the whole and to provide a logical, reasoned and scientific (psychological) basis for further development. Two outstanding thinkers in this field are the Americans Stanley Hall and John Dewey. Neither of these men can be said to subscribe in any way to the Rousseau idea of childhood as the golden age of humanity. What they do, in their different ways, is to note that the human has a much longer period of infancy—when he is dependent for protection on his elders— than does any other member of the animal kingdom, and to conclude that this long period is the vital one in making for the fullest possible development of the human. Thus Stanley Hall the biologist claims that throughout infancy the child is recapitulating in his own play and activities the past stages in the evolutionary growth and development of man, and that this recapitulatory activity is a necessary and vital part of the educative process. No matter how outwardly polite and charming the young boy might appear because of the veneer of good manners and correct social behaviour he has had thrust upon him, he is at heart a savage and needs to be able to live this out healthily and unthwarted. So, for Stanley Hall also, it is necessary that the child should live as long as possible in the country and be able to satisfy those primitive urgings to hunt and to fish, to seek adventure and to " gang up " in various primitive group communities. His school work proper will, in the first instance, be restricted to the acquisition of the basic tools—reading, writing and arithmetic.

John Dewey, a product of the best of the American schooling of the mid-nineteenth century, was a pragmatist and an experimentalist who held that the task of philosophy was not to find out how we know the world but rather how we can control and improve it. His teachings and writings gave full expression to the American " frontier " spirit, and they also came at the time when America was dazedly adjusting herself to cope with the untold mineral and commercial wealth that was hers and learning to cope with the boom and slump periods in economic affairs that were an inevitable result. In consequence, Dewey influenced profoundly the whole of the theory and practice of education in America and was much in vogue in Europe in the period between the two wars for not dissimilar reasons.

Dewey's main thesis—closely and fully, if rather dully argued—

is that life is a self-renewing process " through action upon environment." [1] Nothing is fixed and nothing is permanent, the universe
itself being in a state of flux. Man therefore, if he is to survive,
must struggle to control the process of change, and all he can rely
on in his struggle is his creative intelligence. " Society exists
through a process of transmission quite as much as biological life,"
and education therefore, in its broadest sense, " is the means of
this social continuity of life."

Thus the school is not a preparation for life, but life itself.
Learning by doing must be the keynote, and the ideal school must
be an active, dynamic society in which the child learns through his
experiences. Also, because education is a social process, then the
school must be a democratic community, and the school's chief
function is to make of education a continuous reconstruction of
accumulated experience. " The scheme of a curriculum must take
account of the adaptation of studies to the needs of the existing
community life; it must select with the intention of improving the
life we live in common so that the future shall be better than the
past. Moreover, the curriculum must be planned with reference to
placing essentials first, and refinements second. The things which
are socially most fundamental, that is, which have to do with the
experiences in which the widest groups share, are the essentials."
However, though the teacher may propose what the child is to
learn, it is the learner himself who disposes of it. The teaching,
therefore, must constantly grow out of the child's interests, and the
child must select to suit his needs in the changing world that is
about him. Finally, as it is only by his creative intelligence that
man can hope to be master of his environment, then the school
must carefully encourage creativity, and guide and control it, without using coercion, so that it is not put to haphazard and wasteful
use. Here, there is a very close affinity with the techniques worked
out in some detail by Dr. Decroly which we shall discuss later.

In his experimental school which he opened in Chicago in 1896,
Dewey placed (like Stanley Hall) an emphasis on the early activities of civilized man and introduced weaving, pottery, cooking and
manual work of all kinds. He also announced that the primary
root of all educative activity lay in the instinctive and impulsive

[1] *Democracy and Education*, first published in 1916, is Dewey's classic
work, and should be consulted. The quotations on this page are from the 1930
edition published by Macmillan, New York.

attitudes and activities of the child. In all this there is a definite link with Sanderson and his experiments in Oundle School. There is also an interesting comparative study to be made between the Dewey out-and-out pragmatic approach and the Sandersonian method which still believes strongly (and in the best English tradition) in the value of imparting the accumulated wisdom and culture of past ages. "In this school," says Sanderson speaking of Oundle, "we do not believe in suppression. We must seek out the thing that is good, the desire to grow and to give life and service. This desire we believe is the fundamental creative instinct. We must nurse this desire. . . . We may drive a boy to do what we want but we do not thereby make him a creative soul. We make him a creative soul by giving freedom and light to his own will."[1]

Adolphe Ferrière, who founded in Geneva in 1899 the International Bureau of New Schools, also accepted the theory of Stanley Hall of a parallelism between the development of the individual and the evolution of the human race, agreed with Dewey that life must be a process of continuous growth, embraced Bergson's concept of *élan vital,* and advocated strongly activity methods. Claparède, another Swiss, stressed the necessity for fitting the syllabus to the needs and interests of the child and formulated in so doing his five famous laws: (*a*) *the law of genetic succession* which implies that the child passes naturally through a certain number of stages of development that succeed one another in a constant order; (*b*) *the law of functional-genetic exercise* which states that the exercise of a function is a necessary condition of a child's development and also a necessary condition for the later maturing of other necessary functions; (*c*) *the law of functional adaptation* which claims that action results only when it is necessary to the child's immediate needs and interests—*Pour faire agir un individu, il faut le placer dans les conditions propres à faire naître le besoin que l'action que l'on désire susciter a pour fonction de satisfaire;* (*d*) *the law of functional autonomy* which argues that the child must not be considered an imperfect or an unformed being : he is a creature adapted to the circumstances in which he finds himself—his mental activity is in proportion to his needs and his mental life is thus, within his environment, whole and complete;

---

[1] *Sanderson of Oundle,* Anon. Chatto and Windus, 1926, p. 215. Thring of Uppingham, of course, was the pioneer in extending the interest of the school to all forms of art and craftsmanship.

(e) *the law of individuality* which claims the uniqueness of each individual on both physical and physiological grounds.

In many ways, however, one of the most significant of the European philosophers and educators was Georg Kerschensteiner (1859–1932). His fame resides mainly in the practical application of his philosophical principles to the reorganization of the school system of Munich, and in particular of the continuation schools. By 1895, when after many years as a practical teacher he was appointed school superintendent for Munich, he had a very clear idea of what he wanted. A firm disciple of Kant, he held with Kant that man is the only creature capable of education, and by education he meant the care and attention due to the child in his infancy, the discipline required to make of him a man, and a systematized form of instruction that initiated the young adolescent to a system of values and made him constantly strive to reach a still higher stage of culture. The objective is to make for a cultured community through stressing the value of individuality and of the cultured individual. The type of education envisaged must be the joint concern of home and school, but the school should not " intellectualize " the curriculum and so make its culture content arid. The child must be an active and a willing participant, for " character is only developed through action " and " if the formation of character is the ultimate end of education then the best school organization is that which gives character opportunity for development." The most valuable thing we can give a pupil is not knowledge but a salutary way of acquiring knowledge and an independent way of action.

Kerschensteiner took the continuation school system of Munich and in the space of two short years had effected radical transformations which won the willing support and active co-operation of employer, teacher and townsfolk generally. It should be noted that one of the outstanding features of German education since as far back as the eighteenth century has been the importance attached throughout all the *Länder* to a period of post-primary training for all those who were not embarking on a course of secondary education proper. By introducing his *Arbeitsschule* (activity schools) in 1912, Kerschensteiner made it possible for attendance at a continuation school to be made compulsory (in theory at any rate) in 1914 throughout the whole of Germany.

The first aim of education for those leaving the primary school was for Kerschensteiner " the development of trade efficiency and love of work, and with this the development of those elementary virtues which effectiveness and love of work immediately call forth—conscientiousness, diligence, perseverance, responsibility, self-restraint and dedication to a strenuous life. In close connexion with this the second aim must be pursued : to gain an insight into the relations of individuals to one another and to the State, to understand the laws of health, and to employ the knowledge acquired in the exercise of self-control, justice, and devotion to duty, and in leading a sensible life tempered with a strong feeling of personal responsibility." [1] Again, Kerschensteiner felt strongly that " a man's strongest emotions are always connected with his attainment of the practical ends of life, and if we foster such feelings in a pupil we can win his confidence and make him take pride in his work. And when once this is accomplished, we can make of him not only an efficient hand worker, but a good man and a useful citizen." [2]

The claim is often made that Kerschensteiner drew much of his inspiration from the writings of Dewey. It would in my view be more correct to say that Kerschensteiner recognized quite early that Dewey and he were thinking independently along similar lines, that he valued greatly Dewey's insistence on democracy being regarded as a way of associated living that develops the personality through correctly fostered relationships between the individual and the group, but that he also realized that the practical application of such doctrines as he shared in common with Dewey must of necessity differ in Western Europe from that possible in a new and vitally " rootless " country like the U.S.A. Again, Kerschensteiner is a German reared on Kantian German idealism and a firm upholder of man's duty and all this implies as a loyal member of his *Land* and as a good German.

The scientific trend. So we come to what we may term the final period, that of the development of experimental psychology and of the study of child psychology. Such an approach became increasingly necessary as the idea took hold that all true education must concern itself with the personality and development of the child as a unique personality in his social setting. Neither Rousseau nor his disciples in various lands were psychologists in the accepted

---

[1] *Education for Citizenship*, Kerschensteiner. Harrap, 1915, p. 51.
[2] *The Schools and the Nation*, Kerschensteiner. Macmillan, 1914, p. xx.

scientific sense of the term. Dewey adopted a mixed sociological and psychological approach. So did Kerschensteiner. And the early success of the practitioners of the *mystique* of the new education was due in the main to an intuitive as opposed to a scientific grasp of basic psychological principles. In the U.S.A., however, William James strengthened the position of Dewey with his (psychological) " Talks to Teachers." In France the sociologist Emile Durkheim stressed that no educational system can be an artificial creation of the human imagination, but that its roots are in the history of the people and that it can only satisfactorily be understood by an understanding of man in his social setting. And in France also, whilst Bergson was elaborating his theory of *L'Evolution Créatrice*, Binet (between 1905 and 1911) was devising his scale for the measurement of intelligence. With Binet, experimental psychology was born, and research into child psychology began. Latterly, with the Swiss psychologist Jean Piaget, we have an attempt to show that in the correct social environment the child will spontaneously feel the need to move towards the right kind of self-discipline that is required by man in his social setting. The more the child's individuality is respected— and the more therefore the techniques of the educative process respect his individuality—the more fully will the child be fitted to become an active contributive member of modern society.

Two outstanding names associated with the new psychological movement are those of Madame Montessori and Dr Decroly, both of whom started out their professional life as physicians, and both of whom applied their educational principles in the first instance to the problems of the educability of the mentally defective child. Madame Montessori holds that freedom for the child is essentially biological, his chief requisite during growth being the absence of interference. The only worthwhile education for her is what she calls " auto-education," and she lays special stress on sense and muscle training. Special didactic materials are devised for use in the Montessori school, and the child selects the activity that interests him, working at it without interference. There are definite periods, claims Madame Montessori, in the development of each child. The didactic material is arranged in a systematic sequence to suit these periods. Should a child fail to achieve the desired result with any piece of material that is a sure sign that he is not yet ready to take the next step forward. Gymnastic training is used to make for harmonious development of the whole of the motor mechanisms. Manual work includes pottery and building exercises, and gardening and simple domestic chores also figure on the programme of work. One of the few disciplines imposed on the child is turned into a kind of game : this is a silence period during which the child learns to control his movements by remaining quiet and with closed eyes.

There have been many critics of the Montessori system, and it is mainly attacked for its rigid and somewhat artificial methods of approach. None the less it must be remembered that Madame Montessori made a decisive step forward in proving that the mentally deficient child needs the right kind of education rather than medical treatment, that rapid and sure progress can be made when the child is allowed to be freely active and when the teaching is "functional," and that under modern conditions (when the mother is so often out at work) then the school can make good the deficiencies of lack of prolonged education at the mother's knee. It should also be remembered that in extending her method to the teaching of normally intelligent children, Madame Montessori was catering for poor children in tenement buildings in Rome between the ages of three and seven who conspicuously lacked early maternal care. In her own words, the *Casa dei Bambini*, or Children's House, was designed to " communize the maternal functions."

Dr. Decroly's influence has in many ways been much greater if only because it has embraced the whole education of the child through to university entrance, and because his basic principles (particularly for learning to read and to write) have been largely adopted throughout the whole of the primary school system of Belgium (his native country), have influenced to a great degree the post-war outlook of the primary school in France, and have been " borrowed "—not always with acknowledgments—by education-ists in other countries. He began by interesting himself in the problems raised by the education of the mentally defective child, but the striking results he obtained in this direction led him six years later (in 1907) to open his *Ecole de l'Hermitage*, a co-educational school taking pupils at all ages from the nursery school level to university entrance—that is, from three to eighteen. Decroly's disciples still carry on the school (Decroly died in 1932), Mlle. Hamaïde—the principal assistant and lifelong friend of Decroly—

opened her own Decroly schools on parallel lines (but only at the primary level), and the original school for educationally subnormal children still flourishes.

Decroly always insisted that he was not an inventor, but that he tested out ideas in the laboratory of experience, and to-day it is still stressed that the Decroly method is one of principles rather than one of rules. It is evolutionary, and the method of yesterday is not necessarily the one of to-day, nor of to-morrow. It is not one of dogmatic teaching, but a method which adapts itself to the psychology of the child and his ever-changing environment. Psychological observation of the child is therefore of paramount importance. On a basis of such close psychological observation over a large number of years, Decroly finally elaborated five guiding principles for the satisfactory running of a Decroly school:

(1) The child is a living organism which must be prepared for social living. Hence, education must be for life by living. *L'école pour la vie par la vie.*

(2) The child is a living, growing whole. Every moment marks growth, and at every age the child is different.

(3) Children of the same age differ considerably from one another.

(4) Certain interests are peculiar to each age, and these govern the child's mental activities.

(5) The child's most important activity is motor. Motor activities properly encouraged and controlled by the intellect are necessarily associated with all other activities.

With all this must go an elaborate system of pupil-parent-teacher liaison. From each group of children two representatives are chosen to sit on a central committee which discusses the entire arrangements to be made for the school. This committee meets once a month under the chairmanship of a pupil elected by the whole school, but who must be from a top class. The parents meet with the staff twice a term to discuss their children's problems. Finally, as it is *their* school, the children work for its upkeep, maintenance and general repair. They also run their own workshops and a printing press.

Decroly again concluded that it was indispensable in the educative process to tie together the following activities:

(a) *Observation*, which puts the child in contact with the

material world. Thus there are many pets and domestic
animals and birds in the school, and from the earliest
days there are simple biological studies, observations of
the weather, seasons, etc.

(b) *Association in time and space*, which links knowledge
acquired through observation with more abstract ideas
and helps the understanding of history and geography.

(c) *Expression work* to translate these ideas into action, words
and forms.

To maintain the necessary functional unity of all the various
mechanisms of mind, Decroly adopted as a teaching technique the
principle of centres of interest, but—because the most important
things to be known concern the child himself—the centres of
interest are always based on the child's needs : the need for food,
the need for protection against the elements, the need for defence
against enemies, the need for play, work, rest.

In actual practice, what happens is that until the age of 8
teaching is based absolutely upon the child's own activities and
interests, the teacher watching for interests to emerge or providing
the situations wherein they may emerge and thereafter following
the child's inclinations. After the age of 8, maintains Decroly,
interests naturally direct themselves in the child towards things
social, and prolonged concentration develops. Between the ages
of 8 and 12, therefore, there are guided centres of interest, each of
the four basic needs of the child being taken in turn year by year,
this cyclical study being bound up with social training. From 12
to 16, similar cyclical studies are continued, but becoming more
social in emphasis and more concerned with abstract ideas. At this
stage, one-third of the time is given to synthesizing various topics
previously explored and grouping them for the first time under
their appropriate subject headings. From 16 to 18 the course is
still integrated with a main cycle of interest, but special emphasis
is now placed on preparing the child for the career of his choice,
according to proved aptitude.

The global method of teaching reading that Decroly advocated
has been almost exclusively adopted throughout the State primary
school system of Belgium. Decroly's theory briefly is that, whilst
normally it is expected that the child will want to move from the
simple to the more complex, the contrary is true of learning to read.

Thus in a Decroly school the child is presented with simple sentences related to an action he is performing or an observation he has made. He reiterates these simple sentences, sees them written up on a board, copies them into his own book, and thus gradually builds up his classroom reader. Only when he has " globally " understood does he feel the need to break down a sentence into its isolated words, and later the words into letters. The children are further encouraged in this method by the use of hand printing sets for them to set up their own readers in type on a basis of their own original compositions. By the same token, textbooks in the various subjects taught are *tabu* : each pupil is made responsible for compiling his own *livre de la vie*, the work of both individuals and of groups being of course fully discussed in advance and carefully planned in collaboration with the teacher.

There have naturally been many more experimenters, working along not dissimilar lines, whose achievements we have no space to record here without resorting to a dreary cataloguing of names. For us the essential is to note that all the varied new doctrines and experiments are in effect a criticism of existing conditions as found in the various countries concerned : an over-intellectualized curriculum, lack of real understanding of the child as a whole and as a unique personality, inadequate attention being paid to character training in the schools, and a lamentable failure to educate the child in terms of the changing social scene so that he can be of his *milieu* (without being dominated by it) and remain an individual capable of initiating desirable change. In a world of constantly shifting values it is dangerous to allow the educational pattern to remain too static and uncompromising in outlook. When man is being increasingly shown as capable of most things, then educational effort must match this capacity.

The English Education Act of 1944 and the post-war reforms initiated in the various Western European countries have tried in several ways to ease the way administratively for the better implementation of a newer approach, and also acknowledge that changed and changing social conditions demand a radical overhaul of existing machinery. The four outstanding characteristics of modern society that make change imperative are : the development of the sciences, the consequent demand for higher technical skills in industry, the development of bigger and bigger industrial enterprises, and the complete breakdown of the old distinctions between a governing élite and the working masses. The problem thus becomes one of evolving an educational approach that has due regard for national characteristics whilst educating all, irrespective of rank or fortune, as individuals, to play a full part both technically and politically in the welfare of the State. The old divorce between a liberal and a technical education can no longer exist. Man must rise above both and harmonize both in himself and through himself. Agreed, the present age belongs to science and to scientific and technical pursuits, but if we once lose the idea of man's supreme importance and fail to keep our education humanistic in character and outlook—if, in other words, we forget that man is essentially free and creative and responsible—then we become indeed the slave of this technical age and not its master.

All contemporary societies are preoccupied with this problem. Generally speaking, Anglo-Saxon countries follow the traditional line of continued stressing of the importance of human connexions and contacts, of freedom, and of individual initiative and responsibility—though they have come increasingly to see the danger of a too fluid society degenerating into a homogeneous mass that must lead inevitably to some form of totalitarianism. Totalitarian countries throughout the world are in this sense a timely warning. Countries like France and Belgium which have for centuries recognized the importance to them of the formation of an intellectual élite—in fact the Roman Catholic countries generally—are working out a compromise and a synthesis of the older and newer approaches. The Scandinavian countries are in the happiest position in that geographical circumstances have in the main forced them to organize their whole existence and economy on a basis of small groups, and to maintain their fluidity on such an intimate basis that the inevitable growing activity of the State, the redistribution of power among the social classes, and the changes in occupational patterns are for them not the major problems that other countries must face. Thus the Scandinavian countries can also be said to be a timely example in that they stress to us the importance of the small group which—possibly too much under the influence of Dewey and his idea of a fluid society with people freely intermingling—we have tended to underestimate or to disregard under the increasing pressure of events.

May it not be—as the French Catholic philosopher Gustave Thibon repeatedly asserts—that in this atomic age we are in danger of atomizing ourselves? That in seeking to centralize and so better co-ordinate human effort we do not pause sufficiently to reflect on man's nature and his primary needs? That we forget that man is made neither for solitude nor for multitude, but to live in small communities, his roots in the family and his sense of fellowship arising from undertaking tasks in common with those with whom he is intimately associated?

It will pay us to keep these ideas constantly in mind as we now proceed to consider in some detail the various problems of the organization and administration of education in the various countries with whose peculiar outlook and way of life we are growing familiar.

CHAPTER FIVE

Variant Aims in Education

" The aim of education is to lift the mind out of blind alleys."
—H. G. WELLS.

" Education is the transmission of life by the living to the
living."—THRING.

" . . . securing for everyone the conditions under which
individuality is most completely developed."—NUNN.

" . . . the process of training the industry of man, in its manifold varieties, and in its organized totality, to the highest pitch
of excellence it is capable of attaining."—JACKS.

IT should now be clear that not only is the problem of education
a new one for each succeeding generation, but also that the
various social systems of the European nations as a whole were
more than ripe for change as the last two world wars swept across
them. Again (as we have already seen) the effective agents in this
preparation for change have been: the growth of science; the
growth of invention; the growth of industrial organization; the
extension of education; and an imperative demand for equality of
opportunity for all. There has also been a steady but determined
move towards the idea of an education which will apply to the
whole man : body, intellect, emotion, imagination. In this respect
the twentieth century has heralded the conscious application to
matters educational of our new knowledge of human behaviour, of
child development, of cultural anthropology and of sociology. And
in actual practice not only has the whole field of education (including child welfare) been under review, but close attention has also
been paid to personnel relationships in industry, to community
organization, to government administrative practices, and to the
content of mass media instruction. Our main purpose in this
present chapter will be to show that, as different styles and manners
of thinking are distributed amongst the nations, so are there
different methods of approach adopted towards problems that are

common to all the nations : problems concerning the vast extension of educational facilities that are being planned in all countries without exception; problems concerning the demand for equality of educational opportunity for all; problems concerning the relation of education to society.

For it is evident that education is part of a greater whole and cannot act in independence of it. All life is education, and—as Aldous Huxley pertinently reminds us—" life is a whole and desirable changes in one department will not produce the results anticipated from them unless they are accompanied by desirable changes in all other departments." [1] Education is a part of life which is deliberately controlled, and in which experiences are developed according to a conscious plan. That is to say, the pattern of education is determined by the needs of society as a whole, and that society—no matter how willingly receptive it may be to the ideas of the educational philosophers—cannot wait for the results of philosophical speculation (always changing and always mutually antagonistic) to crystallize themselves out into a conscious programme that can be faithfully applied to serve immediate needs and interests and to meet the challenge of the times. The State must have a dogmatic philosophy and must act upon it, a philosophy which confidently affirms something definite about the origin, the destiny, and the nature of man, and which provides a broad and sure basis for the elaboration of an educational system that will meet to the fullest all the demands the State is impelled to put upon it.

None the less, though because of all this we expect the aims of education to differ from country to country, we must acknowledge —as far as the U.S.A. and the democracies of Western Europe are concerned—that there is a certain common core factor of educational aims typified by what we might describe as Conservatism, Education for Citizenship and Education for Christian Salvation. By the conservative aim we mean an attempt at the conservation and perpetuation of the funded capital of past experience, the assurance of cultural continuity. Education for citizenship implies a firm belief in the democratic way of life and argues that the educational programme shall prepare all future citizens of a given State to play a full and active and responsible part in shaping and controlling the future of that State. Education for Christian salva-

[1] *Ends and Means*, Aldous Huxley. Chatto and Windus, 1948, p. 179.

tion affirms a belief in a way of life which, whilst by no means basing itself on the tenets or beliefs of a particular Christian sect or sects, accepts as a general basis for the good life those moral and ethical standards that have through the centuries been associated with what has come to be referred to in general terms as " the Christian way of life."

The differences in approach to the common problems besetting us all—as indeed in some measure is the case over defining exactly what is meant by " democracy " or the kind of cultural continuity considered most desirable—spring from the way in which the formulation of a political theory must take note of the character of the various social groups that together form the State : their purpose; their relative importance and size; causes of cohesion; the amount of control any given group is allowed to exercise over the individuals forming that group. This can perhaps best be instanced by a quick comparison of the differences in approach between the German and the English peoples.

In Germany the problem of achieving national unity and a unification of the whole country has become for the Germans an historic task, still not realized and which must be courageously and vigilantly striven for. National unity came to Great Britain quite naturally and by a slow, logical procession of events extending from the Middle Ages onwards. With us there has been no real necessity for grim determination; and with us, in consequence, a policy of *laissez-faire* and of easygoing tolerance of all kinds of sub-groups within the main groups has resulted, leading to the foreigners' constant admiration of the Englishman's sense of " fair play " and almost comic perplexity at what he hears expounded by the soap-box orators in Hyde Park and elsewhere. This in turn has influenced the general attitude towards the State. It is a tradition in Germany, extending back in time to the eighteenth century, that the State should be strong and should make itself directly responsible for the welfare of its people. It has now become difficult for the modern German, conditioned as he is to consider himself under the guardianship and tutelage of the State, to see that he *is* the State and to assert fully his democratic rights as a citizen participating fully in the process of self-government. His interest in the State is as real as the Englishman's, but is passively (almost bellicosely) patriotic whereas the Englishman's is critically attentive to the necessity for allowing each and every minority group its say—a process which naturally embraces the mixed blessings of local self-government and of decentralized local responsibility for education. In a word the Englishman's interest in the State machine is that of constantly weakening central authority and not of strengthening it, a process, of course, that is only possible when the question of national unity is once and for all settled beyond any possible doubt. So again is the attitude towards class structure influenced. In Great Britain this has always been rather loose : there has never been a caste sytem, and it has always been possible for the poor boy to rise by merit and ability to the highest and most important positions in the land. In Germany the policy of absolutism that was thought to be necessary in order the better to achieve national unity encouraged a rigid class structure—and such rigidity was subsequently found to be necessary for the perpetuation of the policy of absolutism. Finally, we should note that all these various factors have led in the case of Great Britain to the emergence of the idea that education is afforded as a means of permitting the individual to achieve personal significance, and to participate fully in the social and political life of his country. In Germany, education has been divorced from public life, and the middle classes, finding no place in the political activities of the strong State (and indeed actively being discouraged from so doing) have been driven to achieve personal significance through a deepening of their own experiences—through introspection. Thus, when as now happens the new techniques of scientific industrialism (and of the hydrogen bomb) make their impact upon societies whose organization and habits of thought are adapted to an older system, making revolutionary challenges to the old ordered way of existence, the Germans —too rigidly cast in their mould—feel inadequate and (to quote Professor Spranger) dread the future, an inescapable attitude of mind that is in direct contrast to the prevailing English philosophic balance that enables the Englishman to face the future calmly if vigilantly.

Insular security, of course, has been the chief factor in shaping and determining the characteristic philosophy and outlook of the British people. The insular situation has made political unity a possibility, a rich diversity of flourishing and unfettered sub-group cultures that stimulate the whole nation a reality, a spirit of compromise over burning controversial questions inescapable, a rich common tradition that includes wide ranges of common experience (and that therefore is distrustful of intellectualism and of " professional " interference), the mainspring of all action. In current jargon we tend to be amateurs who muddle through rather than planners with a clearly defined and undeviating purpose in view. We are at our best when improvising, and to improvise we draw on a lengthy tradition of self-discipline and voluntary co-operation. Unlike the introspective German, the Englishman finds his philosophy through action instead of determining his actions by the principles of philosophy. Formal instruction in the schools, therefore, has never been prized as highly as in France, or indeed Germany, and the discipline of experience has been constantly preferred to the discipline of school. For that reason we cannot make the clear distinction between " instruction " and " éducation " as do the French. We educate for personality rather than for literary attainment, and in terms of clearly understood (if not actually expressed) social traditions in which the idea is implicit, as Ruskin put it, that " the character of men depends more on their occupation than on any teaching we can give them or principles we can imbue them with. The employment forms the habits of body and mind, and these are the constituents of man. Employment is the half, and the primal half of education." Or, as Sir Michael Sadler has acutely observed on more than one occasion, just as apprenticeship was the keynote of medieval education in England, so does it remain the driving force behind educational practice to-day.

Nothing can make this point clearer than a close study of John Locke's *Thoughts Concerning Education* and of the influence it has had in moulding and shaping the pattern of a liberal middle-class education throughout the last centuries—centuries during which the ideas of duty towards one's God, of duty towards one's neighbour, of working diligently " in that state of life unto which it shall please God to call me," firmly established themselves and made the State religion more a code of conduct than an act of faith; a resistance to any central unifying tendency on the part of the State an expression of a real belief in the efficacy of leaving as much as possible to individual responsibility and local self-government. It is for all these reasons that there is little likelihood of a uniform educational system ever appearing in Great Britain, and that any Education Act that is to prove acceptable throughout the whole country must be " a flexible statute leaving room for local and regional divergencies . . . (made to) reflect our history and allow for the sensitivities that old conflicts have created." [1]

Ultimately, of course, what is often regarded by foreign observers of the British way of life as an extremely individualistic conception of freedom and of social responsibility stems from a series of historical events that had a heightened significance for the island community they affected. Nowhere else in Europe in the thirteenth century could Magna Carta have been possible. The complete Protestant break from the power of the Holy See made inevitable a new kind of political nationalism and fostered the development of a mercantile economic society based on individual enterprise. The Civil Wars made clear to the new merchant bourgeoisie the importance of tolerance to the island community as a positive good and also as a vital necessity to the new " nation of shopkeepers," and also paved the way for the establishment of the present Parliamentary system of democratic government based on the restricted temporal and spiritual powers of Crown in Parliament.

We have already had occasion in an earlier chapter as well as here to discuss in some detail the forces that have been at work in shaping the essentially different German approach. In the attempt to achieve national unity, education in Germany has constantly been considered as a means of overcoming the individualistic stubborn tendencies of the peoples of the various *Länder* to weld these into *one* nation, *one* culture, *one* State, whilst yet allowing them to preserve as valuable forces for good their present individualistic characteristics. The doctrine of the strong *Land* that really cares for the welfare of its people, however, is still predominant and the problems which have faced post-war Germany in preparing its people for a modern democratic way of life can only be judged in their correct magnitude when it is remembered that Germany, throughout its entire history from medieval to modern times, has been a democracy for roughly only fifteen years (between the Treaty of Versailles and 1933), and then more by compulsion than by spontaneous choice. In the case of Germany the Protestant Reformation did *not* produce democracy, mainly because Luther insisted on a rigid separation between the authority of the Church and the State and taught his Protestants not to interfere in political doctrine. In consequence the rulers of the various *Länder* built on the idea of a German religion for the German people (*cuius regio eius religio*) based on strong autocratic, nationalistic and *Land-*

1 *Education in Great Britain*, W. O. Lester Smith. O.U.P., 1949, p. 22.

centred sentiments.[1] Inevitably, then, education in Germany (apart from being used as a unifying force) became little more than an end in itself, its only practical aim being that of the transformation of man into a worthy being whose life is determined by the desire for values. Hence the prevalence of the ideal of a " general education " (Allegemeine Bildung) which aims at developing a human being *not* primarily useful to the State, useful to society, or useful in his work, but one whose usefulness in different fields of activity is a consequence of his inner worth as a loyal member of his *Land* and of the German race. Even in the case of Kerschensteiner, a close examination of the programmes of work as laid down for the continuation school system of Munich will show this attitude of mind to be prevalent, if not immediately obvious.

Two outstanding names in modern French educational thought are undoubtedly those of Emile Durkheim, the sociologist, and " Alain," the philosopher and schoolmaster, and in their writings both illustrate quite plainly the prevailing and traditional outlook and approach. For Durkheim, education is a process of socialization by which each generation seeks to transfer its own traditions to its successor. " Education," he says, " is influence exercised by adult generations on those who are not yet mature for social life. Its aim is to develop in the child a certain number of physical, intellectual and moral qualities which are expected of him both by political society collectively and by the particular environment in which he is destined to live as an individual." Thus, according to his sociological method, education is an institution produced by society, and the function of education in twentieth-century French society is to turn out men who conform to the ideal type of man envisaged by that society. Each individual pupil, therefore, is entitled to receive the sum of knowledge common to all, but no special consideration is shown for any particular individual as such. Alain, the teacher, gives the practical application of all this. He insists on wide but rapid reading for his pupils, and in the earlier years of books, which, whilst they make an appeal to the imagination, contain some important underlying thought. Latin and geometry teach a child to think, and must be studied before anything else. The more austere the child's surroundings the better :

[1] Echoes of this were to be felt in England when the Hanoverians came over, culminating in the foolish plea : " George, be a king !" that had such unhappy consequences for the monarchy and the country as a whole when George III acceded to the throne.

he will think better. And education is an affair of thought, in the sense that the teacher thinks aloud and comments on a text in the pupils' presence with the object of stimulating in his pupils further thoughts of their own. Every thought should have a solid foundation of fact, for the natural way of learning is to proceed from the fact to the idea. To try to make things too easy for the pupil—to try to sugarcoat the pill to the extent that it is all sugar and no pill —is to do the pupil a great disservice. Alain in consequence looks askance at many of the ideas of the New Education, as he objects to observation lessons (so much to the fore in the Decroly system) on the grounds that they " confine and paralyse the mind." The abstract and the general are much more accessible to the understanding of the child than natural objects which one cannot explain but which one can only dissect or observe. By the same token he deprecates attempts to explain modern theories (such as Einstein's) which can only lead to a superficial knowledge of modern thought, and therefore a dangerous one. Read rather Descartes and Newton and consider them afresh! " L'enfant a besoin d'avenir; ce n'est pas le dernier mot de l'homme qu'il faut lui donner, mais plutôt le premier. . . . Je trouve ridicule qu'on laisse le choix aux enfants ou aux familles d'apprendre ceci plutôt que cela. Ridicule aussi qu'on accuse l'Etat de vouloir leur imposer ceci et cela." [1]

As in the case of Germany, we have already had occasion to discuss at some length (see Chapter Three) the influence of historical and political events on the shaping of the French national outlook. We can therefore content ourselves here with observing that the ideas expounded by Durkheim and Alain are based on the principle of claiming the absolute human value of the individual. If you know the truth you will act rightly. Then, society owes education to the child more for his own sake (as a future French citizen) than for the advantages he will reap from that education. The two important tasks of the school system are therefore (a) integration, and (b) the making of citizens. By " integration " is meant the maintenance of the moral and intellectual homogeneity of the whole nation, and towards this end it has been found that the Napoleonic system of centralization in the long run works best. The central authority recognizes best the general needs of the whole nation, and is thus best equipped for using the schools as an

---

[1] *Propos sur L'Education,* Alain. Presses universitaires de France, 1948, pp. 33 and 35.

instrument for the assimilation of all sections of the population " ad maiorem Francorum gloriam." France educates for individual responsibility within the centralizing framework of the State; Great Britain educates for individual responsibility that makes the State; Germany educates for the strongly unified State.

The Belgian approach to the problems involved in educating for democracy is fundamentally not very dissimilar from the French, except that the Belgian's inherent love of liberty and his almost pathological need to be " up against authority " add more colour and diversity to the picture. Briefly, the attitude taken is that it is the responsibility of the State to provide a sound education for everybody and yet at the same time to sort out most carefully the élite capable of inspiring others by their example to greater effort, and also of dealing intelligently and realistically with the increasingly complicated problems of modern existence as they particularly affect the destiny of a small State that becomes the pivotal point for any major European issue. It is firmly held that every healthy society needs its élite, and that false conceptions over equality of opportunity can dangerously lower standards both of intellectual attainment and also of national vitality. There is no reason, however, why this élite should be chosen from only one class.

The powers of the State are none the less most clearly defined. If it must see to it that all may benefit, and must dispense benefits impartially and justly it must in no sense dictate : " L'Etat ne crée pas; il encourage la création, contrôle et harmonise." [1] Its job is primarily to organize *for* education, to intervene only when the interests of the whole State are imperilled, and therefore in general to ensure that there is a real respect for human personality, a genuine spirit of tolerance, a developing sense of civic pride, and a clear notion in men's minds of their duties towards their neighbour and towards the whole of humanity. Here again, reference to what has already been said of Belgium in the earlier chapters of this book will reveal how historical events have played a full part in determining this approach. The insistence on the State's peculiar function as a harmonizing influence also has its roots in past experience, and in particular in the nineteenth-century struggles between the Liberal and Catholic parties for the control

---

[1] *Esprit d'une politique générale de l'éducation*, Lameere and De Coster, Bruxelles, 1946, p. 23.

of education. Just as it is conceded that the number of groups a person can belong to is bound to restrict his personal liberty in a variety of directions, so it is held that to belong to ONE group only can lead to enslavement to that group. The State's function, therefore, is to see to it that people are not subjected to the domination of one particular social group, but to make for as much diversity as possible within the general framework of government at both local and national levels. " Tout individu est membre d'une collectivité nationale envers laquelle il a des devoirs; mais il est aussi membre de plusieurs groupes sociaux particuliers; il est ou peut être en outre un être qui a sa fin en soi." [1] It is interesting to note that since the passing of the 1944 Education Act and the creation of the Ministry of Education to replace the former Board of Education, the State machine in England has been moving gradually but surely in the direction of a centralization of effort that in many respects would not run counter to what would be approved in Belgian traditional practice.

The aims and aspirations of the Italian people have not much altered since they were first encouraged by Napoleon to achieve national unity. It was grasped then, as surely as it is held now, that education must be the basis of the unified State. What is needed is a common culture that is not so much abstract and academic as concrete and living and in conformity with the soul of the people which it must revive to be successful in the task it sets itself. Education, therefore, must be universal and public—not necessarily the same for everyone, for it is important to sort out from the mass the élite required to guide the country's destiny and shape future policy. Education must also be uniform throughout the country (and here there is more than an echo of French practice as first effectively initiated by Napoleon) because uniformity will ensure an easier control and provide a means for general supervision that alone can make for a satisfactory all-round level of attainment. It follows, therefore, that popular education must primarily be a function of the State, and the State cannot readily surrender this function without surrendering the most potent reasons for its existence. It is also to be remembered that in a country that is so predominantly Catholic, the pupil arrives in school with a mentality that has already been oriented in the Catholic direction. The school's task in consequence is to see to it

1 *Ibid.*, pp. 24-5.

that the forces already set in motion at the mother's knee are not vitiated or destroyed, but elaborated and broadened, once again in an attempt to quicken the soul of the nation as a whole. Religion in this sense (and the Catholic outlook in Italy cannot properly be understood unless this is borne in mind) ceases to be passive submission to an external authority and takes on a fuller and deeper significance, from the point of view of the State, as satisfying the most profound needs of the mind and therefore quickening the national pulse.

In direct contrast to Germany, the Scandinavian countries offer an example of how the Lutheran Reformation, and Protestantism generally, have been used in an attempt to achieve a real working democratic basis for government. We have noted earlier how the Lutheran idea of individual responsibility led in these Scandinavian countries towards the idea of a combined responsibility on the part of the State and Church for education, and how the close bonds between Church and State are still a marked feature of cultural life, thus bringing everybody during the most formative part of the educative process under the influence of the direct teaching of Christianity. When it is also remembered that in Sweden, since the days of Gustavus Adolphus, there have been two guiding principles at work—namely those of a strong State leadership, and of the recognition of education as an important factor in social development and therefore as an immediate objective for State activity[1]—and that the Norwegian and Danish schools have been founded on the principles of freedom of beliefs, thought, and actions within a general framework of service to the community, it will be readily seen that the basic aim in these Scandinavian countries has been to produce a free, healthy-minded generation able to gain an independent outlook on the problems of their time; able to find their true place in society; realizing that they do not live alone in the world but must adapt their lives and actions to serve the good of the whole community from the family through to the nation and finally to all the peoples of the earth. Indeed, no better summing-up of the dominant philosophical outlook of these countries can be found than that published as part of the text of the Norwegian teachers' declaration to their pupils issued on the 9th of April, 1942, as a protest against the attempted nazification of the schools:

---

[1] The creation of the Swedish comprehensive school system is an excellent modern example.

We have been entrusted with the task of giving you children that knowledge and training in thorough work which is necessary if you are to receive full and many-sided development as human beings, so that each one of you can take his or her place in the community for the benefit of himself and others. We have been given this calling by the Norwegian people, and the Norwegian people can call us to account for it. We also know that the sum total of knowledge and labour capacity which a country disposes of are the greatest and most durable of all its sources of wealth. It is our duty to protect those values. . . .

The teacher's vocation, however, is not only to give the children knowledge. He must also teach the children to believe in and desire that which is true and just. He is therefore unable to teach anything which is in conflict with his conscience without betraying his calling. Anyone who does so is committing a wrong both against the pupils whom he should lead and against himself. That, I promise you, I will never do. I will never ask you to do anything which I consider to be wrong, nor will I teach you anything which in my opinion is not in accordance with the truth. As hitherto, I will let my conscience be my guide, and I believe that I shall then be in agreement with the great majority of the people who have entrusted me with my educational duties.[1]

The position in which Holland economically stands in relation to Europe and to the rest of the world has also made the problem of the interdependence of education and society a very real one, and it is recognized that sound educational policy must be based on concrete knowledge of the whole cultural position of the country. It was thanks to the Dutch Reformed Church that the Republic acquired a great number of schools within a short span, after its liberation from Spanish domination, and it was also thanks to the Church—with its extremely democratic organization—that the schools took on from their earliest beginnings their peculiar democratic character that made for real national unity. When, by the Education Act of 1806, the State stepped in to take over general control and to give the schools that national and systematically constructed system the various churches could not themselves provide, the general pattern of thought was already clearly defined. Toleration and a faith in man's ability to rise above himself to even greater efforts if he were given independence and full scope in consequence to realize himself were becoming part of the "feeling-tone" of the whole nation. Discrimination against Roman Catholics and against others who stood outside the Reformed

[1] Quoted by Nils Hjelmtveit, *Education in Norway.* Royal Norwegian Information Service, 1946, p. 16.

Church was eventually rejected and the parents' right to their own convictions in the bringing up of their children came scrupulously to be observed on the principle that national unity can never be attained by identifying one's own convictions with those of the nation : unity to be real and lasting must be based on a recognition of and a respect for variety. None the less the influence of Christianity is inescapably strong in the sense that the parents are still held to be the main if not the sole educators of their children. The Reformed Church was most careful to point out the tasks and responsibilities of parents in educating their children in accordance with the practice of their faith, and this parental sense of duty is to-day remarkably strong even amongst those who would claim the right to move completely outside the sphere of religious observances and practice. Education for national unity, then, is the aim behind the extremely democratic system that has been devised in Holland, it being at all times remembered that the active encouragement of sub-groups in all their diverse activities is a necessary concomitant. Unity out of diversity is the ideal.

We cannot end this analysis without reconsidering once again in some detail the aims of those two great countries that are so diametrically opposed in their views—the U.S.A. and the U.S.S.R. First of all, however, let us try to grasp as a whole and as a pattern what is happening in the Western European democracies. In the most general terms, and with particular reference to the aims of secondary education, the late Sir Michael Sadler once wittily summed up the situation as follows : " The German is apt to ask about a young man, ' What does he know? ' The American to ask, ' What can he do? ' The Frenchman to ask, ' What examinations has he passed? ' The Englishman's usual question is, ' What sort of a fellow is he? ' " [1] In other words, the typical English attitude is one which distrusts intellectualism as such and which aims at producing a citizen type whose sense of justice, and loyalties and " fair play " (so much on the lips of foreigners whenever they discuss the Englishman) is strong enough to make decentralization and local government based on individual enterprise and responsibility really work. The State is very much the servant and never the master of the individuals it purports to represent, and it is very much within the power of those individuals to exact from their

---

[1] Quoted by J. H. Higginson, *An English Scholar's Studies of Education in Europe.* International Review of Education, Vol. I, No. 2, pp. 197-8.

elected representatives a detailed and exact account of their stewardship. In this sense, Great Britain stands very much apart from the rest of Western Europe—as much apart as does Western Germany, though for different reasons of which we have spoken earlier. The remaining democracies of Western Europe stress almost without exception the importance of there being " no better baggage on a journey than much of knowledge," Scandinavia and Holland falling very much under the spell of German intellectualism, France perpetuating the Jesuit cult of scholarship for its own sake and for the intellectual discipline thereby afforded, and Italy rather more diffusely following a path parallel to that of the French but coming under the double influence of the Catholic Church and of the idealistic philosophy of Benedetto Croce. It is over the conception of the relationship of the individual to the State that the most noticeable differences occur, thus giving in each case a slight though important difference to the interpretation of what is meant by a democratic form of government, and thus causing subtle but important differences in the structure and administration of the educational machinery. These mattters we shall discuss later.

The aim of Soviet education can be baldly stated as being the propagation of Communism, in the process of which an élite of leaders for the various Soviets will be found and suitably trained along approved Marxist lines. " It is not the consciousness of human beings that determines their existence," wrote Karl Marx, " but, conversely, it is their social existence which determines their consciousness." In Marxist doctrine a clear distinction must be drawn between society and the State. Society always exists, but the State is a more restricted organization within society, and it owes its rise to an inescapable dialectical conflict of class interests in which those who control the means of production oppress those who do not. The ideal Communist society will be the one in which this apparatus of State power will be destroyed, for only in a truly classless society can real freedom exist, and only a truly classless society is democratic. The U.S.S.R. is seen as in a process of gradual evolution. At the moment private capitalism has been replaced by State capitalism. The ultimate goal is held to be this classless society, and in this important contemporary interim period it is the duty of each and every Russian tirelessly to equip himself, according to aptitude and ability, in order to help his country to move the more swiftly and expeditiously towards that goal. The practical and realist approach towards the pursuance of this ideal is typified by the avowed economic aim of outstripping the most advanced industrial countries in the world, and so freeing the Russian people for ever from the fear of want. Educational theory as such stresses the importance of the individual (within, of course, the framework of the totalitarian State), insists constantly on the possibility for greatness that resides in the ordinary man, urges the release of that creative force which, it is claimed, resides in all human beings and which alone can bring them to the highest peak of human achievement that is necessary to form a truly classless society. Educational practice exacts a materialistic outlook, a stress on socially useful labour, an active participation from the pupils in the building and shaping of their own lives in terms of the Communistic ideal, and a close contact with contemporary life.

It may be argued that the Americans also lay great stress on active pupil participation in the building of their own lives, and on a close contact with contemporary life situations. It is certain that they are just as vociferous as the Russians in claiming that they are educating for a true democracy. It is equally certain that, despite the common language, their whole conception of the educative process is different from that holding in Great Britain, as their culture and civilization are different. We have already seen how American character has been moulded by the necessity of constantly meeting the new situations which arose in the conquest of their frontiers. Resourcefulness and initiative are therefore qualities which the American most prizes in his fellow-countrymen, and a flexibility of mind that will seek successful adaptation to constantly changing circumstances. Thus, where the English stress the importance of character training as the end of education, the Americans emphasize training of the personality. Both countries, of course, seek to promote the fullest development of the individual, but whereas England has devoted the major part of its attention to the training of an élite, America has paid most attention to those pupils of average ability. As Professor Northrop has pointed out, it took one hundred and fifty years from the founding of the earliest colonies in New England for the idea of tolerance genuinely to establish itself in the new and growing continent, and that spirit of tolerance went eventually with Jefferson's belief that the common man would think and act rationally if allowed to do so, and that education's prime task was to give the common man the opportunity for proving himself in this direction; all which means, as de Tocqueville pointed out, that the American, ultimately, is more interested in equality than in liberty. It is this individualistic egalitarian idea—" I'm as good as the next man !"—that leads to a kind of dramatization of the individual at all stages of development; that leads also, economically speaking, to the worship of success ("bettering yourself" and "getting ahead"); that leads, ultimately, to the cult of the average man, which means conformity to the standards of the current majority. It also means that the American people are much more genuinely interested in their school system and what it can be made to do for their youngsters than are the peoples of any of the Western European democracies, though it must be remembered that the American tradition of local self-government (stemming from Jefferson) has been an important factor in this direction. It finally means that America holds emphatically to the idea that the true aim of a democracy should be to adapt education to the ability and aptitude of each individual and to provide for each that education from which he is best able to profit. And America has discovered that a unitary planned system of education best achieves these objectives, and has, of course, a distinct initial advantage over most other countries in that its system has been unitary from the start.

All the other countries we have had under review have for a variety of reasons had nothing approaching such a unitary system, and their present attempts at offering each individual that education from which he and the country as a whole is best able to profit are made primarily on a basis of the traditional approach to which the country is accustomed, and are governed by the kind of system of educational administration the country enjoys. The idea of the education of an élite is still prevalent in all countries, including the U.S.S.R. The Scandinavian countries come nearest to America in spirit, though Russia has adopted completely the unitary system. The English system has developed without any plan, new types of schools being added as the need arose, but without any articulation between them. Belief in a strongly centralized control is much to the fore in Italy and France, and also throughout the various *Länder* of Germany. The importance of a central authority for purposes of co-ordination and general direction is admitted in

Scandinavia, Holland and Belgium, but much freedom and initiative is left to local sub-groupings. The important impact all these differences make will be brought out more fully in our next chapter.

CHAPTER SIX

The Administration of Education

THAT the impact of the political theory of the State is most noticeable in the public supervision and administration of education will be readily understood when it is remembered that political theory must at some point define clearly the purposes of education and then go on to determine the type of administration which seems best suited to the attainment of the citizen type the State wishes to produce. It should, however, also be remembered that it was not until the eighteenth and nineteenth centuries that statesmen decided that universal and compulsory education was a desirable aim, and that even then they were more often than not inclined to leave the actual provision of the schools to someone else, usually the parishes and the local communities. When it became imperative that there should be some centralized control—if only for the reason that to make universal compulsory education a reality and not merely a law on the statute book the State must provide the necessary funds—then the kind of centralized control that was imposed had to take account of the prevailing culture pattern and of the aims and aspirations of the people as a whole as reflected so far in the organization of the school systems in vogue. Only in countries like Russia, or Germany and Italy under the Nazi and Fascist regimes, where a totalitarian system could be imposed, did it prove in any measure possible to impose a rigidly centralized administration to the exclusion of the participation of the public or any of its associated groups. And in the purely totalitarian state, of course, there can be no conflicting opinions and no criticism of theory and practice. Democracy for the Russians, considered from the educational point of view, means training in dialectical materialism and in socialism. Conformity to the Marxist ideal is the aim, and care is taken at all stages and at all levels to control all sources of information which may lead to " the harbouring of dangerous thoughts."

In consequence, the administration of education in Russia, though it is shared by several organizations, is in effect (as far as policies and details are concerned) controlled entirely by the Council of People's Commissars, by the Central Committee of the Communist Party, and by the Central Planning Commission of which each Minister for Education for each of the sixteen republics in the U.S.S.R. is a member. The Minister for Education thus takes part in deliberations and discussions on all national problems, thereby assuring a close and permanent link at the highest administrative level between education and the life of the Communist State. It is the responsibility of the Ministry of Education for each of the sixteen republics to see to the efficient organization of work in the primary and secondary schools, in the teacher-training colleges, in education bureaux, in education laboratories, in educational research institutes, and in the general sphere of adult education. True, there is some decentralization of administration in the sense that local bodies are required to maintain school buildings and approve the appointment of teachers, which is made by the head of the school, who is himself (or herself) a Ministry nominee. They are also expected to take " an active interest " in the provision of facilities for the improvement of the efficiency of " in-service " teachers, and to provide adequate facilities for out-of-school activities. They can have no say, however, in the planning of the school syllabus, in the amount of time that shall be allotted to various subjects at various levels, nor in the approach to the teaching of the subjects on the curriculum, nor in the choice of textbooks.

Indeed, there are common or " stable " textbooks prescribed throughout the whole of the U.S.S.R. to ensure that the basic knowledge acquired is the same throughout the whole union, and that it is consistently up to date in accordance with the latest high level pronouncements. There is also a common syllabus for the whole union, and a fixed timetable, to ensure that the main facts are taught to all children in the correct dosage. Apologists will often argue that much initiative is left to the local teacher to supplement all this as he will in accordance with local conditions and requirements, and that he is encouraged to draw on a wide variety of other material to supplement the textbook knowledge, the choice being entirely his. This is true . . . but he would be a brave and rash man who attempted anything not in strict accordance with the party line and that was not going to win the immediate approval of the inspectorate!

Inspectors to the schools are appointed by each Ministry of Education, after some years of teaching experience during which they have proved themselves to be "sound." Their duties are many and their responsibilities considerable, their main task being that of constantly raising the standard of education and discipline in the schools and of co-operating closely with the head of the school to maintain the school's efficiency and reputation at the highest possible level. This means that they are constantly in and out of the school, listening to lessons and examining the work of the pupils. If an inspector considers that a lesson has been badly given, he will probably go over it in detail with the teacher in private, analysing it to show what was wrong, and then take the next lesson himself to show how it should be done. It is equally the inspector's duty, together with the head of the school, to recommend a teacher for an award or promotion. Finally, in order to ensure that the inspectors themselves do not in any sense deviate from the party line, and are kept constantly informed of the various shifts and emphasis that are from time to time required, there is an institute for the training of inspectors, this training being followed up by regular refresher courses held every three months. As one Russian university professor once put it: "Our education sets itself the task of creating all-round, active, determined possessors of knowledge and of the proletarian world outlook, devoted to communism and communistic morality, builders and defenders of a socialist society." There could be no more direct and simple statement of a completely totalitarian aim.

Of course, several of the Western European democracies—notable amongst which are France, Belgium, Sweden and Holland —enjoy or have enjoyed in varying degrees the mixed blessings of a highly centralized system in many respects not dissimilar from that holding in the U.S.S.R. But there comparison stops short, for the ends to be served in these countries by a policy of centralized control of education are neither political nor ideological, but rather based on a definite theory of education that seems best to suit the peculiar requirements of the country in the light of its past endeavours and achievements. Again, whilst the character of the administrative machine may be authoritarian, authority and controls are limited to the actual work done in the schools and to providing a uniform school system, and are in no sense extended to cover the private lives of teachers, parents, pupils and citizens generally outside the school. A parent or teacher may hold whatever political or religious views he pleases, may freely criticize both the theory and practice of education, and—if he does not like what is provided for him by the State—may send his children to a private " free " school or start such a school himself, subject only to general governmental regulations covering adequacy of buildings and equipment and the employment of suitably qualified teachers, the qualifications exacted from teachers in the " free " schools being by no means necessarily as high as those required for employment under State control. Broadly speaking, such countries among the democracies as to-day have some form of centralization use their powers to make certain that the pupils in the schools have acquired both a certain body of knowledge (for one reason or another considered indispensable) and a mind trained to think for itself. Again, we must remember that without direct intervention on the part of the State the organization and provision of adequate educational facilities for all children would have been impossible in Holland, Belgium and Scandinavia, just as it was proving impossible in England until the passing of the 1944 Education Act which itself proved a step towards a more authoritarian and centralized control.

The advantages that are usually claimed for the centralized system are that opportunities are equalized, and that the rural and more remote areas have as good educational facilities as the more advanced and progressive urban areas; that the quality of education provided is uniform because all schools are provided with teachers possessing the same qualifications; and that the system is efficient because the same standards are set for all schools. This, of course, is only true to a point. All teachers are not of equal calibre even if they have all followed identical courses and passed the same examinations. Nor, in actual practice, do we find the more able and more ambitious teachers willing to bury themselves in remote country areas. Nor, finally, do examination successes show that the same standards of achievement have been achieved in different schools of the same system. A more serious criticism of the tightly centralized system, however, is that local initiative and enterprise is stifled and there is no real incentive to the subgroups seriously to challenge accepted because practised doctrines.

The real vigour of the English educational system has lain in the wide diversity and variety of aims and purposes that have only been made possible through a policy of complete decentralization. The stagnation that has repeatedly been complained of in experimentation in aims and methods in French schools was the inevitable outcome of a strongly centralized system, dating from the 1880's, that whittled away the power and influence of local authorities to virtually nil. It is interesting to note that post-war reforms in English education to be effective have had to initiate a closer control of local responsibility and private enterprise, whereas in France there has had to be a relaxation of control in order to allow what was considered desirable experimentation to take place.

What is obviously wanted in those countries which (unlike America) still believe in the importance to the country as a whole of the formation of an intellectual élite is a careful distribution of functions between the central and the local authorities that achieves real liberty with a high degree of conformity, and it is the proud and justifiable boast of the Dutch that they have managed to do this. The inevitable struggle between Church and State for the control of education led (as we have seen in Chapter Three) to a series of uneasy compromises in the predominantly Catholic countries, but generally speaking these countries—in particular France and Belgium—achieved a working solution to the problems facing them on a basis of what we might call " liberty without the State system." That is to say, the State has undertaken the maintenance and development of a neutral system of education open to all who care to profit by it. Those sections of the community who are for one reason or another dissatisfied with what the State offers may, if they so wish, establish side by side with the State schools " free " schools which become their entire responsibility. In principle the State adopts a passive attitude towards such schools. There is, however, another solution which might be termed " liberty within the State system," and it is this solution the Dutch have sought. Passivity is replaced by active State intervention. Thus the State actively assists the development of such schools as are not neutral, provided certain guarantees are given that the instruction in those schools will be equivalent to, though not necessarily identical with, that given in the neutral schools. Since 1945 both France and Belgium have felt compelled to treat

the Catholic " free " schools in their respective countries on not
dissimilar lines by granting State subsidies proportionate to those
voted for the State schools towards their upkeep and general
maintenance.

Alongside all this, however, Holland has devised her own
peculiar form of decentralization. Though the Ministry of Education supervises the whole system it most definitely does not act (as
in France) as " schoolmaster-in-chief." Its function is to achieve
uniformity of standards and of educational opportunity throughout the country; to pay the salaries of all approved teachers in
whatever school they serve, to regulate the execution of the programme of studies and the timetable of lessons, to see that regulations effecting efficiency in schools are complied with (e.g. that the
number of teachers employed in a given school is not allowed to
fall below the basic minimum prescribed by law), to see to it that
any group of persons legally in a position to demand the establishment of a " free " school are not denied their rights, and to make
a large contribution towards the upkeep of the secondary schools
proper (80 per cent. of the expenses of the commercial secondary
schools is met by the Ministry, which also maintains at its own
expense forty-nine secondary schools in areas where the proper
provision of secondary education by local authorities is difficult).
To enable it efficiently to carry out these various duties, the
Ministry has an inspectorate consisting of three chief inspectors
and fifty-six others assigned to different districts. There are two
architect-inspectors in addition whose sole concern is school buildings, and two inspectors of teacher-training.

The immediate responsibility for the provision of adequate
primary, secondary and technical education falls on the local
authorities, the public schools being managed by the municipal
council and a board consisting of the burgomaster and aldermen,
the " free " schools being privately managed but the local authority
being held responsible for supplying the necessary school buildings. The local authorities appoint local inspection committees on
which parents, teachers and other local citizens are represented.
To sum up, the local authorities pay all current expenses and provide the buildings for all types of schools, the Ministry pays all
salaries and in addition makes adequate grants towards the
efficient maintenance of good secondary education. About 27 per
cent. of the children attend neutral State primary schools, about

28 per cent. attend " free " Protestant schools, about 43 per cent. attend " free " Roman Catholic schools, and 2 per cent. only are in neutral " free " schools—that is to say, schools which belong to no religious body and which equally wish to remain " free " from municipal control. The Dutch love of freedom and independence which probably found its greatest expression for all time in the eighty years' struggle ceaselessly waged to secure freedom from the Spanish yoke finds in modern times its fullest expression in this present system which harmoniously combines the benefits of both a centralized and a decentralized system of educational administration.

As we have already hinted, the situation holding in France is radically different from that in Holland, the local authorities having in effect no say in the policy to be adopted, their functions being restricted in the main to the supply of furnishings, heating, lighting, and so on, and even then being very carefully guided by some specific regulation as to exactly how and when and why and in what measure they shall act. All authority is exercised by the Minister for Education, under the control of Parliament, and by his delegates in each of the seventeen *académies* into which the country is administratively divided. At the head of each *académie* is the *Recteur*, appointed by the President of the Republic and directly responsible to the Minister. Usually he is chosen from among the university professors, but the only qualification he actually needs is the possession of a doctorate degree. The *Recteur* has almost absolute powers within his *académie*, and he directs the whole system of education from the nursery school upwards to the university, and including the general supervision of all private schools. His administrative assistants include, since the last war, an inspector general for primary education, one for youth and sports, and one or more for technical education. Under his control, and representing both the *Recteur* and the Minister, is an academy inspector for each of the *départements* contained within the *Académie*. The academy inspector controls his team of inspectors who are specialists chosen to cover all types of education offered within any given *département*. It should be noted that there is in addition a *départemental* council that fulfils in each *département* the important role of administering the whole of primary education, and in particular holds itself responsible for the recruitment, training and promotion of primary school teachers. This is a traditional arrangement, extending back to the first attempt at organizing primary education in France (that had been entirely neglected by Napoleon) and when the Minister of the Interior, through his *préfêts*, sought an orderly solution.

At the highest level the Minister and his numerous advisers are assisted by a body of special inspectors of national education whose function it is to visit all educational establishments, to report on the teachers therein (in conjunction with the local inspectorate), to keep the Minister constantly informed of the over-all picture of education throughout France, and—most important of all in many ways—to plan the programme of studies for the schools, to think out new lines of approach in view of constantly changing conditions, and to indicate quite clearly and dogmatically what are, in the Ministry's view, the best methods of instruction to be adopted. All these inspectors are, of course, specialists in one given branch, though they may from time to time be charged with a job of work that extends beyond the confines of their speciality. Since 1946 this rigid top-level structure has been to some extent modified by the formation of various new consultative committees on which the actual teaching personnel are represented, and by widening the representation in the teachers' favour on the important *Conseils d'Enseignement* and *Conseil Supérieur* which are concerned with all projects of reform of education. Further, there has been a marked tendency over the last twenty years or so to permit local divergences from the fixed programme of studies, particularly in the last year of the primary school, in technical education, and in advanced and specialized work at the university level or its equivalent.

A further peculiarity of the French system, and one still further accentuating the strongly centralized approach, is that all examinations without exception are State examinations, and not merely school leaving examinations conducted in part or as a whole by the school authorities concerned with the pupil. Any child, provided he fulfils the necessary age qualifications may present himself anywhere for examination in the appropriate subjects, it making no difference whether he has been privately educated at home, or in a State or " free " (usually Catholic) school. Private " free " establishments can, of course, issue their own diplomas, but they have no value whatever in securing one of the innumerable appointments which always specify success in one or a number of State examinations.[1] Naturally, the obligation on everybody to present themselves for the State examinations ensures that the programme of work in all " free " establishments will be the same as in the State schools and that the approach to the teaching of the various subjects will not greatly differ. Finally, there is the *concours* or competitive examination where the number accepted does not only depend on the high quality of work achieved but also on the number of places available—for example, the *concours d'agrégation* for teachers at a secondary and university level.

This principle of the centralization of education was first enunciated by La Chalotais in 1763, upheld by the writers of the French Revolution, and cast in its final practical mould by Napoleon in 1808. And Napoleon quite consciously imitated many of the features of the organization of the Society of Jesus that over the preceding centuries had done so much to create an intellectual élite as a basis for a strongly centralized monarchial regime. As he himself put it, he was anxious to secure for the State all the advantages that were obviously secured for the Church of Rome by the Jesuit organization, and to secure a class of civil servant who would have no other ambition except to be useful, and no other interest except public welfare. " My aim in establishing an educational corporation is to be able to direct political and moral opinions." Not unnaturally we find that, since France was by this time the spiritual leader of the Latin world, most of these Latin countries followed the model set them by Napoleon for the organization of their educational systems.

In Italy, for example, the centralization of administration was introduced as far as the kingdom of Sardinia was concerned well before the Napoleonic reforms. Napoleon's conquest of the Northern Provinces led to their incorporation in the French Empire, and in the south of Italy Joseph Bonaparte and Murat were naturally bound to pursue a policy of close centralization on the approved French model, particularly so when it is remembered that Napoleon owed the germ of his idea for centralization from what he had seen operative in the kingdom of Sardinia. With the founding of the Ministry of Public Instruction in Italy and the passing of the Casati Law of 1859, centralization had been extended to all the provinces, and the Casati Law itself, again

---

[1] Exceptions are made in a few cases, mainly with regard to certain kinds of diploma of a technical nature.

following French practice, left primary education to the initiative of the local authorities and maintained only the secondary and higher schools. Under the Fascist regime Gentile was instrumental in reducing the sixty-nine provinces into nineteen regions that each had their own historical frontiers (an important difference) and in furthering " regional " activities and so allowing each historical region to vary its curricula to suit local bias, local traditions and peculiar outlook. Further, the neutral State schools have never been neutral in the French sense that no religious teaching of any kind shall be done there. It is also to be noted that various attempts made to encourage local self-government in education have proved abortive, and that, mainly for financial reasons, the country as a whole would now seem to prefer the centralized system.

Supreme over all education in Italy is the Minister, assisted by an under-secretary with an educational cabinet of his own. Eight director-generals of education are in charge of general affairs and of personnel, and amongst them cover the whole field of education including university and higher education, antiquity and fine arts, academies and libraries and cultural relations. The highest authority in a province is the Chief Inspector of Studies, who is directly responsible for all matters concerning primary education (including teaching appointments) and who also supervises the secondary schools. The actual task of school visitation, inspection and supervision is carried out by a team of school inspectors. The Chief Inspector of Studies also appoints a provincial school council consisting of an expert in primary education (nominated directly by the Minister), a professor, a teacher, a physician and the chief engineer for public works. This council provides the Chief Inspector with all the technical advice he needs and under his chairmanship deals with questions of school organization, including finance and staffing. The Chief Inspector of Studies is a Ministry nominee and representative.

The slight but important divergences from the French system that have appeared indicate the Italian's historical consciousness of regional differences, reflect the constant striving to make him aware of his national entity, and betray a marked Germanic influence (particularly in the conception of the *ginnasi*) and strong Catholic outlook. In the case of Belgium, with its own peculiar stormy history, its strong Catholic and non-Catholic parties, and the linguistic problems presented by the Flemings and the

Walloons, there are many differences to be noted. By population and tradition, Belgium of course is not a typical Latin country, and the old system of local and provincial self-government is very much in evidence despite the centralized system that is imposed for the sake of uniformity. According to the usual pattern, there is a Minister with his boards of advisers and a ministerial inspectorate with very wide powers of supervision in that they control material organization, curricula, pedagogical methods, and enforce a strict execution of the law as centrally interpreted. When by the law of 1932 Belgium was officially divided into Flemish and Walloon areas, so was the inspectorate divided, though each separate body was subordinated to the central control of the Ministry. Whilst it is generally true to say that, secondary and higher education is administered directly by the Ministry, and that primary education is left as a responsibility of the local authorities and the provinces (under close supervision of the Ministry inspectorate), it must be remembered that several large towns and provinces still cling jealously to their independence, insist on controlling their own secondary schools, and strive often to keep ahead of rival institutions in other towns and provinces in their ability to recruit the best possible teaching staff and to make use of the best and most modern school equipment available. There are in all ten provinces, each with a governor chosen by the King, each with a provincial council elected by popular vote. Similarly, there is in each commune a communal council the executive head of which is the burgomaster assisted by any number of from two to six *échevins* selected by ballot from the rest of the members of the council. Amongst these *échevins* one is responsible for educational matters within the commune.

It is, of course, the boast of the Belgians that in accordance with their constitution all education is free in the sense that anybody can open a school. Education generally, however, is of two types: either " free " or Roman Catholic, or State and therefore secular. School figures to-day indicate that the children are roughly divided between the two types of school, there being quite a number of Catholics attending the State schools. The Belgian insistence on the liberty of the subject is further exemplified by the fact that in the State secular schools two hours per week are left open for religious or moral instruction. According to the wishes of the parents, a priest of the appropriate denomination will attend to give this instruction. Where parents do not wish for this, then the children follow a course of moral instruction given by an appropriate teacher. Again, at the level of higher education, the State provides two State universities, one at Ghent for the Flemish-speaking population, one at Liège for the Walloons whose language is French. The Catholics, however, have their own " free " university at Louvain, and a secular " free " university is established in Brussels. Finally, the Catholic schools have established their right to their own body of inspectors, who naturally follow the main directives laid down by the Ministry.

Further flexibility in the system is to be found in that each secondary school has its own leaving examination, the only State interference being through a *Jury d'Homologation* whose job it is, acting in a general supervisory capacity, to ensure that a certain level of attainment is reached—in other words that the national standards are maintained in all schools. Thus there is nothing as impersonal as the *baccalauréat* in France, and no State system of examinations as such—though the system of *concours* is in existence in certain specialized fields though not in effect in teaching.

It is significant to note that a decentralized system of administration developed almost entirely amongst peoples of Germanic origin or tradition where for one reason or another the Roman legal system did not take deep roots and therefore could not supersede the old customs of self-government. The efforts of the monarchy to achieve a strongly centralized State could not wear down the sturdy opposition of the aristocracy (often of bourgeois and of merchant-trader origin) and of the people. And the Reformation further rendered abortive such efforts at centralization as persisted by the organization of the Protestant churches on the basis of a self-governing parish. Whatever centralization was later achieved was willingly conceded by the people as a whole in the interests of national uniformity, though care was none the less taken to preserve the administrative independence of the local authorities. We have already seen how this has worked out in practice in both Holland and Belgium. We must now examine in some detail the systems of more typically decentralized countries such as Germany, the Scandinavian countries, Switzerland, and of course England.

Germany is in many ways untypical in that the decentralization takes the form of allegiance to the *Land* rather than to a local authority, and the *Land* can often be extremely authoritarian in the control it exercises. The Thirty Years War left the various *Länder* divided amongst themselves and Germany as a whole in a state of political disintegration. As a result the individual *Land*, and not the *Reich*, assumed control of the schools and determined their form and organization, and each *Land* continued to hold and exercise this function until the Weimar Constitution was adopted after the First World War. Articles in this constitution determined a basis for a common school legislation, but nothing was done to implement this, and the *Länder* continued, in the field of education at any rate, to retain complete autonomy. A slight step towards uniformity was taken by agreements negotiated between several *Länder*, when conformity over general standards of education was established. The National Socialists introduced further measures to bring about unification, and created in 1934 the Reich Ministry of Education. The overwhelming difficulties that faced the Germans on the collapse of the Nazi regime, and the complications involved in having to contend with four separate occupying Powers, led once more to the various *Länder* retaining control of school legislation and administration. This time, however, the various Ministers of Education, sensing the need for co-operation between the various *Länder* if the new democratic principles involving a unified Germany were to be realized, formed themselves into a permanent conference which, working quietly and efficiently over the post-war years, has done much towards achieving a uniform purpose in education for the whole country. Thus, general agreement has been achieved on : the adoption of grades of equal value and formulation to be used on school reports and certificates; the introduction of optional foreign language instruction in the primary school; principles of political education in school; adoption of uniform principles of spelling; mutual recognition of certificates of maturity (the *Abitur*) entitling admission to the universities; the methods of professional preparation of secondary school teachers; the standardization of school holidays. None the less, much must still be done before the ideal of real harmony in German education is achieved.

Within each *Land* there are three levels of administration : the State Ministry of Education; the Government-District (*Regierungsbezirk*); and the county level, which is either rural or urban. General school policy, curriculum planning, the setting up of examination requirements, the final certification and appointment of teachers, are all handled at the ministerial level. The Government-District and the county levels of administration have functions of local administration and supervision, the supervision of the secondary schools being separate from that of the primary schools and attaching to the Ministry. Both these school authorities, however, receive their directions from the Ministry, and any innovations they may wish to introduce must first of all have ministerial sanction. They are, on the other hand, held responsible for seeing that school regulations in the primary schools and in the intermediate schools are scrupulously observed, for guiding and advising teachers, for the in-service training of young teachers, and for the licensing of private teachers, including those who wish to " tutor " pupils who need or seek special assistance. As in Belgium, the *Abitur* examination is a more informal and " homely " affair than in France, the teachers in the schools setting the examinations the senior inspector for the *Land* (or his deputy) vetting the questions before they are actually put and having the right of choosing among a number or changing them, and always taking part in the important viva voce section of the examination as chairman of the examining panel.

Thus in this modern attempt to proceed along real democratic lines the German people have recognized the right of the member-states of the Federal Republic to preserve their own particular features of education, and the individual states, in their turn, have devised a working machinery in the Permanent Conference of Ministers of Education for reaching compromises between the administrations of the individual states for the benefit of the cultural way of life of all of them. Diversity, which in the past has so largely contributed to the richness of German cultural life, is maintained; but harmony is encouraged in order to facilitate transfers from the schools of one *Land* to those of another. The goal is not complete uniformity of education throughout the Federal Republic, but equivalence based on a centralized *Land* system.

In many ways Switzerland might be considered purely from the point of view of educational administration, as " Germany writ small." The country is divided into twenty-five independent *cantons*, and within these *cantons* there are about three thousand more or less autonomous political communities (*Gemeinden*), each having considerable jurisdictional authority. Education is consequently the joint affair of the *Bund*, of the *canton*, and of the local community; there is no Ministry of Education, but complete delegation of responsibility to local authorities who have, incidentally, always to consider that there are four official national languages for the whole of Switzerland. As in Germany, the *Bund* places the responsibility on the *cantons* for seeing to it that education is " free, adequate, compulsory and without religious discrimination." No attempt is made in the Constitution to define what is meant by " adequate education." The *canton* must decide that, and should a Swiss in any *canton* feel that education is not adequate he is free to appeal to the *Bund* to seek redress. " Compulsory education " means that the *canton* is responsible for seeing that sufficient instruction is received according to local *cantonal* regulations, but not that children shall attend a State school. All schools, however, whether private or public, must achieve a minimum standard of instruction, and *cantonal* inspectors have supervisory control over the curriculum of both private and public schools. All State primary schools and many of the secondary schools are administered directly by the local communities, and the teachers are appointed locally. The local community also maintains the schools and pays teachers' salaries, though the *cantons* lay down compulsory scales of pay and grant subsidies to their local communities. The Federal Government subsidises teachers' salaries, buildings, welfare work and the preparation of teachers for the primary schools. It also pays about half the cost of vocational training and supervises this.

Obviously the Swiss Republic is the only country in Europe where the old system of extreme decentralization has remained practically unchanged. And equally obviously the Swiss have proved that a really high standard of educational endeavour and achievement can be obtained with such a system, rivalling in all spheres the best in all other countries. Differences of language, religion and cultural traditions, dependent in turn on the geographical configuration of the country, account for the perpetuation of an extreme form of decentralization. Economic circumstances have forced the Swiss to demand a high standard of education from all and for all. Historical events have led to a real spirit of democracy among the people, and this in turn has led to a stressing of the importance of education as a means of producing the good citizen type who will be a well-informed and progressive member of the community.

The Scandinavian countries are constitutional monarchies in which the functions of the Crown are analogous to those of the Crown in Great Britain. The controlling power of government is vested in the people who elect their parliamentary bodies on a principal of universal suffrage. The dissemination of culture is wide, and all classes of people play an active part in community and national life. Characteristic also of these countries is that private capitalism and social collectivism are co-extensive. In Sweden, for example, all public utility services are the concern of either the State or the local government—yet almost all industrial workers are privately employed. Throughout Scandinavia generally the whole of the arable land is privately owned and tilled —and yet the farmers form themselves into co-operative societies to market their produce. Finally, it should be noted that the " welfare state " has been long the concern of these countries as a means of achieving real economic and social stability. Education has been deliberately used throughout the centuries to bring about this high degree of voluntary collectivism, and public education as part of the urge towards popular enlightenment that came with the Reformation has been a national concern since the sixteenth century.

The administration of education, originally in the hands of the Lutheran Church and of local boards, has now become a joint concern of both the State and the local communities. In Norway there is still a " Ministry of Church and Education " which is responsible for all supervision of education, and which for this purpose has a staff of consultants and travelling inspectors for special subjects. The Norwegian " People's School " (primary school) is run by the local authority, its governorship being the direct responsibility of the people. In every municipality there is a school board appointed by the elected municipal council, but which must contain a clergyman of the State Church nominated by the bishop, and a teacher (or teachers) nominated by his own colleagues. This school board is held responsible for the local school administration in compliance with the existing laws of the country. The school board appoints its own teachers, subject to ratification of the appointment by the Ministry. Usually it secures the services of a local school inspector to supervise the administrative as well as the pedagogic side of the school work. An over-all control of primary education is maintained by the Ministry which divides the country into seven administrative districts at the head of each of which is a school director. Any differences of opinion within the school boards, or between the school boards and the directors, may be referred to the Ministry for a final decision. The secondary schools originated from schools opened at the bishops' sees from 1150 onwards, and even to-day still bear in most cases the stamp of their ecclesiastical origins. These schools can be either State or municipally controlled. A State secondary school has a board of governors consisting of the headmaster, a representative of the Ministry, one representative of the teaching staff, and from one to four members of the local authorities in whose district the school is situated. The school boards act as governors for the municipally controlled schools. The final school-leaving examination is the same throughout the country and is organized by a special council of secondary education, the members of which are nominated by the King for a period of five years, and who inspect the schools and act as advisers to the Ministry. The total expenditure on education is roughly divided equally between the local authority and the State.

With only slight, and from our point of view unimportant variations, the same administrative pattern holds for both Sweden and Denmark. One interesting feature in Denmark, however, is that if the parents so desire they may establish a parents' council which shall have the power of school inspection and which may assist the Board of Education in the selection of teachers—this for primary schools only, appointments of staff and general supervision of the secondary schools being the direct concern of the Ministry.

One interesting feature which all these countries so far under discussion share in common is that—no matter whether the administration of education be centralized or decentralized—they have as their aim the formation of an intellectual élite, and they believe strongly in the advantages that can be gained from a strictly academic type of secondary education. As a result, education at the secondary level is generally considered far too important a concern to be left too much in the hands of the local authorities, and the State has increasingly made this type of education its special concern. The contrary can be said to hold in both England and the United States. On the other hand, the chief difficulty in both England and the United States, because of the persistence of their own peculiar traditions of local control of education, is that of implementing the ideal of equality of educational opportunity. All the other countries, centralized or decentralized as their administration may be, are meeting with relatively greater success. It would seem that the most likely explanation for this is that education in these other countries has always been held to be a.1 important instrument in securing the people's allegiance to a particular form of government and to a particular way of life that on its own showing made the people in turn happy, prosperous (to varying extents), and therefore contented. Thus in Scandinavia the decentralized system was imposed on the people by a Lutheran Church which seriously held that Christian salvation came through enlightenment of the people and that the only way to work at the people's level was through the smaller parish community. In France a highly centralized system was imposed *ad maiorem Francorum gloriam*, the hierarchical system of the Catholic Church, and in particular of the Jesuit Order, being the obvious model to follow—as indeed in all predominantly Catholic countries. Russia—the only country to adopt the American unitary system of education—makes it work much more effectively through a form of centralization and through gearing it to the Marxist ideal. Holland and Belgium are in the midway position between extremes of centralization and decentralization, with State control acting as a " harmonizing " influence, and the Germans are hoping to move increasingly towards this.

England and America, each in their own particular sphere, have manifested a widespread opposition to uniformity and educational prescriptions of any kind. In both countries there is strong feeling against delegating the control of education to a central national authority, an equally strong belief in local control as a method of stimulating voluntary effort on the part of the community. None the less, both countries have had to realize that the extreme form of decentralization they have enjoyed has in the long run militated against securing equality of opportunity, and have had to make definite moves towards some further form of centralization to harmonize over-all endeavour. Little more than twenty years ago there existed in the United States 40,605 separate local administrative bodies for education, with more members on the boards of education in some States than there were teachers, and ranging in size from localities with a single teacher school to a system like that of New York City with about 36,000 teachers. In England there were no fewer than 315 local education authorities, some very progressive, some extremely backward. England has now managed to reduce this number of local authorities to 163, and the number of local boards in the United States is being rapidly diminished.[1] In England also, the Education Act of 1944, replacing the old Board of Education by a Ministry of Education, has given greater powers of determining policy to this Ministry which has in turn assumed a larger share in the financial support of education. Over the last thirty years or so moves have been constantly made to secure a greater participation by the Federal Government in the provision of funds for education, but—apart from funds for various special types of education, mainly vocational—any attempts through Federal aid to equalize educational opportunities or to establish reasonable standards throughout the whole country have been resisted through fear of Federal control. The fundamental problems for both England and the United States are thus those of how to increase funds for education from the national purse without interfering with the rights of local authorities to adapt education to local or regional needs, and how also to maintain satisfactory standards of education uniformly throughout the country.

If the American Federal Government has played virtually no part in education, neither can the State governments themselves be said to be in a position to exercise the same control within each state that is exercised by the *Land* within Germany, for example. Within each state there is a Board of Education responsible to the legislative power for issuing general directives and programmes of education for the training of teachers, and for meeting roughly 50 per cent. of the total cost of education. The rest of the money has to be found by the separate L.E.A's which vary greatly in size, population, wealth and efficiency. It is, therefore, the L.E.A. that determines more particularly the actual programme of studies and decides what salaries are to be paid, the local costs for education (about 70 per cent.) being met out of the local rates and taxes on a special budget. This is the direct result of the Jefferson championing of democracy which, it

---

[1] Some 18,000 for the year 1971. In England and Wales further re-organization is now taking place, the number being reduced to 101 (including 8 for Wales).

will be remembered, argued that education was a function of government—of local self-government. In a word, the Jeffersonian approach means that the history of education in the United States is the history of the education of the public itself, and that progress must depend on the ability of the general public to realize education's value and significance. Hence the emphasis, in all local communities, on education weeks, press publicity, school demonstrations, public education meetings, school exhibitions, parent-teacher associations. Education must be kept constantly in the public eye. The taxpayer must know that he is getting value for his money, and a healthy rivalry must be fostered between neighbouring communities both to stir the sluggish and to lead to further experimentation. More recently, as the disadvantages under which the smaller and poorer communities have to work have been more acutely realized, these have been encouraged (wherever practicable) to pool their resources and build a common school to which children may travel from the more distant parts by bus. Where there is no adequate high school accommodation, arrangements are being increasingly made with the nearest authority, capable and willing to absorb an extra population, to take the high school children of the " foreign " L.E.A. on a *per capita* basis of payment. Over the whole of this the Federal Office of Education in Washington keeps an approving eye and confines itself in the main to carrying on the job it was assigned when first created in 1867 : that of collecting and diffusing such statistics and facts as are calculated generally to promote the cause of education throughout the U.S.A.

The central authority over education in England and Wales is the Ministry of Education,[1] with a politically chosen Minister who has a seat in the Cabinet, and a staff of permanent civil servants divided into two groups : those who serve at the administrative central headquarters, and those who act as inspectors and who are assigned to areas administered by local authorities. The Ministry does not maintain, provide, or directly control any kind of educational institution, but through its inspectorate it none the less exercises considerable influence. The work of the inspectors—who are servants of the Crown and not of the Minister—falls into three clearly defined areas : that of inspecting schools, consulting with local authorities and teachers and giving advice where necessary; that of representing the Minister in their local areas on administra-

[1] Now re-named Department of Education and Science.

tive matters; and that of advising the Minister in matters of educational theory and practice and of being responsible for the Ministry's publications. Prior to the passing of the Education Act of 1944 only state-aided schools were subject to inspection; under the terms of the Act *all* schools without exception must be open to inspection and must conform to minimum requirements as laid down by the Ministry. The function of the L.E.A's is to provide a full range of educational opportunity at the primary, secondary, technical and further education levels, and they are responsible to the Ministry for the proper conduct of the schools they establish. Just as each L.E.A. in the United States has its superintendent of schools, so in England there is the chief education officer. The important difference between the United States and England, however, is over the matter of finance : fully two-thirds of the total expenditure on education in each L.E.A. in England comes from national funds; in the United States the Federal Office of Education has until recently contributed almost nil, the local state boards up to 50 per cent., the L.E.A. meeting the remainder.[1]

It is in many ways an interesting object lesson for the Americans to note that, despite the large sums devoted to education from the State funds in England, the L.E.A. still retains considerable independence of action. On the other hand, the Education Act of 1944 brought England much closer to European practice by replacing the former President of the Board of Education by a Minister and a Ministry of Education, and by giving the Minister much more positive functions. In addition to inspecting and allocating grants (as formerly) the Minister is further enjoined to " promote the education of the people of England and Wales." He can compel the L.E.A's when necessary and advisable to adopt a definite line of policy. And the Act itself, in order to iron out glaring inconsistencies, actually commanded local authorities to provide facilities—such as nursery school accommodation and schools for handicapped children—that had not formerly been readily available. It is unlikely, however, that there will be any significant further move towards more complete centralization. The peculiar English traditions of local government and of voluntary service at that level are too firmly entrenched.

---

[1] In 1968 however more than 12 per cent. of all educational expenditure came from Federal funds as opposed to a mere 3 per cent. in the late 1940's.

CHAPTER SEVEN

The Training of Teachers

AS we have seen, every national system of education has some clearly defined objective that is determined for it by the particular kind of political theory considered most desirable by the whole of society. It may be, of course, that society as a whole has preferred to leave the attainment of the ideal state of existence aimed at to the dictatorial powers either conferred upon or usurped by a few, as was the case in Nazi Germany, or that each individual citizen takes an active and personal share and responsibility (as in Switzerland) in matters of government. No matter how practice varies between these two extremes, in the same way as the administration of education is geared to produce the appropriate amount of responsibility (or docility) in the citizens of the State, so is the training of teachers inevitably an important element in maintaining the State ideal. As is the school, so is society. And as is the teacher, so is the school. Thus no country can afford not to give particularly close attention to this problem, and the different ways in which the problem is faced by the different countries once again give a key to national aspirations and afford some explanation of the divergences that exist between nation and nation in seeking to resolve some major issue that is the common concern of all.

The United States and Russia, for example, both vaunt the importance of their common school systems as being a prime factor in achieving real equality of opportunity within the particular form of democratic government they prize. Both are insistent on the equal importance of teacher-training at the primary and secondary school levels. In Russia, however, it is clearly laid down for the whole of the Soviet Republics exactly what shall be taught in the training colleges, and in what proportion. In the United States there are considerable divergences from state to state, and there is unlimited freedom for experimentation which is constantly and actively encouraged. Again, countries like France and Belgium which still lay great stress on the formation of an intellectual élite have by no means accepted the necessity for any form of serious training for future teachers in the academic type of secondary school, though they have given much thought and care to the formation of the teacher who is to instruct the child of primary school age. Where the dual system of education still persists in the minds of men despite the post-war reforms that have attempted to eradicate its evil effects, there is still reluctance to concede that to learn the craft of teaching is as necessary to the " professeur " as to the " instituteur." This attitude of mind springs also, of course, from the persistence of the dichotomy between " instruction " and " éducation."

Indeed, we must remember that until the mid-nineteenth century, when the ideas of new education began to make themselves for the first time heard in the schools, the general techniques applied to teaching had not changed much since Sumerian times. That is to say, the adult was expected to break down his subject matter into what to his adult mind appeared to be the necessary digestible elements, and then to compel his pupil to master by heart these elements. Hence, for example, the persistence of the idea in English schools until relatively modern times of learning by heart the dates of kings and queens of England; of capes, bays and estuaries around the coast of our islands; and of intricate rules of French grammar and of irregular plurals of all kinds. The teacher instructed and disciplined his pupils, and " éducation," in so far as it was held to be the concern of the school, was held to be a by-product of this necessary instruction. It is to Pestalozzi and Froebel (and the many other reformers, some of whom we have discussed in detail in Chapter Four) as well as to Herbart, who based his educational views on a new and carefully worked-out psychology, that in Western Europe in particular we owe the shift in emphasis to the child, the recognition of the need for an understanding of the child, and therefore of the need for adequate teacher training that goes far beyond the former practice of instilling into the would-be teacher sufficient knowledge for him to parcel out in appropriate doses to his charges. It is to John Dewey's penetrating criticism of Herbartian methods, which led finally to the formulation of his own doctrines, that we also owe much of the present-day " child-centred " approach to teaching that always closely follows the most recent findings of the psychologists.

The necessity for effecting a complete change in whatever teacher training methods were in vogue really came, however, with the spread of free, compulsory and universal education. And this only was realized when governments at last understood that in the new technological and scientific age that was heralded into real being with the turn of the century it was most important for the masses of the people to have a kind of education that went beyond the acquisition of mere literacy and simple number. Similarly, as the children in the schools had to be given opportunities for proving their aptitude for a variety of different pursuits, all demanding an increasing amount of skill and intelligent understanding of what was involved, so did it become necessary to cease recruiting teachers at the primary level from amongst those who had themselves little more than a primary education. He who would educate others must himself be educated, and have a broad background of general cultural training, for it is only the teacher who has himself enjoyed a broad liberal education who can hope to avoid the pitfalls of routine pedestrianism and show resourcefulness and enterprise in his work. Again, just as the responsibilities of the teacher to-day transcend the mere imparting of subject matter and demand of him that he have a knowledge and understanding of the place and function of the subject he professes in preparing his pupils to lead a full and meaningful life (as well as an economically useful one), so do they make of him a still more important cog in the machinery of good government, still more obviously an instrument of society. In actual practice this is shown by the way in which he is expected in a variety of ways to be a diagnostician : to keep records about the health, environment, social background and mental testing of his pupils; to mix freely with parents in parent-teacher associations and discuss with the parents problems which were once thought to be the sole concern of the parents and are now accepted as the joint concern of both. Open days at school, school exhibitions and displays of all kinds, school journeys and excursions and visits to factories and works which bring the pupil into ever closer contact with the realities of modern existence amid the baffling perplexity of increasing specialization—all these are part of the routine of the modern teacher. To sum up, the teacher to-day in the various Western

European countries is being forced by the sheer pressure of industrial advance and technological change to follow much more closely the example set by the United States; by the necessity in this new age for educating all children for responsibilty, to abandon much of the ivory tower academic approach. Before we consider how each of the European countries with which we are familiar has set about the task of teacher training in the light of the problems with which it is faced it will therefore pay us best to see first what has been done in the United States.

The U.S.A. We have seen that the underlying principles behind American public education can be summarized as decentralization, free, compulsory and universal education, one educational ladder (involving one system of articulated schools leading from the kindergarten to the university), and equality of educational opportunity for all—though this in practice, due to the policy of extreme decentralization, is not generally realized. Thus, the great variety of practices and standards which as a result of this policy prevail throughout the educational systems of the United States lead to as great a variety of standards in the training of teachers. In effect, all kinds of methods of teacher preparation are found from high school classes which maintain courses in school law, teaching and psychology, to local and state normal schools, to teachers' colleges, and to education departments in colleges and universities. And these divergences from state to state and from local authority to local authority are due to the wide divergences that prevail in economic conditions, in the popular attitude to education, in the effectiveness and inspiration of local control, and in the social status that is accorded a teacher. Inspired and go-ahead authorities consider the teacher a king-pin in the social system and do their utmost to recruit the best and to give them a thorough training. Others treat the teacher as someone appointed to " deliver the goods " as in a factory or business concern, and until relatively recently it was no unknown thing for teachers in certain districts to have no security of tenure, or to be appointed on a contract for one year only with no knowledge as to whether that contract would be renewed. In too many areas they are still far too much at the mercy of the local superintendent of schools, who in turn must see that the rate and taxpayer is satisfied that he is getting value for the money spent on education. Thus, statistics of the average length of service for all teachers throughout the United States are very revealing : in 1914 it was four years; in 1941 it had only risen to nine years. It should also be noted that teaching is primarily considered a woman's job in the United States, men who enter the profession usually staying there only a few years before passing on to administration, which is considered their *forte*. It would seem that as America developed historically as a nation, and passed from the period of national expansion to that of economic expansion (see Chapter Three), so were the early ideals of people like Thomas Jefferson to make of education a civic force betrayed (or at least pushed into the background) in favour of ideals of materialism and individualism.[1]

There is, of course, another and more important side to the picture. It was during the period of national expansion that the first normal school (called a " normal school " after the *écoles normales* introduced into France by Guizot in 1834) was established in Lexington, Massachusetts, and this in 1839. By 1850 most of the New England states had established similar institutions, and by the end of the century every state in the union had at least one such normal school. The high schools also were devoting their attention to the problem of teacher training, but, with the rapid new provision of high schools that came with the twentieth century, intending primary teachers came to be required to graduate from high school before passing on to the normal school. Such graduation was made compulsory in 1890 in New York, in 1894 in Massachusetts. Thus, though the American teacher training college had been originally modelled on the European pattern, it quickly developed in a distinctively American way and planned from the first its curriculum and methods to meet the needs and ideals of the American democratic way of life, paying much closer attention to education as a science and carrying the professional training much further forward than was usual in Europe. Again, the rapid expansion of the high school system meant that a more competently trained recruit to primary teaching could be secured than before, whilst it also ensured quite early in the present century (when in most European countries primary teachers were still in effect debarred from any form of secondary education) that the primary teacher achieved freedom from his purely primary environment. The next logical step was for the normal schools to insist on their ability and on their right to prepare teachers for

[1] Consult Raymond E. Callahan's *Education and the Cult of Efficiency*, University of Chicago Press, 1962.

service in all types of public education, since there was but one educational ladder, and this led to their transition from two-year normal schools to four-year degree granting State teachers' colleges. Some of these newly formed colleges have remained as purely teacher training institutions; others, for a number of reasons (often economic), have become multiple-purposed and admit students who have no intention of teaching to a variety of different courses. It is also becoming an increasing practice for intending primary school teachers to be trained in university departments of education.

The interest shown by the universities in teacher training goes back to the year 1873 when the University of Iowa founded the first permanent chair in education in the United States " to prepare students for *advanced* schools." The New England states seem to have been content for the time being with the normal schools that were in existence, though it is interesting to note a project of New York University in 1832 to establish a chair in education to instruct " teachers of common schools." However, though the idea was firmly rooted that the normal schools did and could provide adequate teacher training for all types of schools, and though some of them quite early did become attached to universities, the lead given by Iowa was soon followed by other universities who were immediately faced with the problem (by no means unknown in Western Europe to-day) of persuading other faculties that education was and could be a serious academic subject. Fortunately for America in many ways, the influx of new ideas in education from Europe coincided with the need to stake an academic claim for education, and fortunately also there were men willing and able to meet the challenge. Degrees in education were soon established as a matter of course. Men of the stature of Dewey and Stanley Hall, Thorndike and Charles H. Judd, perfected the techniques of a science of education, started an educational psychology movement, a child study movement and an educational measurement movement and gave a new and vital impulse to the whole problem of teacher training and the study of education just at the time, again, when the country—undergoing as it was a vast industrial development—was ripe for it. It may be that as a result of this urge and necessity to " establish " education America has gone too far in the direction of a purely scientific approach and neglected the social values by which Dewey himself set much store. It may be also that from the point of view of purely academic studies the ground is " thin." None the less, we in Western Europe in comparison have still a long way to go with our post-war reforms at the teacher training level, and we can learn a lot (both of what to emulate and what to avoid) from a close study of present American practice.

Nowadays, the minimum requirement for admission to normal schools and teacher training colleges is graduation from the high school, and whilst four years of training in a recognized college is a standard requirement for secondary teaching, some states (now generally in a minority) only exact two or three years for teachers in the primary schools. It is, of course, widely held in the United States that there is no one way to educate teachers and that no one type of institution is best suited to the job. Experimentation is important. Thus, curriculum and methods of training vary from institution to institution. Generally speaking, however, it can be said that there is a broad basic course consisting of general education, general and educational psychology, general and special methods of teaching, and practice teaching. The course in general education is obligatory for two years, and the University of Minnesota, for example, states that " the purpose of general education is to help you to take your place in contemporary society, whatever your occupation or your interests may be." The courses in general education are centred on the major areas of human knowledge : the humanities, the social sciences, the natural sciences. In addition, much attention is usually paid to what is termed " communication "—that is to say a study of the English language expressly from the teacher's point of view, and involving both composition and speech. There is naturally an opportunity for specialization, both for secondary and for primary school teachers. The latter more usually take a special course on some aspect of child development or methods of teaching; the former will tend to specialize in one particular academic subject or subjects.

Increasing attention is being given to the periods of practical teaching in the schools. A typical practice is to send the student in the third year for a nine-week period in charge of a suitable " critic " teacher, the student's work being planned by his college adviser in conjunction with the critic teacher, and frequent conferences being held amongst all three. A student must then apply for a practice period in the fourth year, and this application is most carefully considered in the light of his past achievement. A further period of nine weeks' continuous teaching then results, and at the end the various reports of the supervisor, of the teachers concerned with the student, and all other relevant information gleaned will be taken into consideration for giving a final assessment which must be confirmed by the State Commissioner for Education. The teacher will then receive from the State authorities, *not* a " life " certificate to teach, but one that is valid for usually three years and subject to renewal. Neither mediocrity nor excellence are accepted as something necessarily static and unchangeable. Hence, the extreme success of courses for the " in-service " training of teachers, for summer schools for teachers, for workshop conferences and the like during all of which the teacher may not only broaden and bring up to date his professional background but also prepare for further degrees at the master's and doctorate levels.

Thus the final picture that emerges is one of apparently healthy dynamism and drive, of experimentation and eagerness to press onwards, of training (at least academically) in breadth rather than in depth. Education is looked upon ultimately as an important means of helping individuals to meet effectively their personal and social needs which are in a constant process of evolution as they and their society mature. There is no better illustration of the way in which American national character determines the form and content of the educational process than that afforded by the approach to the training of teachers. Nor, for that matter, is there a better illustration than in teacher training generally of the truth of Sir Michael Sadler's constant belief that " England stands half-way, as it were, between the American and the German ideals " in education, and that therefore " Great Britain is one of the bridges between East and West."

Generally speaking, the European system of teacher training throughout the nineteenth century was based on the fact that pupils from the State primary schools did not proceed to any form of secondary education. It was the custom, therefore, to recruit the teachers for the primary schools from amongst those who had progressed towards the top of the primary ladder, and no degree of culture or of academic knowledge was required of them. The teachers in the secondary schools were likewise products exclusively of the type of school in which they taught, and all that was required of them was the possession of a good university degree. Again, the more authoritarian the country, the more closely was the primary teacher confined to the subjects he was to teach and to the level at which he was judged fit to teach them. At the primary level, and in order to cope with the shortage of teachers that became apparent with the spread of free and universal primary education, for the first half of the century a system of " mutual instruction " (based on the Bell and Lancaster system) was much in vogue. By 1850, however, this had been generally abandoned in favour of some system of State licensing either after a period of training in a normal school or after a period of real apprenticeship on the " pupil-teacher " system, this being a Dutch invention and much in favour in both England and Holland. Holland took the lead by opening the first normal school in 1816 and by developing an inspectorate which had amongst its tasks that of seeing that pupil-teachers were adequately and properly trained. Before 1835 France, Scandinavia, Prussia and Switzerland had all established publicly controlled normal schools. In 1840, but only on a semi-official basis, came the Battersea Normal School in England. It aimed at " reconciling a simplicity of life not remote from the habits of the humble classes, with such proficiency in intellectual attainments, such a knowledge of method, and such skill in the art of teaching, as would enable the pupils selected to become efficient masters of elementary schools." [1]

England. Following this pattern, training colleges for primary school teachers in England continued to spring up in an individual and haphazard way, being at first established by voluntary or religious bodies, and much later by local education authorities. Gradually—though the pupil-teacher system perpetuated itself in varying forms well into the twentieth century—the system settled down to an acceptance of two years' professional preparation at a training college after satisfactory completion of a secondary school course, though insistence on adequate preparation at a secondary level did not become in any way general until well after the passing of the Balfour Act of 1902. Even then, however, the kind of preparation offered from training college to training college varied enormously both in quality and in standards of performance expected of the students. There was no over-all co-

---

[1] Quoted by H. C. Barnard : *A Short History of English Education.* U.L.P. 1947, p. 118.

ordinating policy, little vital contact between college and college, and—what was far worse—a feeling of inferiority engendered in the training college student *vis à vis* his more academically or financially fortunate school mate who managed to secure for himself a university education on a promise to teach on the successful completion of a four-year course (three years to a degree and one year post-graduate training in the university department of education) paid for him by the then Board of Education.[1] There was, of course, no contact of any real value between the training colleges and the universities. It was a dual system of teacher preparation, a cleavage equally as strong as that holding in France or Belgium (or indeed most of the Western European countries) and lacking the merits of uniformly high standards of preparation that a highly centralized system could exact.

The first attempt made at securing professional training for secondary school teachers came with the foundation of the College of Preceptors in 1846 and its establishment of the first chair of education in 1872, which was in existence for only four years. University chairs in education were established in 1876 at Edinburgh and at St. Andrews. In 1878 the Maria Grey Training College for Women was founded. In 1879 a teachers' training syndicate was started at Cambridge, and a Cambridge training college for women was opened in 1885. In 1890, university day training departments were opened, primarily for the training of future primary school teachers (who could also read for a degree) though they increasingly reacted in favour of training teachers for the new secondary schools that came to be established in increasing numbers after the Balfour Act of 1902. As is still the case in Belgium, those who read for a degree in these day training colleges ran their professional training concurrently with the academic work. This unsatisfactory system was not changed until 1911 when the present system of four-year courses started.

It was obvious, therefore, that with the passing of the Education Act of 1944 a system of teacher training that should have more organic unity became a necessity. In 1926 a move had been made in this direction by the Board of Education's decision to delegate the responsibility for the certificate examination of training college students to regional boards on which the universities and the local

[1] This unsatisfactory method of recruiting secondary school teachers by paying for the whole of their university education and exacting a promise to teach at the end of it came to an end only in 1951.

education authorities were represented, and by the association of a group of training colleges for this purpose with a university (or universities). The McNair Report took the necessary and decisive step forward by recommending the establishment of area training organizations involving the pooling of resources and facilities by the universities, the training colleges, the local education authorities, into a teacher training centre based administratively on a university and to be known as the university's institute of education. Seventeen such institutes were created. Their functions can be described briefly as supervising the course of training in their member institutions (of which the university department of education was one); to recommend qualified students for certification as teachers; to plan the development of all kinds of further training at all levels in the area; to provide an education centre not only for teachers in training but also for teachers in service; to provide opportunities for further study, to encourage research, and to organize courses for teachers in service. Thus, the university became (as never before) the focal centre for the training of teachers of all kinds and (if the institute was properly directed and used) a constant source of help and inspiration to all teachers working within the institute area.

The importance of the reforms following the recommendations of the McNair Report is that not only was a truly decentralized system of teacher training evolved, reducing governmental and ministerial control to an absolute minimum, but also that general agreement on curricula in training establishments as well as a uniform standardization was achieved whilst allowing an absolute maximum of freedom for experimentation and pioneer work. On the other hand, it cannot with any truth be claimed that the dichotomy between the training colleges and university departments of education did in actual practice disappear. Similarly —and this has its bearing on relationships between departments of education in universities and training colleges—the country as a whole was by no means as yet convinced that a fourth year of professional study was absolutely necessary to the graduate who had studied his subject in depth and who wished to go on to teach it in the academic type of secondary school. Until 1973 there was still no legal requirement for a university graduate to possess a teaching qualification before taking up a post in any type of school, though many local authorities had begun exacting such qualifications. And university departments of education are still striving hard to get education recognized as an academic subject at the university level. Recent moves in the right direction, however, have led to the extension of training to three years for primary teachers (1960), and (on the recommendations of the Robbins Report, 1963) the re-naming of teacher-training colleges as Colleges of Education. By the same token schools of education were established in the universities to integrate more closely all teacher-training and educational studies and also to make it possible for the more able students from Colleges of Education to read for an appropriate university degree.[1]

To-day there is a grand total of 211 institutions devoted to the education of teachers, and, with the University Departments of Education being unable to cope with all post-graduates now obliged to seek professional teaching qualifications, Colleges of Education have been encouraged to admit up to 30 per cent of their total intake for one-year post-graduate certificate awards—this proving a very healthy step towards further bridging the gap between the colleges and the universities. Colleges of Education have also been able to raise the minimum standard requirements for entry to approximate more closely to those exacted by the universities, whilst the creation of the B.Ed. degree (awarded by the university with which a college is associated by virtue of its membership of an Institute or School of Education) has considerably enhanced their reputation for academic "respectability".

The James Report of 1972 on *Teacher Education and Training* was eagerly and passionately debated and resulted in the publication of official governmental policy at the end of the year in a White Paper, *Education: A Framework for Expansion*. Briefly, the recommendations are that following governmental reorganization of local authorities into larger units there shall be a parallel re-structuring of area training organizations to make for greater efficiency at all levels of higher education; that Colleges of Education shall develop into Liberal Arts Colleges awarding a Diploma of Higher Education after two years' initial study—it also being hoped that universities may wish to award the same diploma;[2] that those students who wish to teach may add a third

---

[1] There are now 22 Institutes or Schools of Education.
[2] Note the parallel here with university reforms in France.

year to obtain an *ordinary* B.Ed. degree, and a fourth year to convert this into an " Honours " B.Ed.; that those not intending to teach may leave with the possession of the Diploma in Higher Education, or convert it similarly into other kinds of degrees; that for newly qualified teachers there be an " induction " year of further training on the job under the close supervision of competent tutors;[1] and that every seven years teachers shall be released for one term for further study and training.

Germany. The growth of education in Germany was conditioned by the stress of Germany's change from an agglomeration of farming provinces to an empire based on industry and trade, by the domination of a strong ruling Prussian group, and by the development of a highly efficient armed force. Coming late in the field to an industrial switch-over, Germany had to develop very early an efficient educational machine and had therefore to give much serious thought to the preparation of teachers at both the primary and the secondary level. In 1810 Humboldt raised the profession of the *gymnasium* teacher to a high level of dignity and efficiency by introducing the measure (still in force to-day) that all secondary teachers should be required to do two years' probationary work in the schools on the completion of their degree course and at the end of that time should submit themselves before final acceptance as a teacher to a test both as to competence in the subject professed and as to ability to teach. As the training colleges for primary teachers grew in number and importance, the State, made increasingly apprehensive by the growing associations of primary school teachers and by the revolution of 1848, and increasingly convinced that the people must be thoroughly drilled to play their part as the docile yet necessary partner in a growing imperialistic national outlook, took more and more concern over details of curricula and preparation of primary teachers for their admittedly important task. And so it was that Matthew Arnold in his report to the Schools' Inquiry Commission in 1866 could write that " the school system of Germany in its completeness and carefulness is such as to excite the foreigner's admiration." Obviously, he saw but one side of the picture, and that its administratively attractive side. Efficient preparation of intending teachers was turning out really skilled craftsmen, but their studies at the primary level were severely limited and curtailed to that amount

---

[1] This approximates to what has long been German practice.

of knowledge they were required to put over in the classroom. Again, there was a distinct cleavage between the kind of work done in the training colleges and the university training given to future teachers in the *gymnasien,* and this cleavage was further accentuated by the liberal and free outlook that the universities, as independent institutions, could enjoy. The training colleges were subtly geared to reconcile the interests of the primary teachers with those of the State; the universities enjoined their students to pursue knowledge in depth for its own sake and to eschew political matters as not being primarily the concern of the intellectual. It is true, of course, that the regulations enforced by the State of Prussia on the whole of Germany rigidly to control the work of the training colleges were modified in a more liberal direction in 1872 (when the University of Leipzig made it possible for the best students from the training colleges to embark on university courses) and that further modifications in the curriculum came in 1901. None the less, the " two-track " system of education and of the preparation of teachers remained more or less cast in the same rigid Prussian mould until the German Republic, under the Weimar Constitution, sought to liberalize the teaching generally and to prepare their primary school teachers " according to the principles which apply generally to higher education " (Article 143 of the constitution). Though the attempted reforms were greeted with great optimism and though newer and progressive methods came in with the introduction of outdoor activities and projects that went with an expanded curriculum, they were finally killed by the gradual reversion to force culminating in Hitler's rise to power. It was left to the new German Federal Republic of the post-1945 period firstly to clear up the educational chaos into which the country had been plunged and then to try and pick up the story all over again from where the Weimar Republic's liberalizing movement had failed.

One of the first steps taken was for the whole of the *Länder* to agree at least in principle at a meeting of the Permanent Conference of Ministers of Education that the education of future teachers in the primary schools should be raised to university level, and that satisfactory completion of a full secondary school course should be a prerequisite for embarking on the training course. Training courses for primary teachers are now given in what can be generically termed pedagogical institutes (the one in Hamburg is closely connected with the university)[1] and the duration of these courses is either of two or three years, dependent on the different regulations in each of the *Länder*. The university practice of freedom of learning is followed as closely as possible, and though not much time can be allotted to scholarly research, certain limited research projects are undertaken by all the students under the guidance of their supervisors. The course of studies is designed to give the student a thorough training in one special field of knowledge of his own choosing, and includes a solid grounding in educational psychology and various methods of teaching as well as pupil observation and periods of practical teaching.

At the end of his course the student takes his first teachers' examination and is then assigned to a school in the normal way. For the next two years,[2] however, he works under special supervision and guidance and has to attend regular study-group meetings directed usually by an experienced teacher delegated for that purpose by the Ministry of Education. He then presents himself for the second teachers' examination for which he has to submit a thesis treating some phase of educational practice and a report of his experiences during the period of his in-service training. The core of the examination is composed of two trial lessons, one of the candidate's choice, one set by the examiners. An oral examination follows; thesis, report and trial lessons are discussed, and the successful candidate is then awarded his certificate of qualification to teach in a primary school and made eligible for permanent appointment.

Primary school teachers who have thus successfully qualified may, after gaining what is judged sufficient practical experience, then present themselves for a similar examination to allow them to teach in the *Mittelschulen*. Some *Länder*, however, consider that a three-year special university course in school subjects and education should be the minimum basic training for the middle school teacher.

Students heading for a career as grammar school (*gymnasium*) teachers must have studied for at least four years at the university or (for subjects such as mathematics, chemistry, geography, geology, etc.) at an institute of technology. There is then the usual final university examination to test their proficiency in their chosen

---

[1] Since 1964 this is also true for Hesse and Bavaria.
[2] In some *Länder* the probationary period lasts three years.

academic field. Some universities (notably Hamburg) insist that during this time intending teachers must serve short periods in different types of schools in order to make quite sure that they feel fitted for teaching. On completing his university studies proper the candidate is then admitted to a two-year period of in-service training in appropriate secondary schools (usually one year in each of two schools) where he has to observe the instruction given by experienced teachers and do some carefully supervised teaching himself. In addition he has to attend seminar sessions every week where the problems of practical teaching are related to educational theory and at which seminars he must present appropriate papers for discussion. The final examination consists of two trial lessons, the presentation of a thesis, and (usually) an oral examination on his knowledge of educational theory in general and of the methods of instruction in his particular subjects. The successful candidate is then eligible for appointment on a provisional basis, being what is termed a *Studienassessor*. Usually, he has to wait several years before the authorities confer upon him the title of *Studienrat* which gives him recognition as a fully qualified teacher of civil service status.

All primary and secondary school teachers naturally have the same official standing once their appointments are confirmed. They are civil servants, however, who owe their allegiance to the *Land* which employs them, pays them, and secures for them professional advancement. It is as rare (though now possible) for a teacher to move outside his *Land* as it is for an intending student to seek his training under some other authority. For despite sincere protestations of the necessity for moving towards a real democratic way of life that shall embrace the whole of the German Federal Republic, the various *Länder* jealously guard their autonomy and their age-old responsibility for the welfare of those who comprise the *Land*. It should further be remembered that the Germans are still proudly conscious of the fact that the training of the primary school teacher has always been made to reflect the cultural aims of the whole country as that of the *gymnasium* teacher has been devised to secure that the work done in the *gymnasien* shall be of the highest possible level of intellectual attainment. The easing of the way for all classes of children to be able to profit from a *gymnasium* education does not mean that standards in the *gymnasien* are in any way going to be lowered. Thus, at the primary school level there is an insistence on a really sound and comprehensive general education that will adequately prepare for entrance to the *gymnasium,* and an equal insistence on having the primary school teacher better trained than before. All of this leads to clearly defined hierarchical divisions between teachers in the primary schools, in the middle schools, and in the *gymnasien*. If the aim of the ambitious teacher in the French *lycée* may be said to be that of securing eventually a university post, so in German schools do teachers look far too frequently to bettering their position by moving from the primary school to the middle school, or from the middle school to the *gymnasium*. Salary scales, of course, have much to do with this, but salary scales are not the whole story. As in Holland, education means a lot and status based on educational attainment and position is real and much prized.

However, with the schools in Germany beginning to be re-organized (as elsewhere) on comprehensive lines, the necessity for training a " comprehensive " teacher is now being empha-sized. A parallel problem is an acute shortage of teachers due in part to the population " explosion " but also to the rigid " class " differentiation between teachers. In 1970 the Ministers for Education of the various *Länder* agreed on proposals for the harmonization of teacher training and of teachers' salaries. In future teachers will no longer be distinguished by the type of school in which they are trained to serve, but by the age or grade level for which they are recognized as competent to teach, the traditional terms *Volksschullehrer, Realschullehrer* and *Studienrat* disappearing. Training itself will comprise common basic studies in education for *all* and specialized studies in one or two particu-lar subjects, the minimum duration for any course being three years. Again, *all* newly-fledged teachers will have to undergo a supervised probationary teaching stage of eighteen months.

France. Proof of the statement that the character of a people is revealed in its institutions could hardly better be found than in an examination of the conditions governing the recruitment, training and eventual status of the French primary school teacher. Because he is regarded first and foremost as responsible for handing on knowledge, high intellectual qualifications are required of him in proportion relative to those required of the teacher in the *lycée*. Because he is a civil servant and part of an efficient and highly organized and centralized bureaucratic machine, then entry to the teaching profession is on an entirely competitive basis as with all other civil service appointments. Because primary education is provided free of charge to all schoolchildren, those who wish to teach in primary schools are almost entirely supported by the State during their period of training and (since 1947) they also receive a modest salary from the moment they set about practice teaching in the schools. Because the country as a whole is still firmly wedded to the idea of *instruction du peuple* and *préparation d'un élite* and cannot see how the two can properly be mixed, the traditional distinction in status between the primary and the secondary teacher still remains. True, the Langevin Commission for the post-war reform of education insisted that the preparation of primary and secondary school teachers was one and the same task and that they should in consequence be all educated to university level. This recommendation, however, remains more or less a dead letter. All that has been achieved is to raise the standard of recruitment for entry to teachers' training colleges, to ease the way for really promising students to take university courses (or their equivalent), and to organize some sort of professional training for the university graduate who wishes to teach in either the classical or modern sections of the *lycée* or *collège*.

By 1869, France had established efficient training colleges for primary teachers in every *département*. By 1879, it was made compulsory by law for each *département* to maintain one training college for women as well as one for men. In 1886 and 1887, the general character and constitution of the training colleges was fixed and they were decreed lay institutions. None the less, in keeping with the French spirit of toleration, private religious bodies (usually Catholic) have been permitted to open their own colleges which must be efficiently run according to specific governmental regulations and which can prepare their students for the State primary teachers' qualifying certificate if they so desire. The majority of these students, however, take only the special college certificate and then pass on to teach in private denominational schools. Students in these private training colleges are either fee-payers or are given a grant from diocesan funds, this on a promise to teach in church schools for a number of years.

We have seen in discussing the administration of education in France (Chapter Six) that in each *département* there is a Council responsible for the whole of primary education including the recruitment, training and promotion of primary teachers. What happens in effect is that each *département* is held responsible for the provision and maintenance of the training colleges whilst the Ministry of National Education pays the salaries of the staff, prescribes the course of study and general timetable divisions and supervises the conduct of examinations. All students in a training college are resident members of the college. The governing body of a college consists of the *Recteur* of the Academy, the responsible inspector of the *département*, two representatives of the *départemental* Council, and four members (including the principal of the college) chosen by the *Recteur*.

Each year it is the duty of the *départemental* Council to decide what teachers will be required in the *département* four years later and so fix the number of places that will be open to public competition in that given year. It is a firm principle that all primary teachers must give evidence of *culture générale et savoir professionnel*. To this end all intending teachers now must hold the *baccalauréat* before embarking on their professional studies proper. Students enter the college between the ages of 15 and 17, and the work of the college divides itself usually into (*a*) a period of three years' preparation for the *baccalauréat* followed by (*b*) one year's professional training. In some cases, however, it is two and two years. Thus, not only is the academic and intellectual level of the future primary school teacher raised to that of the entrant to a university, but it is also possible as never before for a pupil to take his *baccalauréat* at a *lycée* and then to proceed to a training college for his professional studies only. Such an entrant will be required to do two years' study usually. Most of the entrants, however, have not fully completed their secondary school courses and enter either from the former *cours complémentaires* (now renamed *collèges d'enseignement général*) or from the former *collège moderne* (now a modern section *lycée*).

The competitive entrance examination is one part written and one part oral and practical. Candidates proceed to the second part only if their written papers are deemed satisfactory. The written papers consist of a spelling and dictation test (including handwriting), comments on a French text, two mathematical problems to be solved, and a translation into French from a modern language. The oral and practical examination consists of the reading of a French text and questions on its content and meaning, two questions in mathematics, the reading aloud of a literary or scientific passage to the students on which they take notes and which they have then to reproduce in their own words as a written exercise and hand in together with their notes, freehand drawing, simple sol-fa musical notation and singing, handicraft for boys and needlework for girls, and physical training. Most obviously these are, from every point of view, searching tests designed not only to discover the knowledge already possessed by the candidates and their particular abilities, but also their sensibility and mental alertness as well as a gift for clear and lucid exposition.

The training college authorities seek to awaken among their students a spirit of initiative and a sense of responsibility, to inculcate " *le goût de la tolérance à l'endroit des êtres et des idées . . . la connaissance et le gouvernement de soi.*" A further important postwar reform is that once a brilliant student has obtained his *baccalauréat*, or later his *certificat de fin d'études normales*, he can obtain scholarships to continue his studies at a higher normal school and push on to the *agrégation*, or to C.A.P.E.S. (see below), and so to an assured and coveted place as a teacher at the *lycée* level. In other words, the training colleges are no longer recruiting solely from amongst the best pupils in the primary school streams and returning them to teach solely in the primary schools. In preparing for the *baccalauréat*, however, since most students will teach in primary schools, they choose the modern scientific section which was originally created in the modern type *lycée* (see page 229). The first part of the *baccalauréat* is completed in the first two years. In the third year the majority of the students in the training college will take the experimental sciences section for the second part of the *baccalauréat*, whilst the few brilliant ones we have already mentioned will opt either for the philosophy section or the mathematics section, and will then present themselves as candidates in the competitive examination for entry to the higher normal school.

The French still believe firmly in the value of demonstration and observation schools (*écoles annexes*) that are attached to the training college, but they also make use for purposes of demonstration of other schools and particular teachers selected by the inspector. The students themselves are required to do one continuous month of supervised teaching in each of the three terms of their final year. At the end of his course the student sits the usual written and oral examinations in principles of education, history of education and psychology and is also required to give proof of ability to teach *any* of the classes that fall within the province of the primary school teacher, as well as the general range of subjects, including physical training and music. This final practical test usually takes place after a probationary period as a full-time teacher in a school. On the strength of it the student is awarded his *certificat d'aptitude pédagogique* which completes his *certificat de fin d'études normales* (awarded on the theory work) and entitles him to appointment within the *département* to whatever vacancy there exists. He cannot choose his own post, nor can he be moved from the post to which he is appointed unless he asks for it, or unless he incurs disciplinary punishment for some kind of proved incompetence or unprofessional conduct—a rare occurrence.

There can be no doubt of the thoroughness of this training, and there is throughout the whole course great stress placed on the social value of the teacher to the whole community. All teachers' training colleges are resident in order the better to inculcate the values of community life and to make the students constantly aware of the role they will be called upon to play, as primary school teachers, in the community in which they will later live. It is to be remembered that France, even to-day, is primarily a country of very small townships and that almost 50 per cent. of the population is to be classified as rural. Thus, the primary school teacher is expected to organize all kinds of activities and to take a full and active part in local administration in the area he serves. He needs both social insight and a good and sound general education. The training colleges make it their proud boast to deliver the right kind of man or woman. And—be it noted—this highly centralized system which directs a teacher to fill a vacancy wherever it occurs ensures that the remote and probably unpopular areas are not denied (as in countries like England and the U.S.A.) the services of the best men and women the colleges can produce.

The picture is by no means so happy and of a piece regarding the training of secondary school teachers. Even to-day, France remains the chief protagonist among Western European countries of the idea that the strict academic training the future secondary school teacher receives in studying his subject in depth is sufficient to enable him to teach the nation's élite that will be drawn off to the academic type of secondary school. A weakening of this attitude has come about, resulting in several important post-war changes, mainly through the necessity for creating new types of secondary schools designed to have less of an academic and more of a scientific or technical bias. In France these are the former *collège moderne* (now modern section *lycée*) and the *collège technique*. None the less, the traditional outlook of the *lycée* as constituted by Napoleon still dominates the whole educational scene at the secondary level, and we must make therefore the *lycée* our starting-point.

Traditionally, the teaching staff of a *lycée* consists of *professeurs*, *adjoints d'enseignement*, *maîtres d'internat* and *surveillants d'externat*. These last two categories are really responsible for out-of-school discipline and general supervision. The posts are held on a temporary basis and are usually given to young men and women pursuing their studies beyond the *baccalauréat* with the later intention of entering secondary school teaching. The first quali-fication required to embark on a secondary school teaching career leading to the coveted position of *professeur agrégé* is a university degree awarded in a special combination of subjects chosen to fit in with what will later be taught in the *lycée*. Such a young gradu-ate may then hold the post (on a temporary basis) of *adjoint d'enseignement*. The next step for the graduate is to present him-self on a competitive basis for the *agrégation*, success in which en-titles him to nomination on a permanent basis as *professeur* of his specialist subject in a *lycée*—not necessarily the *lycée* of his choice, but the one anywhere in France where the appropriate vacancy occurs. As *professeur* he is required only to teach, and his teaching hours may not exceed between fourteen and sixteen per week, this leaving him ample time for keeping up to date with his subject and for pursuing his own private research in it. The goal of the ambitious *professeur* is ultimately a university appointment. He may also, of course, become the head of a *lycée* or a secondary schools' inspector.

Those presenting themselves for the *agrégation* must already hold the *diplôme d'études supérieures* as part of their full degree qualifications and must also have taught for at least six weeks in a *lycée*. In actual fact, of course, many have taught much longer, for it is no uncommon thing for a candidate to present himself years running before obtaining his *agrégation*. There is, however, an upper age limit of 30. Again, the examiners for the *agrégation* are so determined that the standard shall not fall that it is equally no uncommon thing for them to refuse to fill all the places vacant in any given year on the grounds that the quality of the candidates presenting themselves is not of a sufficiently high standard to warrant this.

The most usual method of preparing for the *agrégation* is from the *école normale supérieure* (two establishments for men, two for women), entry to which is again on a strictly competitive basis. Candidates must be between the ages of 18 and 23 and already in possession of their *baccalauréat*. They may not compete for a place more than three times. Usually, the candidates follow a special preparatory course lasting two to three years, and directed by the *lycée* they have been attending, before presenting themselves for this competitive entrance examination. We have already noted that post-war reforms have made it possible for the brilliant student in the *école normale*, who might originally only have intended to teach in primary schools, to prepare for this examination from his *école normale*. The ordinary degree work is done at the Sorbonne, and the *écoles normales supérieures* concern themselves with preparation of the students for the *agrégation*, and for the preliminary *diplôme d'études supérieures*. The course is thus of three to four years' duration : two for the university degree, and two for the remaining studies. All students are compelled to reside in the *école normale supérieure* for the full duration of their studies, except in very exceptional circumstances. All expenses incurred by the student are covered by the State. It is naturally possible to prepare for the *agrégation* from any of the universities without entering the *école normale supérieure*. To-day, little more than 17 per cent. of teachers in the secondary schools of France hold the *agrégation*, the remainder being absorbed into rapidly expanding university education.

The wider post-war extension of secondary educational facilities has also given rise to a new kind of certification of secondary school teachers that at present is held mainly (though not exclusively) by teachers in the former *collège moderne*. This is known as C.A.P.E.S., or—to give it its full title—*Certificat d'Aptitude au Professorat de l'Enseignement Public du Second Degré*. Preparation for this qualification ensures that in some measure there shall be some serious preparation of the teacher professionally along lines suggested in the Langevin plan for reform. Candidates must be under 30 years of age and in possession of the appropriate university degree. If they already hold the *diplôme d'études supérieures* they start with an advantage in that bonus marks are awarded them. The examination—like the *agrégation*—is on a competitive basis and the examiners also reserve the right not to fill all the places vacant in a given year if the quality of the candidates does not seem to warrant this. There are two distinct parts to the examination : a written and oral part in which the candidate is examined on the subjects he wishes to teach (as with the *agrégation*), and a practical part consisting of one year's professional training. Candidates can prepare themselves for the examination either in the university or in one of the *écoles normales supérieures*. Entry to these training establishments is also on a competitive basis, and preparation for the entry examination is either done in special classes held in the *lycée* or in the *école normale*. The course in these higher training colleges lasts three years normally, but an extra year is added for those who are preparing the *agrégation*. As with the other higher training colleges already mentioned, all student expenses are met by the State, and they are residential establishments.

Candidates for C.A.P.E.S. who are pronounced successful in the written and oral part of the examination are then assigned to the regional education centre (*centre pédagogique régional*) and there receive a small salary for professional and practical training, unless they are resident in an *école normale supérieure,* when all is already paid for them. Each student in this practice year is under the guidance of a *conseiller pédagogique*, usually a teacher of long standing and of outstanding ability. At the end of the year's practical training there is the passing out examination of at least two lessons with different classes given before a special examining body. Possession of C.A.P.E.S. entitles the teacher to a permanent appointment. Such a teacher differs in status from the *professeur agrégé* in that he receives a lower salary and is required to do a minimum of eighteen hours teaching per week.

The reader who has not given up in despair at this point in his attempt to understand teacher-training in France will appreciate what a highly complicated and highly centralized business it all is, and yet how subtly varied it all can be, with all kinds of nuance creeping in and every attempt made to sieve as finely and as intellectually equitably as possible. The aim is undeviatingly that of securing the best possible teacher in the right place, and "best possible" means always, of course, *ad maiorem Francorum gloriam*. The *lycée* has the reputation of producing an intellectual élite and jealously protects its reputation. The primary school is vowed to a *culture générale* that shall be a basis for producing the élite. The new schools that have come into being midway between the primary school and the *lycée* must also produce their particular élite. That is all there is to it, and a steady flow of ministerial circulars and directives regulates and controls the whole and leaves no individual teacher in doubt as to what is expected of him, or what is his hierarchical place (and duty) in the profession he has embraced.

It should in conclusion be mentioned that bewildering changes in the re-organization of post-primary education together with an over-all shortage of teachers at all levels has led to a number of makeshift and not entirely satisfactory situations. Primary teachers have had to be recruited straight from passing the *baccalauréat* and be given a certain amount of on-the-job training. The newly created secondary schools have absorbed into one body former higher primary school teachers, craft teachers, holders of C.A.P.E.S. and also of the *agrégation*, and the mix has not always been either fruitful or happy: the headmaster of a former higher primary school, made head of such a new secondary school, can be made to feel inadequate or even redundant as I have personally witnessed in the *Pas de Calais* area. True, such former training college products are encouraged (on a basis of in-service training) to upgrade themselves in academic respectability by taking the C.A.P.E.S. examination, but in 1971 only about one-third of the entrants were successful, whilst the figures for the same year for the C.A.P.E.S. by the traditional route only registered a success rate of 43 per cent. What are termed auxiliary teachers (those working whilst hoping in due course to achieve C.A.P.E.S. or even the coveted *agrégation*) must make up at least 30 per cent of the total teaching force in the total secondary sector.

Meantime, plans are afoot for a revision of the whole system of teacher education to bring it more closely within the university framework. As a start it is hoped in 1973/4 to set up centres for the professional training of secondary school teachers (C.F.P.M.—*Centres de Formation Professionnelle des Maîtres*), entry to which will be based on a competitive examination to sort

out some 3,800 students. Successful students will prepare for
C.A.P.E.S. and can hope to qualify in exactly the same way as a
person reading for an ordinary university degree. Thus, *competition at the end of the course* is eliminated, and C.A.P.E.S. will be
the equivalent of the *maîtrise* or master's degree. For the time
being, needless to say, the *agrégation* remains sacrosanct.

Belgium. Though the Belgians are equally insistent on preparing the educational élite in their academic grammar schools
(*athénée* for boys, *lycée* for girls, *collège* for the privately controlled
Catholic schools), and though they give as little attention to the
training of the grammar school teacher as the French, they are
much more insistent on asserting their local rights than the French
can ever be, and the school system—despite its superficially
centralized form—is much more elastic and much more provinci-
ally controlled than would at first sight appear, much more
ruggedly individualistic. Thus, the various teachers' unions are
represented on all local bodies and examine all government proposals as to salaries and to conditions of work, acting always in a
real consultative capacity. Again, the provinces of Belgium often
make themselves responsible for their own schools—as do the
wealthier communes—and until 1945 (and after) it was no unusual
thing for independent-minded and enterprising provinces and
communes to pay higher salaries than the State laid down and so
vie with one another and with the State in order to attract the best
teachers. Many still hold strongly to the view that they should
have the right to appoint their own teaching staffs, and in some
cases they even insist on holding their own competitive examinations to decide who shall be appointed.

The training colleges for primary teachers in Belgium are run
either by the State, or by provinces, or by large townships, or by
religious congregations.[1] To ensure uniformity of standards of
training, all are inspected by State inspectors and the final
examinations proceed under State supervision. None the less, the
considerable freedom that they can enjoy makes for much healthy
experimentation and there is considerable rivalry between colleges
that has an over-all beneficial result. The training is most thorough
and modern in outlook, and aims at providing a course which will
not only complete the education of the student, but also make him

[1] There are sixteen State colleges, five provincial colleges, seven colleges
run by L.E.A's, and fifty-three " free "—i.e. mainly Catholic.

a knowledgeable citizen and therefore a proficient teacher. The teaching staff of the training colleges must all be university graduates—though exceptionally a brilliant teacher who has only trained for two years at a middle school training college (of which more later) may be appointed—and they all must pass in addition a further examination to prove their aptitude and right-mindedness for the job.

Entry to training college is not, as in France, on a competitive basis except in so far as the number of applicants exceeds the number of places available in a given college. Of course, the candidate's previous school record and the recommendations made on his behalf by his teachers—as well as his behaviour in a simple examination and at an interview—are taken into consideration in deciding who shall be chosen. There are in all three distinct types of training college : the *école normale gardienne* which admits girls only from the age of 15 to train them for nursery school teaching; the *école normale primaire* for boys and girls who also enter at 15 to prepare themselves to become primary teachers proper; and the *école normale moyenne* (middle school training college) which takes boys and girls on the satisfactory completion of their secondary studies at the age of 18, or when they have obtained their teacher's certificate from the *école normale primaire*, and gives them a two-year course before graduating them as *régents* to teach in the *école moyenne* (middle school). Such students may be termed non-graduate specialists, and their teaching is done mainly in the *école moyenne* or possibly in the lowest forms of the secondary school.

The girls who train as nursery school teachers follow an intensive course of study and practical work—much of it on the job in a nursery centre—for three years. The course in the *école normale primaire* is of four years' duration. Usually the training colleges are residential establishments, and boys and girls are therefore educated separately. Those in the Flemish areas have particularly in mind the training of boys and girls who must later take a really active part in instigating and promoting cultural activities in the rural areas, but all training colleges are noteworthy in that they pay particular attention to the local customs of the area in which their students are later likely to serve. Thus, town and country brass bands are an especial pride of many areas of Flanders. The training college of Blankenberg is particularly proud of its own very efficient and competent brass band, and serious training in this particular kind of musical activity is much to the fore in the curriculum. In all training colleges much attention is also given to all forms of artistic expression, and students are taught in particular to use a blackboard artistically and with telling visual effect.

Plans for the reform of the educational pattern were first mooted by the minister Bovesse in 1936, though they were only implemented after the last war. These reform projects draw their inspiration mainly from the writings and teaching of Dr. Decroly and can briefly be stated to advocate : (1) the global method of teaching how to read and write; (2) the adaptation of all teaching to the social and regional environment; (3) direct contact with the outside world in which the basic material for living lessons can be found; (4) that each lesson should be, as far as possible, a response to the native interests of the child; (5) that confidence should be placed in the child's instinct for freedom, and that an appeal should constantly be made to his own individual efforts.

Not only is this teaching, therefore, very much to the fore in all training colleges, but the fuller post-war implementation of the Bovesse reforms has now led to the fusion of the general management of the State training college with that of the primary schools. Thus, a single line of policy is followed by the school in which the teacher has been trained and by that in which he will have to put into practice what he has learned in the training college. Furthermore, a director-general of teacher-training encourages the setting up of educational study circles, open to practising teachers, and placed under the direction of the inspectorate and of the staffs of the training colleges.

Intending teachers in the secondary schools must be in possession not only of a university degree in the subjects which they wish to teach, but also of the title of *licencié-agrégé*. In theory this implies a further year's study beyond the four years normally required to complete the degree course proper. In practice the law allows intending teachers to run this professional training course parallel with the last year's work for the degree. The disadvantages and drawbacks of such an arrangement will be obvious, but it must be said in fairness to those students who have made teaching their vocation that their interest is genuine and they usually work hard to give of their best. It will be noted that there is no competitive examination like the *agrégation* in France. The usual theoretical courses in principles of education, history of education, psychology and methodology are followed, there are certain practice periods set aside for teaching in the schools, and at the end of the course, to qualify, the candidate must receive a satisfactory mark on two lessons given by him before an examining board, the lessons being indicated by the examiners.

There is no highly centralized control and direction of teachers to their appointments as in France. A teacher is appointed by the authority responsible for the school : the State for State schools, the Church for Catholic schools, the provinces and the communes for their own schools. In effect, therefore, a teacher is not appointed to a particular school which he might have in mind, but rather to one of a system of schools in which his diplomas entitle him to teach. For these reasons mobility from school to school is greater than in France, though nevertheless restricted. This holds for primary as well as for secondary school teachers. Secondary school teachers are on probation during their first year out from the university and are placed under the guidance and control of a " mentor " during this time, the " mentor " being a member of the teaching staff of the school. It should finally be noted that education in the training colleges and the university is not free as in France. True, scholarships and loans are made to all necessitous students in training, but the amount usually available is hardly ever sufficient to cover more than the bare necessities of living.

Holland. Equally independent-minded as the Belgians, and equally anxious to tolerate all possible points of view, the Dutch manage to maintain ninety-three separate training colleges for primary teachers (as opposed to the eighty-one existing in Belgium). Twenty-two of these are State colleges, three are run by local authorities, and the remainder (with the exception of two non-sectarian colleges) are maintained by one or other of the religious bodies—Catholic or Protestant. The course lasts five years and intending students are admitted at the age of 15. Provided a student holds the leaving certificate of the advanced elementary school there is no entrance examination. In addition, a pupil who has satisfactorily completed a full secondary school course may enter a college for the last two years of the course. In point of fact very few do this, as their leaving certificate automatically entitles them to admission to the university.

As in the case of both France and Belgium, the training college is expected to complete in a most thorough way the secondary education of the student, and the curriculum comprises : the Dutch language, Dutch history, general history, geography, natural history (including hygiene), singing (including wherever possible the study of the piano or the violin), drawing, manual training, gymnastics, French, German, English, mathematics, and (for girls) needlework! The main teacher-training is done in the third and fourth years of the course, and comprises the usual run of theory one would expect. A primary school is sometimes attached to a training college for practice teaching and observation of teaching along certain approved lines, but the majority of the colleges rely on the primary schools of the district.

Upon completion of their studies and practical work the students are examined for the teacher's certificate by their own lecturers and tutors, under general supervision of delegates appointed by the Ministry of Education. It is also possible—and this is a unique feature of Holland—for private persons to train for the teacher's certificate without being in attendance at a college and whilst carrying out some other job. Such persons are, of course, examined by special examiners from the Ministry of Education.

Another interesting feature is that certain of the training colleges have attached to them a special section for those who are already in possession of the teacher's certificate, and doing a full day's teaching, and who wish to take the State examination to become a head teacher of a primary school. Many teachers also take this course though they have no intention of becoming a head teacher : possession of the additional certificate brings them in a considerable increase in salary. The course lasts two years and classes are held in the evenings. The programme of studies comprises pedagogics (including methods of teaching), Dutch language and literature, history, geography and natural history. Many teachers also take supplementary diplomas to qualify them to teach, for example, modern languages or advanced mathematics, and the possession of these additional certificates secures them a place in the higher elementary schools.

It will be obvious that there is definite disparity of status between not only the primary school teacher and the secondary school teacher, but also between the primary school teacher and the higher elementary school teacher. On the other hand, every opportunity is given teachers to improve their professional status, and so increase their salary, and it is traditional for most ambitious Dutch teachers to do this, and in their spare time. It is no unknown thing, for example, for a primary teacher to acquire patiently over the years a whole series of diplomas and extra qualifications so that finally he is appointed to a secondary school, and even to the head-mastership of a secondary school.

There is no kind of compulsory training of teachers for the secondary schools, the traditional emphasis being on instruction rather than on education in the English and American accepted sense of the word. Most teachers (though as we have seen above, not all) in the secondary schools hold a university degree—a doctorate or the candidate's preliminary certificate leading to the doctorate. Those who possess no such qualification must hold the special certificate for secondary education which can be taken at the university or privately. Most universities offer courses in educational theory to those students who are interested enough to attend them, and a regulation of 1953 laid down that university-trained teachers must comply with certain minimum requirements with regard to a knowledge of pedagogy, adolescent psychology and special methods of teaching.

As is common in most Western European countries, the real interest in education and educational experiment and development centres on the primary school, and is stimulated by the primary school teacher. The lecturers in education in the various universities have turned this interest to good account by forming an association which—in co-operation with the Ministry of Education—awards two types of diplomas in education, A and B, at different levels, and for which anybody is entitled to sit who gives proof of a good general education and of ability to read a book in at least two foreign languages. Four non-university institutes of education are also co-operating with the venture. Thus, if the university undergraduate is at present chary of courses in education, the universities themselves are seriously tackling the problem at the primary school level and creating institutes of education that will eventually be not dissimilar in function from English institutes of education, though more free and elastic in their possibilities.

Norway. We have already noted how the schools in Scandinavia are in a very real sense the people's schools and how deeply rooted in tradition, extending back over 400 years, is the idea of the home's responsibility for education as it is the teacher's responsibility faithfully to serve the community to the best of his abilities through his school. None the less, the approach to the actual business of teaching has remained traditional, and firmly wedded to the idea of knowledge as indispensable to the good citizen of a Scandinavian democracy. Progressive education, therefore, has gained little ground in these countries, and reforms in education have been mainly directed towards making the people's schools more surely common or comprehensive than before, and ensuring that the teachers are adequately trained to cope with changing circumstances.

In Norway the basis of all education is the common seven years' school (from 7 to 14) that every child must attend. The primary school teacher is in consequence important and much attention is given to his training. The first teacher training colleges were established in the 1820's and the 1830's and ran two-year courses for those who had satisfactorily completed their primary school education. The course was extended to three years in 1902, and to four years in 1930. Nowadays, candidates for entrance must have completed a full primary school course and spent at least a further six months in some kind of post-primary school. The minimum age for entering a training college, however, is 17, and statistics of recent years show that the majority of those who are accepted for training are between the ages of 18 and 25. A marked contrast here with practice in France, Belgium or Holland—or indeed any other European country! It is also interesting to note that *increasingly* students from the secondary schools known as *realskole* (a grammar school for modern subjects) are entering primary teacher training, and in 1951 accounted for 47 per cent. of those who were accepted.[1]

Entry to the four-year training college is on the basis of a written and oral examination designed to test a candidate's maturity and knowledge of the basic primary school subjects. There are no fees, and the State will always provide bursaries to necessitous students. The course itself provides a mixture of general education and specialized training. Instruction in the theory of teaching begins in the second year and practical instruction in the third year. Whilst some of the training colleges have their own practice schools, most students go for their practical teaching (usually one

[1] Details of most recent changes are given on pages 179–181.

morning a week throughout the school year, though there can be many variations from this—e.g. periods of " block " teaching away from the training college in a country school) to recognized schools where the teachers are solely responsible for them to the point of lecturing them on methodology and granting their practical teaching mark.

Since 1930 there has been a popular addition to the four-year training college in the shape of a two-year college for those students who have successfully completed their studies at the *gymnasium*. This two years' course concentrates mainly on the theory and practice of teaching, but also adds additional practical subjects (singing and music, drawing and needlework), and scripture to counterbalance the essentially academic nature of the studies in the *gymnasium*. There is much discussion as to which is the better form of training : *gymnasium* first followed by two years only at the training college, or the traditional four-year course. The supporters of the two-year course argue that by founding all teacher training on the *gymnasium* the entire educational system will be more unified and more in keeping with the traditional ideal of education common to all. Supporters of the four-year college maintain stoutly that it has a definite function to fulfil, and that it must continue to exist since it draws its students mainly from the thinly populated areas in the country districts lying far from the nearest *gymnasium*. Again, many of the students in the four-year college have worked for several years at agricultural or other practical pursuits before seeking college entrance, and it is claimed with justification (cf. the recruitment of emergency teachers in England after 1945) that these mature students have a valuable contribution to offer unlike, but just as important as, that of the academically trained *gymnasium* student.

All training colleges—there are eleven in all—are State colleges under the centralized control of the Ministry of Ecclesiastical Affairs and Education, and the training given, therefore, is of a uniformly high standard. Every student takes the same subjects and submits the same curriculum for examination, but individual and special interests are catered for through the preparation of a thesis in part-requirement for the final examination. Needless to say, lecturers in training colleges must all be in possession of a university degree covering the academic subjects they teach, and they must have qualified at the university level in education to teach principles and practice of education, psychology, etc.

All teachers at the *gymnasium* and the *realskole* must have a university education and must therefore have passed through the *gymnasium* and taken the qualifying leaving certificate. An examination for a teacher's degree at the university covers three or four subjects. The reason for this is primarily that, in Norway, there are a number of small secondary schools in the small towns and country districts, and therefore only a small number of teachers at these schools. Usually on the arts side an intending teacher will choose his three subjects from : Norwegian, Latin, Greek, English, French, German, history, geography. On the science side he will often take four subjects from : mathematics, physics, chemistry, zoology, botany, geography, astronomy, mechanics. There are two kinds of degree, known as the lower and the higher. Preparation for the lower degree lasts from four to five years, and for the higher degree from six to seven years. Most students eventually take the higher degree.

On the completion of his degree course the intending teacher then spends six months in the university department of education. His course is very much the same as that of a graduate in an English department of education. As in the case of the primary school teacher, he does his teaching practice under experienced teachers in either the *gymnasium* or the *realskole*, and these teachers who supervise him are responsible for assessment of the final teaching practice mark. In 1938 an important step forward in treating education as a serious academic and university subject was taken by the creation of an institute of education at the university of Oslo, and the numbers of students availing themselves of the opportunity for thus including education as a subject on the degree course have steadily increased.

The same conditions as outlined in some detail above may be said to hold (with relatively unimportant variations) for both Denmark and Sweden. In Denmark, however, it should be noted that of the twenty-nine training colleges in existence, eight only are run by the State, the rest being private institutions subsidized by the State. In Sweden, considerable thought has been given to devising methods of testing an applicant's suitability for the teaching profession, but it is admitted that nothing conclusive has so far resulted from experiments carried out. In Sweden also, there is no real final examination for the teacher's certificate other than a test lesson of thirty or forty minutes' duration. For the rest, his performance over the whole course of study is assessed. On the other hand, a primary school teacher undergoes a period of probation in that he cannot be appointed to a permanent post without having first taught for two full school years.

To sum up, we can state that the aim in all three Scandinavian countries is that of developing the best possible mode of life for both the individual and for the group. In consequence, democratic living, participation in citizenship and community, and real belief that all this will be achieved as the people gain more and more knowledge will be found to be at the heart of the entire educational programme, the primary school (or rather common school) teacher being the king-pin of the whole.

Switzerland. It is a well-known fact that education in Switzerland is accorded a degree of importance equal to that in the Scandinavian countries, and that the democratic ideals of the country (as well as economic circumstances) demand high standards of education among its citizens for the performance of the duties of citizenship. The pattern of recruiting teachers is very much the same as in the Scandinavian countries, and we need not, therefore, linger too long in discussing Swiss education at this stage. As in Scandinavia, the primary school is the bedrock of all further education, and at least 95 per cent. of all Swiss children pass through this school. Primary school teachers must likewise have spent two to three years in some form of post-primary education, and their training college course is of four to five years' duration. One democratic feature peculiar to Switzerland, however, is that the appointment of a primary school teacher to a post depends on the local commune, which has considerable authority also in deciding hours of work, length of holidays, and even pay. The mode of election of the primary teacher varies from commune to commune : it is done either by secret ballot, by decision at a general meeting, by the local council, or by the school authorities. The same applies generally to secondary school teachers, who must all have the appropriate university degree(s). Again, teachers are elected for certain lengths of time : in some areas it will be for life, in others for a term of eight, six or five years—or even less.

Italy. Of Italy I propose to say little at this stage, simply because the principles behind teacher training derive mainly from the French pattern, and also because the present regime is still struggling desperately to clear up not only widespread illiteracy, but also the burden of poverty and the problems of achieving economic stability. There is also the added complication of the autonomy of local authorities for their primary schools and the large number of private schools which are nearly all Catholic Church schools. The general pattern, however, is that primary school teachers must possess the middle school leaving certificate gained after at least three years of post-primary education in the middle school. The course in the training college is of four years' duration, and the larger part of this time is devoted to completing the student's secondary education. The general criticism of the course is that, whilst the student acquires a fair humanistic culture, he lacks sound practical experience. Teachers in all types of secondary schools must hold a university degree or its equivalent. There is no professional training as such, though a few university courses do exist to prepare for a teaching career. Neither the possession of a university degree, however, nor of the teacher's certificate, entitles the right to teach. Appointment to a permanent teaching post in both cases is on a competitive basis on the results of an examination set by the various regional authorities every few years. All Italian citizens between the ages of 18 and 45 who possess the required preliminary qualifications may present themselves for such an examination.

U.S.S.R. So finally in this survey we come to the country which lays supreme store on the quality and importance of the teacher as a most essential cog in the whole complicated business of government along preconceived lines and devotion to a Marxist way of life. A seventeenth-century Russian maxim held that " as is the teacher so is the child," and to-day Lenin is repeatedly quoted as saying : " We must raise our teacher to a height such as he has not attained and never will attain in a bourgeois society." Soviet propaganda constantly stresses that without teachers there can be no education, and that without education the standard of living cannot be raised and the people freed from insecurity and poverty. The whole process of Soviet education is likewise inspired by the cult of work which Stalin in 1952 defined as not only " a means of supporting life but life's prime need."

Thus, the training of teachers in the Soviet Union has two main purposes : first, to make certain that they are politically reliable;

and second, to make sure that they illustrate constantly through their teaching the relationship between general education and the economic life of the country. It is equally important to note that, unlike most other countries, the Soviet Union maintains entirely separate training institutions for the teachers in the different types of schools, notwithstanding the existence of the common or comprehensive school system. The one common basis for the training of teachers at all levels is the study of the science of society from the Marxist-Leninist point of view.

There are three distinct types of teacher training institutions, corresponding to the three clear divisions made in the general educational programme: the primary school which now comprises the first three years of study between the ages of 7 and 10; the secondary school, compulsory for all, which adds five further grades to the primary grades and thus takes the pupil up to fifteen years of age; the final secondary schools taking pupils up to the age of 19. There are obvious comparisons to be drawn in this method of school organization with that holding in America : the six years primary school followed by three years in the junior high school and three years in the senior high school.

Until 1954, teachers for primary school (now the first three years of study) had a four-year course on completion of their secondary education. In 1954, because of an acute shortage of teachers at the primary and kindergarten levels, this was reduced to two years as an emergency measure. As these " cram " courses have faded out there has been a return to four-year training on lines not dissimilar from earlier practice, but with the exception that these new four-year courses are gradually being absorbed into the Pedagogic Institutes. These originally only trained teachers for work as specialists in the upper forms of the secondary school, but turned their attention from 1952 to the training of teachers for lower secondary school work, and are now obviously seeking to unify the whole teaching profession and to attract more highly qualified recruits. Teachers' salaries generally have been increased by some 20 per cent. (1973) and at the same time the school leaving age is being raised from 15 to 17 and a new ten-year school syllabus introduced. It is claimed that this is being done to secure many more able recruits for developing industries, to gear education to a constantly expanding technology, and to intensify ideological training.

Amid all this change the Pedagogic Institutes are growing both in numbers and importance and come increasingly to resemble more closely in function the Faculty of Education of an American university. They are still, however, *not* university institutions in their own right. Originally designed (as we have said) to train highly specialized teachers, they had until 1956 a four-year course only, for students who had satisfactorily completed a full ten-year school course. Reorganization in 1956 gave them a five-year course (in common with most other higher education institutions) and so brought them into line with the thirty-one universities throughout the country who virtually did the same job—though the universities provide less teaching practice and insist on study in greater depth of the chosen specialist subject(s). Now they have become comprehensive teacher training establishments.

Until reorganization in 1956 specialist teachers in the Pedagogical Institutes were required only to study one subject. Since that date suitable combinations of school teaching subjects (as in Europe generally) are required. Thus, a modern linguist will study two foreign languages; Russian language and literature will be studied along with history; a mathematician will also study physics, and a chemist biology. In addition to the study of his specialist subjects a student is also required to follow a political and general course of instruction and a course in pedagogy. The general course concerns itself mainly with sport and recreational activities, mastery of the Russian language and of one foreign language. The political and general course together account for about 6 per cent. of the curriculum, and up to 20 per cent. of the remainder is devoted to pedagogy which almost always includes some study of comparative education. Practice teaching is required in the last two years of study and works itself up from observation to continuous periods of teaching under normal teaching conditions in appropriate schools. It is also obligatory to have spent a minimum of three weeks in a summer vacation as a youth leader in one of the Pioneer Camps for youngsters. It is interesting to note that future modern language teachers may spend as much as 70 per cent. of their time on their specialist subjects and are often trained in separate language institutes.

Entrance to a Pedagogical Institute is competitive on the basis of an examination, references as to suitability for training, and priority. In consequence relatively few students enter directly from school. Most have had some two or three years' work experience on farms or in factories, and quite a number have already qualified at the primary school level, have taught there for a few years, and now seek to improve their qualifications and standing. Some will also have qualified for entry by correspondence courses whilst being gainfully employed in a non-teaching capacity. In a word it is stressed again and again that a good teacher must know much more than the subject he teaches. He must know the world into which his pupils will have to fit. And he must understand his pupils and their individual backgrounds.

Nor does it all end there. Education, like industry, needs research and further inspiration to keep it alive. There is in consequence an elaborate system of in-service training of all teachers. Those at the highest level are encouraged to go further with their studies as are those at the lowest, and the Ministry of Education and institutes for educational research are constantly publishing manuals and records of individual experiments carried out in the schools for the benefit of all. All schools have their methodology groups for discussion of current problems, and in each suitable region functions a teachers' co-operation service for the general pooling and passing on of experiences at the regional level. It is the proud boast of the Russians that none of this in-service training is compulsory, but that all teachers, filled with zeal and ardour for their important task, rush both to avail themselves of it and to contribute to it what they have to contribute. This is undoubtedly true. But could it possibly be otherwise?

CHAPTER EIGHT

Pre-School Education

THE expression " pre-school " has increasingly come to be
used as a blanket term to cover all forms of organized
groupings of children under the starting age of compulsory
education. In most European countries the starting age is 6 or
even 7, though by 1980 Western Germany hopes to have lowered
this to 5 and so conform with practice in Great Britain. Usually,
however, three basic divisions are to be noted in this pre-school
period. First there comes the *crèche* or child-minding centre for
the working mother. Next is the kindergarten where children
mainly develop sensory-motor and aesthetic capacities through
play and are helped to become socially acceptable. Lastly, we
have the nursery school proper which often resolutely prepares
the child for entry to the primary school by developing his
linguistic and mathematic abilities. We can very roughly say
that the *crèche* handles the child from about the age of 6 months
up to 3 years of age and that thenceforward, as more and more
children flock to some form of pre-school education, the lines
between kindergarten and nursery proper merge at about the
age of 5. It will therefore be more convenient for the purposes of
this short study to lump kindergarten and nursery education into
one and refer only to nursery schools, categorizing these as
accepting children between the ages of 3 and 6 or 7.

Reasons for the growing popularity of nursery education over
the last fifteen to twenty years are many and varied, and a comparative study of the rate at which these schools have tended to
grow in popularity will indicate what factors have been at work.
It will equally reveal that, whilst in the first instance such schools
were (as in France) institutions for children whose homes were
unsatisfactory or whose mothers had to go out to work, more and
more has been demanded of them as new education techniques

have made their impact throughout the pre-secondary system and as newer ideas on mental health and growth have emerged from the findings of child psychologists. At a severely practical level, the main reason for children entering nursery school is to ensure as far as is possible that adequate basic preparation is given to obviate the necessity to repeat classes in the primary school and thereby make for early self-assurance in the school situation. Allied closely to this, of course, is the problem of the culturally deprived child—a problem which led America to launch its Head-Start programme. With increasing democratization of education right through the secondary level it became clear that no real identity of opportunity could exist for children entering the main school streams who were already culturally or socially deprived. It became equally obvious that the sooner diagnosis of individual handicaps was made and dealt with the better, and thus the nursery school came to the fore as a place where early diagnosis could be made and proper remedial treatment given.

All this in turn, whilst focusing attention on the nursery schools as being important institutions for rescuing deprived children, raised the question as to what exactly was meant by the word " deprived ". To think of the deprived child as coming from poor, feckless and/or illiterate families was soon seen as being only part of the total picture. It had to be recognized that deprivation can be psychological and emotional as well as economic. The spoiled only child of a well-to-do family can be psychologically " deprived ". The unwanted child of any family, rich or poor, can be emotionally " deprived ". And " unwanted" must now cover the increasing number of cases where the mother goes out to work NOT because she has to. She goes to work because she is bored with being a housewife and a mother, and she seeks her own independence alongside her husband. So are family ties weakened. So are the rich emotional responses needed by the child in his early formative years diluted and many important experiences denied within the family circle.

Again, growing prosperity in this post-war period has led to the replacement of many small towns by a concentration of the population in rapidly growing and large urban centres, and this phenomenon of concentration is still going on. As people flock to large towns and cities so are they obliged to live in tall blocks of flats or crowded housing estates. In both instances play space and play facilities must be strictly limited. In such a setting not even the best of parents can stop their children from being in some measure " deprived " in the broad sense in which I have defined deprivation—or from being starved of those enriching experiences the nursery school sets out to offer.

The problem, then, is primarily an urban one in most places. Everywhere in the Western World much more attention is being given to nursery education. Everywhere the nursery school is being called upon to play a more important and decisive role. Everywhere it is recognized that urbanization and the tempo of modern life disrupt family life and reveal inadequacies in most families which were not hitherto suspected. Even more important, parents themselves are coming to realize that modern conditions of home life are not always the best for a child beyond a certain age; that all children can benefit from an experience which guides natural play and interests towards the development of skills which are going to be of real importance later; that by involving their children in a nursery school situation they can themselves become involved (and are wholeheartedly encouraged to do so) so that the whole process becomes a happy partnership leading the parents in particular to greater understanding both of their children and of what the complicated modern educational process is about. The ideal is the " educative family " with the young mother playing as full a part as possible in the nursery school situation.

Belgium. The modern tendency is perhaps most sharply defined within Belgium in that to-day virtually all children between the ages of 5 and 6 are in nursery schools, thus bringing Belgian practice (on a non-compulsory basis) closest to the English compulsory starting age of five.[1] Latest released figures show that well over 85 per cent. of children between the ages of 3 and 6 are also in attendance. In addition *crèches* exist in all the large industrial towns in which mothers who must go out to work

[1] The position in Great Britain is the most unsatisfactory for the whole of Western Europe. Whereas before 1900 half a million children were registered as attending school earlier than 5, the figure had dropped to 23,000 in 1964. Only now is it slowly beginning to rise again with roughly 8 per cent. in the 3–5 age range voluntarily in attendance. There are, as yet, just not sufficient schools nor sufficient qualified staff. True, Great Britain aims at small classes whilst the Continent tends to cram children in almost regardless of class size. French nursery schools in Paris in particular are hopelessly over crowded.

can leave their infant earlier than the age of three for the whole of the working day. These *crèches* are provided by a variety of public or private bodies and fall under the general umbrella of the *Oeuvre Nationale de l'Enfance* which dates back in origins to 1919 when it was founded to care primarily for war orphans. Nursery schools may be maintained either by the State, or the province, or the commune, or the Catholic Church, or by private persons (in which case a fee is charged). The schools themselves are attached to a primary school, or to the primary department of such secondary schools as still run a primary department, or to a model primary school annexed to a teacher training college. Inspection of the schools is carried out by the appropriate primary school inspector. It should also be noted that if more than thirty parents petition for the setting up of a nursery school within their commune, then there is a legal obligation upon the commune to provide these facilities.

All this means that no longer are the schools frequented mainly by children of the underprivileged but by children drawn from every social group and are (in the best sense of the word) democratizing institutions. Parents have come increasingly to realize that modern conditions of home life at every level militate against proper social adjustment and the individual development of their child. Only by freely mixing with their peers away from the boredom and often inescapable petty restrictions of home life for a number of hours each day in the kind of calm and relaxed atmosphere that the trained kindergarten teacher engenders can children at the pre-primary ages find proper self-fulfilment in relation to themselves, to others, and to the exciting world about them. Only by such a pre-apprenticeship is the child prepared fully to benefit from his primary school education by being given a wider cultural background than the home can ordinarily provide. At the same time the schools (mostly indirectly) are educating parents at all social levels in proper child care—particularly is this so in the *crèches* for children of working mothers—and stimulating parental interest in the total education of the child at a time when growth in material wealth is leading to a lessening of family ties and substituting a variety of interests that money can afford that are no longer primarily centred on home life.

All nursery schools since 1880 have been run on sound progressive Froebel lines, and the latest recommendations (October 1950) incorporate the main ideas of Madame Montessori and Dr. Decroly. Thus the schools seek to develop in the child powers of observation, to correct and improve his speech, and to give him a sense of discipline. The development of an aesthetic sense and of physical dexterity are encouraged by simple handicrafts such as paper cutting, bead, raffia and wool work, clay modelling, dancing, singing, rhythmic exercises of all kinds, and by story telling. Normally the child will not be taught to read and nothing will be attempted that could in any way encroach on the work to be done later in the primary school.

France. In France the *école maternelle* has a long and glorious history extending as far back as 1837 and it is justifiably proud of the role it has played (and continues to play) as an important social force in caring for the children of working-class parents. Because of the unique nature of this task, and also because of the marked success the school has had in extending most subtly its influence from giving simple child care to becoming an instrument of positive help to all deprived children (and of instruction to their parents), it has been allowed to experiment freely and has acquired to itself its own specialized inspectorate although it falls directly under the control of the Ministry of Education. Today it is usual to find one such school in every community of more than 2000 inhabitants, and the work of these schools has been further supplemented by the creation of kindergartens by the Ministry of Health (usually fee-paying) which are attached to large industrial enterprises or factories.

Increasing use has been made of the facilities available since World War II and for much the same reasons as in Belgium. Latest figures (1973) show that almost all French children are in nursery school between the ages of 5 and 6, and that the national overall average for children between 2 and 6 is about 70 per cent. Of these children over 87 per cent. attend State as opposed to private (Catholic) institutions. Any *commune* which so wishes may open a school, but if it does so it pledges itself to operate it for thirty years. In return the State will pay all teachers' salaries and up to 85 per cent. of the cost of the school, the *commune* thereafter being responsible for general maintenance. Thus the nursery school in France is a school in its own right and has more clearly defined functions to perform than the Belgian school. It is primarily still a school for parents of children of necessity deprived of what in modern terms would be considered a satisfactory home background and this explains both the earlier starting age and an overall percentage of attendance of almost half that in Belgium. The flight from the land has also helped to characterize the school as predominantly working-class: in 1800 agricultural pursuits occupied 85 per cent of the total population; this figure had declined to 27 per cent. in 1954 representing a grand total of some five million agricultural workers; by 1965 a further million workers had left agriculture, and the drain continues.[1] This again obliges many nursery schools in industrial areas to open as early as 6.30 a.m. and to stay open throughout the day, arranging their schedule to fit in with factory hours.

Educationists are usually quick to point out that the French nursery school does not follow any one educational method but that teachers must experiment to find the approach best suited to their charges. Nevertheless the influence of such personalities as Madame Montessori, Decroly, Piaget, Claparède and Ferrière is much in evidence. The French tend perhaps to look on the school (for obvious reasons) much more as a social service institution than do the Belgians. There is specific training in hygiene habits, both for mothers and children; there is some rudimentary instruction in ethics; and every effort is made to give each child a good fund of general knowledge. In all other respects activities are much the same as in Belgium or in any other well-run and modern nursery school. The slant, however, is different in that the school has the avowed aim of preparing the youngsters for their primary school career. It is this fact that explains the sharp rise to full attendance between the ages of 5 and 6, for in the last year in the nursery school all children are initiated to the rudiments of arithmetic and are taught both to read and to write. That the figure between 2 and 5 years of age is not higher than about 60 per cent. can be attributed to the fact that France is still basically Catholic in outlook and still looks to the Church and to the family as the most important influences in the life of the young child. Nor can the marked working-class origins make an easy appeal to the still class-conscious bourgeoisie with its conception of an intellectual *élite* that only the most famous (and exclusive) schools can properly train.

[1] Consult Louis Cros: *L'Explosion Scolaire*, Paris (1961).

Unlike Belgian schools, therefore, which really supply the felt needs of all social groups, the French nursery school recruits to it mainly the children of the working class and (at the 5 to 6 level) the children of the lower middle class—teachers, tradesmen, minor civil servants who are anxious to miss no opportunity of giving their children every possible advantage in the gruelling scholastic course that lies ahead. It is such parents who still stolidly resist any reforming tendency to reduce the emphasis on reading, writing and arithmetic in this last year in the nursery school. Time and the present reorganization of the whole post-primary school structure will no doubt change this attitude. Experimentation in the schools is going on ceaselessly, one of the most interesting of recent developments being the teaching of English and German on the oral method in pilot areas. It is this freedom to experiment which makes the schools resilient and hopefully confident that they can more than meet the demands the present critical phase of educational reconstruction must eventually make of them.

U.S.S.R. Many points of similarity can be found between the system holding in France and in the U.S.S.R. *Crèches* exist for children from the age of six weeks up to three years and are often run by factories, offices and collective farms (when they will be of a seasonal nature). Nursery schools proper, for children between the ages of 3 and 7, may be again run by industry or farms, or by a local education authority. Since 1956 all new apartment housing developments are required to build and operate a nursery school. In certain circumstances between 65 per cent. and 75 per cent. of the cost of the school will be borne by the State, but in all cases fees are charged commensurate to the parents' ability to pay. The schools are open all day for six days a week and hours vary (as in certain French schools) to fit in with factory shifts. *Crèches* fall under the supervision of the Ministry of Health and nursery schools are the province of the Ministry of Education. Despite the fact that the schools are fee-paying they are in great demand and there are still not enough places to meet the demand. Usually children of parents who both are out at work and who do not have a grandmother (or some other competent relative) to look after them are given priority. Statistics are difficult to come by. At a guess one would say that about one in every five Russian children has been in regular attendance at these schools, and we are informed that urgent attention is being given to improve this ratio.

The Russian attitude would seem to be that you cannot start too early in training up the child in the way in which he should go, and they have capitalized on the ever present need for both man-power and woman-power in their attempts to popularize these schools. They are conscious of the need to educate the parent in proper child care and upbringing and all good schools have parents present during both play and activities to show them how the trained teacher deals with various problems that can arise in the handling of their children. Parents' corners in schools can also be a feature, designed to instruct the parent in how to give his own child his own corner in the home and choose for him suitable play and reading materials. The actual proramme of school activities is much the same as elsewhere except that much more attention is paid to the child's health. Emphasis is given to acquiring a good command of the mother tongue, and the child is expected on leaving the school at the age of 7 to be able to do simple oral arithmetic and to read and write. Some schools (again as in France) are experimenting with teaching a foreign language by the oral method. Such experiments are proving popular and are likely to be on the increase over the next years. The ultimate aim of the schools would seem to be to over-come as far as possible the disruption of family life caused by economic pressures by making parents supremely conscious of the importance of their role as parents and as citizens of the U.S.S.R. Parental authority, they are repeatedly told, rests on love and respect, and is determined by the moral pattern and the behaviour of parents both at home and at work. It is not a bad directive in any present-day democracy

U.S.A. If nursery schools did start in the U.S.A. primarily as laboratories for psychological studies and observation rather than anything else they have none the less become more popular and today about 50 per cent. of children go to such schools from the age of 5. Like the sixth grade (first year of compulsory education) they only work a morning session of three hours and the nursery year is looked upon as a period of careful preparation for happy and fruitful social integration into the primary school proper. These schools seek to explore learning experiences (along the usual modern lines) to form a sound base for a more formal education. Very few children at the moment attend nursery schools between the ages of 3 and 5 and such schools as do exist try to offer what homes and parents (for one reason or another) are unable to provide as well as to extend whatever experience has been gained in the home. Many such children are organized into play groups similar to the park playgrounds that are to be found in Norway. It is assumed that, since the passing of the important Elementary and Secondary Act of 1965, money will be available under Title One of the Act (provision for educationally deprived children) to establish more nursery schools for the whole range of 3 to 6 years of age. Like the Russians, the Americans are now feeling the necessity for more adequate pre-school care and preparation (and parent-training) in proved cases of what we might call social deprivation in preparing to-morrow's citizens for the tasks that lie ahead. The issue, however, is still the subject of much debate. The home is still considered the most important and natural formative influence in these early years, and only time can show to what extent the ambiguous term " educationally deprived " will be fully extended to nursery schooling.

Scandinavia. Scandinavian countries share the generally accepted American view that the most formative period of a child's life is at the mother's knee and in the home even though compulsory education does not begin until the age of seven. None the less problems have been created in all three Scandinavian countries as a result of industrialization and the growth of urban centres. There is an increasing tendency for the mother to go out to work coupled with a tendency for families to be smaller in size which restricts proportionately opportunities for desirable social experiences for the child. As one authority puts it: " The (nursery school) in Norwegian cities is meeting a real need in those areas where the families live in block houses having small apartments and little play space. For a mother with no maid, the centres for child care and education answer one of her most pressing needs ".[1] The fact has to be faced that to-day there are houses which are not homes and housing estates which are in no sense communities.

Tacit recognition of this difficulty has been given by the grow-

[1] H. Huus: *The Education of Children and Youth in Norway* (Pittsburgh, 1960), pp. 24–25.

ing practice of allowing certain children to begin their compulsory schooling one year earlier—at the age of 6 rather than at 7. It is, however, incumbent on the parents to show that the child is ready to start school by submitting him to a kind of " maturity " examination. Is he sufficiently socially mature for formal schooling? Has he had adequate playway experiences in the home? How well developed are his powers of observation and memorization? Such nursery schools as exist do, of course, develop all these sides and base their approach on approved Montessori, Froebel and Decroly methods. Norway admits children to nursery schools between the ages of 3 and 6. So does Denmark, but it also has *crèches* for children up to the age of 3. Sweden runs nursery schools for children aged between 4 and 6 and will only very exceptionally admit earlier than 4. By the same token it gives priority to children who have attained six years of age and wish to spend one year there prior to beginning formal schooling. Schools are either privately run or by the municipality, and fees are charged. Private institutions may be subsidized either by the municipality or by the state. Fees paid in any school do not normally meet more than about 30 per cent. of the total cost of maintaining the school. A rough calculation based on averaging the attendance at nursery schools in the main towns where they are situated shows that no more than about 10 per cent. of children between the ages of 3 and 6 frequent them. The Danish *crèches* work out at an allocation of one place per thousand inhabitants.

Germany. Nursery schools exist in Western Germany for children between the ages of 3 and 6 and are administered by *communes*, Churches, welfare societies, industry or privately. Parents who can afford to do so are expected to pay between two or three marks per child per week and the rest of the cost is met partly by the founding organization and partly from grants approved by the Youth Office. They are mainly Montessori and Froebel-inspired, and as in Belgium aim not so much at preparing the child for entry to the primary school as at improving his physical, moral and intellectual development. A special kind of nursery school can be found in the larger towns which deals with the problem of the slow developer and takes children only at the age of 6 (the beginning of compulsory schooling) with the specific intention of fitting them for transfer to the primary school proper as speedily as possible. Entry to such a school is on the recommendation of a medical officer who will have put the child through a series of routine tests and checks.

Statistics for present attendance at nursery schools are difficult to come by because of varying regulations holding in different *Länder* and because of the number of agencies providing this service. To date there must be about 16,000 nursery schools with place provision for some one million children—this representing a 34 per cent. attendance for the 3 to 6 age group. The new Structural Plan for Education, however, agreed to at a joint meeting of Ministers for Education from all the *Länder* in 1970, recognizes the urgent need to improve offerings at this level if other developments envisaged are to be smoothly effected. Thus, whilst by 1980 a full compulsory ten-year schooling is to be introduced, this will depend on dropping the age of entry to primary school to 5 by 1980. By the same token, it is hoped to have at least 75 per cent. of all 3–4 year olds in nursery schools by 1980 and to have achieved the target of virtually 100 per cent. by 1990.

Holland. In Holland nursery schools cater for children between the ages of 4 and 7, the higher age level being concerned (as in Western Germany) with the slow developer. Not unnaturally, in a country where so many of the schools belong to private trusts, to towns, to communes, or to religious bodies, and where State control is limited to general inspection, only 20 per cent. of the nursery schools are government controlled. This has meant that standards have varied considerably from school to school in the past, and to overcome this a special act on Infant Education was passed in 1956 taking the schools out of the supervision of the primary school inspectorate and creating a specialized inspectorate consisting of one Chief Inspectress assisted by 24 Inspectresses and 2 Inspectors. In addition, one Inspectress is responsible for supervising the training of all nursery school teachers and Headmistresses. A parents' committee is also attached to each school and in towns possessing several schools a joint parents' committee is established for general oversight and coordination of policy throughout the town's school system.

All but necessitous parents are required to pay a weekly contribution varying between 40 cents and 2.50 florins, the bulk of the cost being met mainly by the State and to a much smaller amount by municipal councils. The majority of the schools

(84 per cent.) employ the Froebel system as opposed to that of Madame Montessori, though more modern influences (such as that of Decroly) are to be found everywhere. Latest available statistics show that roughly 50 per cent. of all children between the ages of 4 and 7 voluntarily attend such schools.

Italy. The powerful hold the Catholic Church has on education in Italy led to the fall of the government in June 1964 over a proposed increase in state subsidies for non-state schools and again in January 1966—this time over a proposal to set up State nursery schools. At present only a very few nursery schools that are attached to teacher-training institutions are State-controlled, and this government defeat would indicate that the recommendation made as early as 1947 in the so-called Gonella Plan to extend nursery provision to the poorer and more remote areas of Italy by making it compulsory for all communes to establish such schools where they are needed, with State financial assistance, has again been indefinitely delayed. Such nursery schools as do exist for children between the ages of 3 and 6 are to be found in the larger and more wealthy towns and communes, and they can be divided into two distinct types: those which look after children whilst the mother is at work; and those which, following the most modern ideas, give an education comparable with the best done elsewhere in Europe. In addition they are of especial benefit to children of poorer parents in providing free lunches and free medical treatment. Statistics are difficult to obtain, but Italy, with a total population of almost fifty-one million has about the same number of children in nursery schools as Western Germany (population fifty-five million).

To sum up, we can see that everywhere in the Western world the nursery school is being called upon to play a more important and decisive role in proportion as the tempo of modern living disrupts family life, or (perhaps more important still) reveals inadequacies in the family which were not hitherto suspected. The findings of child psychologists have had their part to play both in pin-pointing these inadequacies and in securing more thorough and professional training for nursery school teachers. Professor Bloom of the University of Chicago, for example, has shown that the most important years for a child's intellectual development lie between the ages of 0 and 8, and that all which comes after is dependent to a large degree on the foundations then laid. Similarly, most countries now recognize that the child must spend longer in school than ever before if he is properly to cope with the complexities of modern living, the prolongation being at both ends, as it were: it is most important that the child's mind be properly awakened and he in consequence culturally and socially prepared to enter on a lengthy period of formal schooling. In the meantime, families in many countries are reminded by having to pay fees for the attendance of their children at nursery schools—even though these fees can only be reckoned as token—that such schools are rendering them an important family service. It may be that future generations of parents will, by measures now being taken in the field of pre-school education, be ready once again to accept the full challenge of parental responsibility and to create all over again a suitable family nexus to cope with problems of living in the century that lies ahead.

CHAPTER NINE

Primary Education

W E have noted elsewhere in this book how the changing
character of industry in the nineteenth century brought
about an imperative need for a better trained worker, and how in
consequence the idea of universal, compulsory and free primary
education established itself. In almost every Western European
country without exception, however, this primary education—or
elementary education as it was so often called—was a kind of mass
education, intended solely for the working class, and it was kept
quite separate and distinct from the kind of primary education
received by the boy or girl of non-working class parents which
usually started in the primary department of a grammar school (or
lycée) and so led naturally and easily into the main fields of
academic work. The boy or girl educated in the elementary school
moved rarely (and then with great difficulty and often inade-
quately prepared) to the secondary school. The elementary school,
in effect, led nowhere. Once a child's education had been completed in it there was little or no further full-time education for
him, unless he elected to train as an elementary school teacher.
Only gradually, throughout the first decades of the twentieth
century, was the way made easier for the elementary school child
to transfer to the secondary school. And only in this present post-
war period have the rigid barriers of the dual system of education
been finally lowered.

"Open a school and close a jail" became the nineteenth-
century slogan, and the elementary school was expected to produce not only a more literate and capable workman, but also to
discipline him and shape him both morally and socially for his
lowly task. The three R's—reading, writing and arithmetic—
were the basic tools needed by the future employee in industry,
and it was generally held that the methods employed in teaching

the three R's (the dunce's cap and the twitching cane) were salutory. An intellectual and moral discipline was expected to result from the effort required at learning by rote and from constant repetitive drilling. Order and method was the watchword. Flushed by victory over the French in 1870, the Prussians felt that the qualities the German army sergeant had shown during the campaign should not be wasted, and they therefore recruited such men to teach in their elementary schools. And most other European countries—if less openly and usually to a lesser degree—followed suit through the strict regimentation they imposed on the training of the elementary school teacher either at pupil teacher centres or in teacher-training colleges. There was one undeviating way of doing things. The " fold-your-arms-school," as it has been often called, was not interested in the child but in the techniques involved in teaching children *en masse*. Good figuring, well-kept exercise books, copper-plate handwriting, were essential parts of the drilling of the child, and the copy book used by the child gave him a whole series of moral maxims to be copied laboriously many times, and therefore (if indirectly) fixed for all time in his mind : " Knowledge is power. Honesty is the best policy. We reap what we sow. Look before you leap. A stitch in time saves nine "—and so on.

It was only at the very end of the nineteenth century that new subjects crept into the curriculum in the shape of history, geography, elementary science, and what came to be called " object lessons "—usually some simple form of nature study. Even then, however, the emphasis was still on imparting skills and information : a child would be shown a sticky bud and brought to study its growth and development day by day—but he also had to draw what he saw (and what the teacher made him see) with exactitude and meticulous detail. He had to learn by heart the names and dates, in strict chronological order, of kings and queens and decisive battles. He could chant like a litany the names of bays, capes, promontories and great rivers around his native country.

The shift in emphasis from the teaching of a subject to the education of the child came in the first place, of course, through the pioneer efforts of those educationalists whom we have discussed in Chapter Four, and from all the new information on the child that came pouring in from the psychologists. Men of calibre like the

Englishman Herbert Spencer who dared to ask the question :
" What knowledge is of most worth? " also had their influence.
Herbartian psychology became fashionable in Germany and
America, and later in England. But education for living, as we have
called it in Chapter Four, became only a reality in proportion as
the various countries were in a position, economically, to make
enforcement of their laws on compulsory primary education really
effective. A gradual reduction in hours of labour, thus making
for more leisure time for all, was also a prerequisite. To make the
teaching child-centred and to give each child the individual attention he needed demanded a much longer period of schooling.
These are important points that are often overlooked.

Again, if the child was to be given " new things to love and
admire," as Sir Michael Sadler put it, then radical changes had to
be effected in the attitudes adopted towards teacher training.
Economical and technological reasons might demand that the
teacher should be really skilled and well versed in the subjects he
taught. But it had to go much further than that. Beauty and truth
(aesthetic, moral and scientific) are in the eye and brain of the
beholder. Then the teacher must be trained to perceive, and in
consequence given an education that taught him to see so that he
might bring others to see. It is at this point that the philosophical
ideas of Henri Bergson have a particular relevance. Similarly, it
was necessary that the elementary and primary schools should
cease to be grim barrack-like buildings, and should be transformed
—if they could not entirely be abandoned—into something gayer
and freer and that really would help to open the windows of the
mind.

But none of this—as I have said—was possible until compulsory primary education for all became a reality and until
the school-leaving age could be extended to give the child
at least eight full years of education. It is significant to
note that the school-leaving age was raised to 14 in Belgium
in 1914, in England in 1918, in France in 1936, and that
not even to-day can Italy (particularly in Calabria) compel
full attendance much beyond the years of primary education
(5 to 11). Even in America it was not until 1920 that Mississippi
came into line with the other states by making its primary education at long last compulsory for all. On the other hand, America
has been the pioneer for the gradual raising of the school-leaving

age, and the ultimate aim has been the education of all to the age of 18. It is nowadays rare for an American child to leave school as early as 14, and most children stay on until their junior high school course at least is completed. America, therefore, is the obvious starting-point for our survey of variant aims and practices in the primary (elementary) school.

U.S.A. If the American public school is to be considered the foundation of American democracy, then the elementary school—which is a common school attended by over 90 per cent. of American children—is looked upon as the keystone of the whole educational structure. In most states compulsory schooling begins at the age of 6, and, whilst the length of time devoted to elementary education may vary from state to state (and even within one state), two main practises exist : either an eight years' elementary education followed by a four-year high school course, or a six years' elementary education followed by six years to be spent in the high school—usually divided into the junior high school and the senior high school.[1]

The elementary school is looked upon as the place in which the child gains the fundamental knowledge, skills, habits, and ideals of thought, feeling and action which are considered necessary for all American citizens regardless of social status, vocation or sex. Obviously, the work of John Dewey has much influenced the pattern of work in the elementary school and equally obviously the elementary school has been used for educational experiments of all kinds—not always with fortunate results. Indeed, one main criticism levelled at the schools to-day from within the U.S.A. is that the children have been too much considered as guinea pigs and too little as human beings, and that a kind of spurious science of education has been erected which ignores humanistic values and the great cultural heritage of the American nation. Teaching is as much an art as it is a science, and in any case deals with a different kind of material than that with which the scientist deals in the fastness of his laboratories.

The Dewey approach was a revolt against the formalism in education which favoured the establishment of the " fold-your-arms " type of school of which we have spoken. It led to the estab-

---

[1] What is called the 5–4–3 plan (5 years Elementary, 4 years Intermediate, 3 years Senior High School) is now being introduced. New York City favours a 4–4–4 plan.

lishment of the one-time fashionable " child-centred " school which in its turn has been criticized as much too individualistic and concentrating too exclusively on the immediate needs and interests of the pupil to the detriment of the community's interests. Nowadays the fashionable catchword is " the community-centred school " which is defined as aiming at giving the child an appreciation and understanding of his environment, a sense of civic and social responsibility, and a feeling of loyalty to the American democratic ideal. There is also another outlook—that of the " essentialists " as they are sometimes called—which claims that the prime function of education is that of transmitting the cultural heritage of the American people. Though the " essentialists " are attacked as being primarily concerned with the content of education, they start none the less from the principle that the teacher should base his work on the interests of the child, whilst insisting that through those interests the child must be prepared for community living as a free and responsible citizen, and that this can only properly be brought about through making him conscious of his heritage. In any case, in all three groups of thought—child-centred, community-centred and " essentialist "—the emphasis tends to be on group-learning and co-operative effort; topics for study (rather than subjects) are selected at local, national and world community levels; and all have to agree that the basic skills of reading, writing and arithmetic must first be taught.

In all state-maintained schools there is a complete absence of any general religious instruction or school worship, but on the other hand all kinds of means (direct and indirect) are used to inspire the work of the schools with moral and spiritual values. Slogans on the walls—such as " Don't make excuses, make good!" —abound, and every effort is made through literature, music and the arts generally to develop standards of good taste and appreciation. In literature the twelve-year-old will have read the usual myths and folklore (including stories from the Bible) which have an appeal for children, and he should know how to use reference books to extend his knowledge on a basis of his interests, and how to set about using libraries to widen his reading. In history, he should know something of the biography of outstanding historical characters and the stories of a few of the more important historical events, present and past. In the liberal and practical arts he should be able to sing and draw and should be showing the beginnings of an interest in some of the best music, pictures and other forms of art. He should possess information in nature study, and, if possible, have a definite interest in some phase of nature study as a scientific pursuit that will help in the proper utilization of his leisure. He should possess the ability to do simple constructive work and be able to make some of the things he is interested in. He should know something of the several industries that are the concern of the locality in which he lives both through visitation and through participation on a limited scale wherever possible.

The promotion of good physical and mental health is also a major concern of the primary school, and in a sound progressive school the child of 12 should have had training in the fundamental habits of exercise, cleanliness, eating and sleeping; he will play several games and belong to one or more societies, as for example the Boy Scouts.

Finally, it should be noted that the still prevalent European custom of class examinations held at the end of the academic year in order to decide who shall be promoted to the next class have in America long since been discarded almost everywhere. For this traditional type of examination, what are called achievement tests are substituted, and much energy has gone into the compilation of such tests which are of the true/false kind, or of the completion kind, or of the multiple kind, all calling usually for one-word answers. It is interesting to note that such methods of testing have crept into the kind of " intelligence " test set in England at the eleven plus examination for admission to some form of secondary education, and that the same criticisms are now being levelled at achievement tests in both America and England : that for mere factual information and cut-and-dried instances of right and wrong such tests have their place, but it is a strictly limited one; for the more subtle kinds of discrimination and evaluation they are a danger in that they lead the pupil to over-simplify and do not train him to think in sentences or to develop a simple logical argument. The value of the achievement tests, of course, in a large country like America, is that they set up comparable standards of achievement in the teaching of a given subject throughout the whole country, and they also help teachers to discover the weaknesses in their own methods of instruction as well as the difficulties the children are likely to encounter. It should also be noted that it is important in America to discover and isolate such weaknesses because of the general marked reluctance to keep a pupil down in a class to repeat the work all over again if it can possibly be helped. Discouragement, frustration and a sense of failure are at all times to be avoided. All well and good. But the cumulative effects of this policy repeatedly make themselves felt at the high school level and prove often embarrassing if not disastrous. On the other hand, we must admit that the common school principle behind American education which makes it automatic for every boy and girl to pass from the primary school to some form of secondary education in the high school frees both parents and children from the anxiety neuroses which abound in Europe wherever the kind of secondary education a child shall have is determined by some kind of examination hurdle at the completion of the primary school course.

Nevertheless, much serious thought has been devoted to the problem over the last decade or so, and one of the most interesting suggestions emanating from the influential National Education Association is that the practice of starting school as late as 6 is " obsolete ". Education should be from the age of 4. The Association claims that " a growing body of experience and research demonstrates that by the age of 6 most children have already developed a considerable part of the intellectual ability they will possess as adults " and that it is during the first four or five years of a child's life that physical and mental growth is not only most rapid but also most susceptible to influence by environment. This recommendation is, of course, in direct line with the trend we have noticed everywhere to more nursery school education, and it underlines this by emphasizing that the school for the under-sixes would not have to be a place where the rigid three R's curriculum was provided, but would have an " open " curriculum at the infants' level.

Further recommendations have resulted in much more up-to-date equipment in the elementary school; the beginnings of the teaching of a foreign language together with the supply of all the latest language laboratory equipment; more academic pressure for excellence.[1] This last requirement is often achieved by inviting parents of promising children to send their youngsters to special summer vacation classes as they near the end of their elementary school career, thus giving them more adequate

[1] All this pressure for academic excellence was originally sparked off by the Russian launching of Sputnik in 1957.

preparation for embarking directly in the high school on an academically biassed course. Ultimately, of course, it is recognized that the able child needs a programme which extends him more than at present; that parallel to this there must be a more adequate provision for the culturally deprived child; and that nothing of lasting value to the whole nation can be achieved without more *national* financing and control of education. As things are, it is estimated that fully 30 per cent. of those in elementary school will never complete a high school course.

The National Defence Act of 1958 (one year after Sputnik) gave direct Federal grants to encourage excellence in the study of the sciences, mathematics and languages in schools and colleges, to re-train science teachers, and to support new programmes in mathematics. Extended in 1963, it made student loans for the first time available for any form of higher education, whether public or private. In 1964 the Economic Opportunity Act launched the so-called " War on Poverty ". Children between the ages of 3 and 4 were recruited into " headstart " classes to overcome cultural deprivation due to home circumstances, and it has been estimated that by 1968 there were at least one million children in attendance in nursery schools on this federally financed scheme. Educational opportunities were also made available for their parents and other deserving adults. Special opportunities for help were given to High School students from culturally deprived homes and, by the Advanced Placement Scheme, the ablest of High School students were enabled to collect credits for university work whilst still at school and so skip some of the Freshman year on entering university.

Finally, on 11 April 1965, President Johnson made the symbolic gesture of signing the Elementary and Secondary Education Act outside the one-roomed schoolhouse he had attended as a boy —a law which terminated almost a century of effort to persuade local authorities to accept Federal aid to equalize educational opportunities as far as possible throughout the whole of America. At long last had come agreement (however grudgingly accorded from some quarters) that there are poor and rich states in America—under-privileged Negroes, coloured, and poor whites —and that America cannot play the major role in world affairs she is now called upon to play without a major *national* effort to improve education all round and so assure that every American child everywhere is given the opportunity to develop his inherent mental capacities to the full; recognition that only by means of a large Federal grant scrupulously administered and judiciously distributed can inequalities from state to state and from authority to authority properly be ironed out. At the same time, however, it is strongly emphasized that real responsibility for planning and action must rest with local authorities and state agencies who are equally charged with ensuring that private educational establishments are not left out of consideration when determining the needs of the culturally deprived child. One-sixth of the money available can be used for library resources, textbooks and other instructional materials; for supplemental educational services (guidance, counselling, adult education); for promoting educational research and training in research techniques; for strengthening state departments of education to cope better with planning —which covers such things as improving the quality of teacher preparation. The bulk of the money is earmarked to be used for school construction, for varieties of curriculum aids and equipment, for textbooks—and even for teachers' salaries. As time passes, it will be interesting to study the impact the passing of this first Federal Bill on education will have had on improving quality of achievement at all levels of instruction, but particularly in the elementary and high schools.

Scandinavia. The idea of a common primary school with well over 90 per cent. of the total child population in attendance is just as dear to the Scandinavian people as to the Americans. Frederick VI of Denmark, for example, was well in advance of other countries when in 1814 he made schooling compulsory for three days a week between the ages of 7 and 14 and insisted that every township must have its elementary school. In 1849, compulsory schooling was extended to cover a full six-day week. Norway has had compulsory schooling since 1739, extended its duration from five to seven years in 1860, and finally in 1959 gave its blessing to a nine-year school. Sweden inaugurated compulsory schooling in 1842, developed it on a six-year basis until 1937, added a seventh year then, and finally (1962) scrapped the whole for a unitary nine-year school system, this being given the over-all title of *Grundskola* (in contra-distinction to the general meaning attached to the term elsewhere in Europe).

Misgivings felt in SWEDEN about the wisdom of initiating what is frankly admitted as being a purely political decision to implement a unitary school system stem partly from traditional teacher-resistance but mainly from the unease felt by a people who still hold fast to the implications behind the well-known Scandinavian proverb that " there can be no better baggage on a journey than much of knowledge ". To put it another way, the American and Scandinavian conceptions of the role of the common school differ considerably though America, if anything, is moving somewhat nearer to the Scandinavian position. There is in Scandinavia no desire to be other than selective of the academic élite at a given point in the child's school career. Scandinavia feels an acute need for such an élite and makes no bones about educating for it within a truly democratic framework. The question is, when shall this selection take place? And which is better and more democratic—an elective school or a selective school? The defenders of the unitary school system in Sweden opt firmly for the elective school which they maintain will produce various and much-needed kinds of élites for the modern age. Thus, on the basis of the new school law of 1962, 80 per cent. of pupils were in attendance at the unitary school by 1964 and over 90 per cent. by 1966, the target being 100 per cent. for 1972.

The nine-year unitary school admits children from the age of 7 to be taught for the first three years of their school life in the lower school by a fully (two-year) trained woman infant teacher. Classes are held only in the morning (a common practice throughout Scandinavia) and are limited to 20 periods weekly in the first year, 24 in the second year, and 30 in the third and final year. No class may exceed 25 in numbers and classes move up together to the next grade. Guidance and remedial work is carried out on both an individual basis and (where numbers demand it) in special remedial classes. Swedish and mathematics are taught along the most modern lines. Art, craft and music are properly stressed. Social topics (history, geography, civics) are grouped as one subject. Courses in religious instruction and regular periods of physical training complete the curriculum.

As the child moves to the middle school—again of three years' duration—he is taught by either a man or a woman trained elementary school teacher. Here no class may exceed 30 in number. Classes are again mixed and unstreamed and the only specialist teachers employed are those who teach crafts—

20 periods in each craft per year. The children have 34 periods per week in the fourth grade of which two are devoted to English. In the fifth grade they have 35 periods (5 in English) and in the sixth and final grade of the middle school they again have 35 periods (four in English). The latest audio-visual aids are used in teaching a modern language and a modern approach to mathematics teaching is in full use. In the Spring term of the final year of the middle school parents and children are invited to choose options on which they hope they may specialize on entering the upper school. Optional groups must operate as long as five pupils want a course. Most common options are: German/French (5 periods a week); German/French (3 periods) with Swedish/Mathematics (2 periods); German/French (3 periods) and typing (2 periods); Crafts/typing (3 periods) and Swedish/Mathematics (2 periods); Handicrafts (5 periods).

The attempt to make a unity of schools in DENMARK and to coordinate the work of both the primary and secondary schools began as early as 1903, and it was left to the Education Act of 1937 to make secondary education for all a reality. The Education Act of 1958 still retained the period of compulsory education as being from 7 to 14, mainly because of the vested interests of the farmers who have looked to the Folk High School to provide any further education in farming pursuits, and also because of the traditional importance attached to the village school. On the other hand, the law has insisted on a comprehensive form of education for all up to the age of 14 (as opposed to hiving off the supposedly academically-minded at 11), has made the school of origin (*not* the receiving school) responsible for selection for some form of post-primary work, has given added status and importance to the seven-year school, and yet does not disparage the village school. It was a shrewd compromise respecting the views as far as possible of all sections of the community—and critics of the Swedish parliament's bull-dozing tactics are not slow to draw the comparison. Where small village schools still exist, children may attend them for the first three years of their school life and must then transfer to a central receiving school with a wide catchment area.

The first five years of schooling give the common basic groundwork. After this there still can be what is best described as " mild differentiation ", the non-academic pupils following one stream and the academically-minded another, though once again local authorities are left to decide how best to arrange this according to the man-power requirements of their respective areas. In the sixth year in all schools physical sciences are introduced, along with the teaching of one foreign language, and woodwork for boys and housecraft for girls. The seventh year is concerned with rounding off the education of the many children who will be leaving school for good in the predominantly rural areas; with organizing the curriculum in terms of local opportunities for employment and in accordance with the child's aptitudes, ability and desire for some form of continued education; with beginning the teaching of a second foreign language and the addition of more mathematics for those who wish to pass on to an academic secondary education. Periods are also devoted in these last two years to what is termed " family knowledge "—preparing the child to lead an active and useful life in terms of the democratic society of which Denmark is justly proud. Schooling is for six days a week from 8 a.m. to 2 p.m. with a break for lunch at 11 a.m. when children either eat their own food or buy open sandwiches and milk in the school canteens.

In 1972 the school leaving age was extended to 15 with a further extension to 16 envisaged for 1973–74, and schools must now prepare themselves to offer an optional further year's study to the age of 17 for 1974–75. And, since well over 90 per cent. of all pupils have been voluntarily staying on beyond the age of 14 anyway, the Danish parliament, whilst still allowing pupils to leave at 14 provided they are going on to some form of regular vocational education, now envisages the future introduction of a full twelve-year system with built-in vocational training and no selection to be made before the age of 14. In a word, Denmark has now brought herself into line with Norway and Sweden by establishing one single *folkeskole* (people's school) and has followed a general Western European trend in permitting differentiation only after the age of about 14.

By the School Law of 10 April 1959 NORWAY made a serious attempt to overcome geographical and regional obstacles to securing the best possible education for the masses of the children now seeking it in an extended form. Over the past forty years or so the standard of living had more than doubled, and as a result over 75 per cent. of the children in school were now voluntarily prolonging their schooling beyond the basic seven-year " people's" school which had so proudly served the people's needs since its creation in 1889. On the other hand, it had to be remembered that only 3 per cent. of Norwegian territory is inhabited and that this thinly-spread population (27 per square mile) had led to the development of small rural schools which were becoming increasingly backward in respect of those subjects requiring modern teachers and modern teaching devices. To put it briefly, teachers no longer wished to serve in outpost territories away from the amenities of modern civilization. How then was the rural child not to be disadvantaged in competition with the city dweller?

The law began by recognizing that to secure the best possible post-primary education for all children meant that primary education (*not* post-primary) must have prior consideration, and that sensible changes made there must have a beneficial effect higher up the educational ladder. It reinforced (as in Denmark) the function of the common primary school as being that of developing abilities and aptitudes and giving a good basis of general knowledge so that its pupils may become good members of the community. At the same time, bearing in mind the evergrowing difficulties of handling rural education adequately, it insisted on uniformity throughout the whole school system and carefully laid down fixed standards for the teaching of each subject on which the higher schools might rely as pupils were fed to them. To this end also the various local school boards, in consultation with the teaching staff, must decide on the textbook to be used for each subject, and this choice must again be approved by the Central Ministry of Education.

Experiments with a nine-year common school began in 1954, and the law of 1959 invited each commune now to consider extending its " people's " school to a full nine years. A year later there were 17 such schools in existence. By 1963–64, 105 communes out of a total of 525 had introduced the new type school, and by 1971 the change-over was virtually completed for the whole country. In the more sparsely populated areas the principle of simply adding a further two years to the original seven-year school is followed. The normal pattern is now a six-year primary school (*barneskole*) followed by three years in a comprehensive lower secondary school (*ungdomsskole*). The timetable for the first six years stresses the teaching of Norwegian, arithmetic, religious studies and arts and crafts. For the first three years there are home environmental studies superseded for the last three years by history, civics and geography. Housecraft (for girls) is introduced in the last three years. Everybody studies natural science for these last years, and in grades five and six English is taught for four periods a week.

Strictly speaking, pre-secondary education ends with the completion of the first six grades, but the Norwegian intention to " shape a unity school for youth up to the age of 16 or 17 which can be a democratic society in miniature ", and the insistence on giving a complete, all-round education to everybody, makes it convenient to consider at this stage the kind of course which follows on in the three-year comprehensive lower secondary school. The seventh grade allows for no free-choice subjects, but in grades eight and nine pupils are divided into broadly-based theoretical and practical sides of instruction, and necessary remedial work is undertaken with the most backward. The arrangement for electives is complex. In the eighth grade a second foreign language (German) is allotted five periods a week for the more academically minded, others taking a more vocational elective. In grade nine there are further modifications depending on whether Science, English or German is to be pursued, the academically inclined (some 20 per cent. at the moment of writing) opting for the stiff course of two modern languages. Here, up to twenty periods a week can be used for electives. There are three clearly differentiated levels of instruction for mathematics, Norwegian and English, and two for German. Those pupils wishing to proceed to the academic *gymnasium* must take two foreign languages and the stiffer courses in other basic subjects. Thus, roughly six different lines of preparation emerge: general theoretical, commercial, agricultural, domestic subjects (for girls), industrial, fishing and seafaring.

U.S.S.R. Naturally, the idea of a unitary school is part of the whole way of life of the peoples of the U.S.S.R. but there has been much shifting of position as to how long the period of basic (pre-secondary) schooling should last. Originally the Russians opted for a seven-year school (from the age of 7) leading to a further three-year course in what was to be a full ten-year school. In 1955 it was decided that every child must complete a full ten-year course, but Kruschev's school law of 24 December 1958 declared this ruling unrealistic and impracticable, and ordered the phasing out of the ten-year school by 1963. It was replaced by a compulsory eight-year school, termed a school of " General Education, Labour and Polytechnical Studies ", and it sought to bring the programme of studies into closer contact with the realities of life in the modern technological age. Kruschev's policies were attacked mainly on the grounds that his reforms had led to an increased number of drop-outs (probably over 25 per cent. leaving school at 15) and that workshop practice twice a week in factories for upper school pupils uselessly cluttered up factories, overloaded academic training, wasted too much valuable time, and resulted in too narrow a vocational approach too early. With the fall of Kruschev there came in June 1964 a revision which firmly placed workshop practice within the school itself, insisted that the eight-year school gave only an " incomplete " education, and provided three clearly distinct lines for further study for at least a further two years. The result has been that by 1970 fully 70 per cent. of pupils were prolonging their studies to the age of 17 (or beyond), and the current five-year plan (1975) optimistically expects 100 per cent. such enrolment. Workshop practice within the schools has now largely been abandoned on the grounds that the business of schools is to provide a *general* education. Syllabuses have been re-drafted to provide what can best be described as a somewhat traditional curriculum to meet the demands of a scientifically orientated society, and in 1969, to this end, primary grades proper were reduced from four to three.

The avowed aim of the Russian school system, however, remains the same. All children are deemed educable, though there are special schools for educationally sub-normal children and special classes for children retarded in some branch of their work. There is no streaming of pupils and they are required, grade by grade, to go steadily through the school course together. A boy cannot get ahead, however good he may be in some subjects, the argument being that the Russians do not want to produce a boy brilliant in mathematics only (for example) but one who has received a properly rounded education. If a boy is outstandingly good at one subject only the chances are that he is weak in others. The best pupils must help the weaker, and mutual aid and instruction of this kind is encouraged. School takes place usually in the morning only, for six days a week, and the children spend their afternoons in the pioneer palaces and in all kinds of clubs and societies, academic as well as aesthetic, or purely recreational. Until 1957, yearly examinations were set to move from grade to grade, but the first state examinations now take place only at the end of the eighth grade.

During the first three years of schooling, apart from such specialisms as physical education, a teacher is responsible for teaching all the subjects and usually moves up with her pupils. Most schools are co-educational and there is a predominance of women teachers. The Russian language and literature, mathematics and natural science (starting on a regional basis) form the core of the curriculum. Singing and the fundamentals of music are also taught, whilst manual work consists mainly of " self-help ", household tasks (such as sewing), working a garden plot, technical modelling and work with cardboard and paper. From the fourth grade to the eighth, natural science is taught as separate subjects (geography, biology, physics) and a modern language is added. Emphasis is placed on Russian (or another native language) and on mathematics. Chemistry is introduced in the seventh grade as the teaching of art, singing and music are phased out. Manual training in school workshops occupies two hours per week, and the study of history and literature begin to receive special attention,

Boarding schools were first opened in 1956–57 primarily to relieve crowded home conditions, but also to release parents for productive work. They have usually been run on a weekly basis, the child spending the weekend with his parents who, it was argued, were far too busy during the week to give their children the full attention they need and have the right to demand. Over the next decade or so they became so popular that demand soon outstripped places available and special reigonal commissions had to be set up to try to establish priorities. Whilst it is difficult to discover exactly on what basis selection is finally made, it would seem that orphans, children with only one parent or children of ailing parents, and children from large families receive most favourable consderation. What is certain is that in almost every school there will be found sons and daughters of professional people—politicians, diplomats, doctors, lawyers, actors and ballet dancers—who are deemed to be so busy as to be " disadvantaged " from the point of view of properly running a home. The schools are co-educational. All clothing (uniform and non-uniform) is supplied free, and, whilst the poorer children pay nothing, the average fee charged to parents seems to vary between three and fifty dollars a month according to parental income. Present information, however, would indicate that such establishments are beginning to be frowned upon except for children who must be boarded if they are to receive a proper education—which means genuine orphans and those from the remote and rural districts where adequate modern schooling on a full ten-year basis is not possible.

Germany. The organization of education throughout the German Federal Republic favours the common primary school (the *Grundschule*) but leaves each individual *Land* to control and direct as it best thinks fit. The post-war organization has stated quite baldly in Article 7 of the Basic Law that :

1. The entire educational system shall be under the supervision of the *Land*.

2. Religious instruction shall form part of the curriculum in State schools, though those entitled to bring up children shall have the right to decide whether their children shall participate in it.

3. Private schools must have a State licence, and this will only be granted if the State is satisfied that (*a*) the curriculum conforms to the basic minimum required in State schools; (*b*) the academic staff is competent and qualified by State standards; (*c*) the wealth of parents is not made a criterion for entry to such schools.

The aim, of course, is to ensure that the *Grundschule* becomes the foundation for all instruction for all classes, and to try to make education in some measure compulsory between the ages of 6 and 18. The idea of the *Grundschule* is no new one. As early as 1920 the Weimar Republic, in its campaigning for the *einheitsschule* (comprehensive school), decreed that there should be a basic and compulsory four years' schooling in an elementary school before any child be allowed to pass on to any form of secondary education, and to further this aim it discontinued all preparatory schools attached to the grammar school proper. To-day there is a distinct divergence of opinion throughout Germany as to how long the period of common schooling should last. Many *Länder* are in favour of the original four-year school, but Hamburg in particular has advocated a six-year school on the grounds that four years of elementary education is too short when it is remembered that 90 per cent. of the population of the *Grundschule* will be passing on to some form of further education that is not academic; it is folly to sacrifice the mass of the German people for the doubtful benefit of pushing further forward a mere 10 per cent. élite who will attend the academic grammar school. Upholders of the four-year *Grundschule* argue that six years of primary education dangerously shortens, in this age of acute specialization, the period of secondary education and holds back unnecessarily the gifted child.

In any case, it is generally held that the function of the *Grundschule* is to recognize, cultivate and develop a child's natural gifts and to give him a thorough instruction in the basic essentials of a good general education. These essentials are variously listed as : confident oral and written use of the mother tongue; assurance with figures; familiarity with the objects and workings of nature; appreciation of poetry (and the arts in general); a sound religious grounding; a knowledge of history that will gear itself closely to the study of the workings of a democratic society. And all this time the school will be on the watch to distinguish as well as possible between what the Hamburg system defines as the practical, the technical and the academic talents of its individual pupils. Free tuition for all pupils following a course of elementary instruction has been common usage in all schools for at least seventy years. It has now been extended in all *Länder* to cover the part-time vocational schools (which we shall discuss in the chapter on technical education).

Growing dissatisfaction with the traditional *élitist* structure of German education led in 1953 to the appointment of a commission to advise on the reform and unification of the whole school system. The commission's *Rahmenplan* (master plan) was published in 1959. It was quickly followed in 1960 by the Bremer Plan (sponsored by the German Teachers' Union). In the late 1960's came the Martin Plan proposed by the influential Christian Democratic Union political party, and it in turn was countered by the Evers Plan proposed by the Social Democratic Party. Eager debate which followed the publication of each separate plan led to no real positive action except on the personal initiative of a few progressive Länder. And then finally, in 1970, came the Structural Plan approved by all the Ministers for Education and which it is hoped speedily to implement. The *Grundschule* will be a four-year school taking pupils between the ages of 5 and 9. There will then be slotted in an orientation stage (between the ages of 10 and 11) when there will be the same studies for all pupils and no possibilities for specialization. This orientation stage is described as providing facilities for the pupil " to recognize his own learning possibilities and fields of interest in order to prepare for the later choice of a suitable main (and specialized) course of instruction ". Doubtless there will be some modification and even elaboration of this simple outline as the practicalities of the situation are grappled with. But, as the provisions made in the Structural Plan for the reform of secondary education only too clearly show, the Germans (like the Dutch, the French and the Belgians) will continue to stress the *suum cuique* rather than the *idem cuique* and to pin their faith in the first instance on a " common " primary school geared to give a sound, basic and thorough general education.

Switzerland. Primary education has been free and compulsory in Switzerland since 1874. There is, however, no Swiss education as such since each of the 25 *cantons* into which the country is (mainly geographically) divided has its own local government with its own constitution. The position of the schools in each *canton* is the result of its particular history, of its religious and cultural development. However, to secure overall harmonious balance the confederation of *cantons* has agreed on four basic educational principles to be universally applied. These are: that elementary education must be obligatory, free and adequate; that all public schools must be under the direction of the cantonal authorities; that freedom of conscience in religious matters must be guaranteed; that physical education is compulsory for boys up to the age of 15.

Some of the *cantons* are Protestant, some Catholic, some mixed, and they all jealously safeguard their autonomy in educational matters as in all other spheres of activity. There are four distinct linguistic groups, but though German speakers predominate (72 per cent.) amity reigns. The French-speaking population (21 per cent.) have the prestige the French language holds throughout the world, and the Italian group (5 per cent) and the Romansch speakers (almost 2 per cent.) feel in no way disadvantaged.

Compulsory education begins with the primary school, but the age of entry varies according to cantonal law which also governs the duration of the primary course, fixes the length of school holidays, the size of classes, the content of the curriculum, makes itself responsible for social welfare and the training of teachers, and also decides as to whether schools shall be co-educational or single-sexed. Children start school at the age of 6 or 7 and the period of compulsory education varies between seven and nine years. The primary school course proper may last for three, four, five or six years, after which pupils pass either to some form of general purpose education (which can be carried on in the same school buildings) or to the *gymnasium*. The acknowledged aim of primary education is to educate all children without distinction and by methods carefully adapted to their stage of development and talents to prepare them for the activities of everyday adult life. Thus there is emphasis on education for citizenship, and insistence on character training which is held to be primarily the responsibility of parents, the school (as in many other European countries) being considered essentially a place for learning. It is traditional for the Swiss peasant to be an educated man and to be afforded the fullest opportunities for ensuring the education of his children to the highest possible level required for the job they will take up. It is also the proud and justifiable boast of the Swiss that they owe their political stability and their sense of balance and proportion in all things—as well as their drive—to the sound educational background which, over the centuries, has made each and every Swiss supremely conscious of his own value to the community, no matter what his employment. Or, as Rousseau put it in 1758: " Consider what a difference there is between our artisans and those of other countries. A Geneva watchmaker is presentable anywhere; a Parisian watchmaker can only talk about watches. The education of a workman in his craft trains his hands and no more. Yet there remains the citizen to be considered." It is at the level of the primary school that the Swiss insist this problem be seriously tackled and so give the *Grundschule* a special emphasis. Curriculum-wise, Swiss schools have much in common with Scandinavia or Germany and likewise place insistence on a thorough grounding in basic subjects.

France. Within the framework of the highly centralized system that (despite recent moves to grant more local autonomy) still holds in France, the primary school has an important part to play both in helping to form conscientious and loyal citizens to perpetuate the glory that is France and also in giving the pupil the elements of that practical knowledge necessary for him in the performance of his daily task as a worker. Existence for the Frenchman has always been a serious matter, and he has always insisted (and will continue to insist) on the necessity for a sound, intellectual training at all levels in the school system. It is equally recognized that the majority of pupils passing through the primary schools (even when the latest reforms are taken into consideration) will move on to some form of manual or agricultural work, though it has been estimated that by 1975 only 15 per cent. of the population (as opposed to 85 per cent. in 1800) will be actively engaged in agricultural pursuits. By the same token, 40 per cent. will be in industry as opposed to 5 per cent. in 1800. Other estimates indicate that even after the latest reforms to keep all children together in a " common " school until the age of 15 become fully operative, only some 35 per cent. will then opt for an academic course. Some form of technical/commercial instruction will be followed by 45 per cent., whilst the remainng 20 per cent. will form an unskilled labour force.

Primary school begins at 6 and now ends at the age of 11. The aim is to pick up where pre-school education ends and to teach not a great deal but teach it well. The school is still organized on a basis of a thirty-hour week (six hours a day for five days) and is geared to give thorough grounding in the three R's, with insistence on ability to handle the French tongue expertly and elegantly. A little time is devoted to the teaching of history and geography, centred almost exclusively on France, and a little elementary science is crammed in where possible. Five periods a week are allotted to physical education and recreational exercises, and there is one hour of moral instruction. Old, well-tried and proven successful methods of instruction are not abandoned, but continued side-by-side with the more modern " activity " approaches and the introduction of the global system of teaching to read and to write. There is still much learning by heart, but alongside this one can easily find group work and group discussions, creative writing, studies of local interest, and the delivery of lecturettes by individual pupils to the rest of the class designed to encourage the development of some particular and personal interests. And, though the practice of setting homework was abandoned in 1956 along with the abolition of an eleven-plus examination for transfer to some form of secondary education, children whose parents are anxious for them to succeed may have up to five hours of private supervised study each week on school premises.

On 6 January 1959 it was decreed that the school leaving age throughout France should be raised from 14 to 16 by progressive stages—this merely regularizing a general trend since at that time it was estimated that for the whole country easily 65 per cent. were prolonging their education beyond the age of 14 (and over 80 per cent. in the larger towns)—and that the changeover should be completed by 1967. A more realistic target date of 1972 was finally decided. In January 1960 De Gaulle also signed a bill which attempted to put an end for all time to the struggle between Church and State for the control of education. The bill was tacit recognition of the fact that roughly 43 per cent. of Frenchmen would prefer to send their children to Catholic schools could they afford to do so;[1] that 16 per cent. of children of primary school age were in Catholic schools anyway; and that 30 per cent. of pupils in technical or academic secondary education were again in the private sector. Put very simply the bill has allowed all accredited Catholic schools (i.e. those with qualified teaching personnel) to enter into contracts with the government whereby all teachers' salaries are paid by the government whilst day-to-day running expenses of the schools become a charge on the local authority. No fees may be charged in any school at any level except for religious instruction and incidentals (such as music) and even then permission must be sought from the Ministry.[2]

Belgium. The organization of primary education throughout Belgium derives from the reform plan put forward by the then Minister for Education, Bovesse, in 1936, but not implemented until the end of the Second World War in 1945. The plan aimed at bringing harmony, cohesion and simplicity into the entire school system; at ensuring that every child received the kind of education for which he was best suited; at extending the facilities of the already well-developed system of child and vocational

---

[1] *Le Monde,* 16 June 1959.
[2] For a fuller and more detailed account see my essay in the *World Year Book of Education for 1966,* pp. 67–77.

guidance; at the establishment of parallel classes of study to make for easy change from one type of education to another; at replacing the workshop apprenticeship system by vocational education which did not neglect the cultural aspects. Over the years the Bovesse Plan, has been carefully amended and elaborated so that firstly there is to-day no examination hurdle of any kind to secure that form of post-primary education the parents want for their child. Secondly, there has been a gradual move towards establishing a common secondary school for all between the ages of 12 and 18 without necessarily following the fashionable swing to comprehensive education in some form or another. Thirdly, whilst there is talk of progressively raising the school leaving age to 18 (it is at present 15), no one worries much since the bulk of the pupils are already in school on a purely voluntary basis to at least the age of 16. Fourthly, all school fees (abolished for children up to the age of 14 in 1947) have since 1959 been abolished in every kind of educational institution except the universities.

The real problems for educationists turn on the thorny question of religious and linguistic differences. It has to be remembered that education in Belgium is " free " in the sense that a parent may educate his child as he wishes, even to the extent of employing a private tutor (though this is now rare). What in practice happens is that the State itself has no monopoly in education (as in France), more than half the pupils electing to be taught in Catholic schools, and considerably more than half being Flemish as opposed to French-speaking. Schools, therefore, are maintained either by the State, or the Catholic Church, or by a province, or by a *commune*. A new school law of 1959 sought to end the century-old quarrel between Church and State, the Catholics at long last accepting the State's right to create and maintain its own schools, and the Liberals and anti-Catholics (left-wing usually) according the Church parity of esteem and complete equality alongside the State system. Briefly the law authorizes an equitable distribution of State grants for education to all kinds of schools recognized as efficient. Parents are perfectly free to choose between the neutral State system and the Catholic schools, and the State's prime responsibility is to ensure that the type of school a given number of parents requires is provided. The abolition of all fees in all schools in both the public and private (i.e. Catholic) sectors has been matched by the State making itself responsible for paying all salaries to all teachers, and ensuring that pension rights and sickness benefits are again the same in all similar types of school. Traditional Belgian individualism is reflected in a further clause which leaves each authority (State, Church Province or Township) free to decide its own teaching techniques and to draw up its own syllabus and time-table distribution of hours allotted to each subject in accordance with minimum over-all requirements as laid down by the Ministry of Education. Finally, any new regulations concerning the schools must be implemented on a basis of common agreement amongst Catholics and Christian Socialists, Liberals, Socialists, and the Provinces and Townships.

The delicate and more explosive problem of linguistic differences has been aggravated by the fact that modern industrial development has firmly shifted from the French-speaking south to the Flemish-speaking north. The Walloons feel aggrieved and almost deliberately disadvantaged. The Flemings feel they are at last coming into their birthright. To solve the language dispute at the schools' level a new law of 1962 declared Brussels a bilingual capital city, insisted that all schools in clearly defined Flemish areas must teach in Flemish, and that in Brussels there must be a sufficient supply of Flemish-teaching schools, the decision as to whether a child attended a French or Flemish school there being dependent on the language spoken by the father. A further law of 1963 abolished such schools as were still giving parallel classes in French and Flemish. All teaching personnel in a given school must now speak the same language. And by the same token a dual Ministry of Education has been instituted with each French-speaking administrator having his Flemish opposite number. Since the war it had become customary for children in the primary school to begin a foreign language (usually English) from their fifth year of studies. The 1963 law now substitutes the other mother language for a foreign language proper (three hours per week) in strictly unilingual areas. Along the linguistic frontiers and in Brussels the other mother language must be introduced in the third year of studies (three hours per week) and then stepped up to five hours from the fifth year.

Primary schooling starts at 6 and now ends at the age of 12. Co-education is frequent in villages but not in towns. The programme is divided into three cycles of two years each, the teacher moving up with his children for each cycle and a child being required to show he has fully mastered the work of his present cycle before advancing further. Remedial teaching takes place to obviate as far as possible having to hold a child back. Much freedom is allowed the teacher, though in 1958 it was found necessary to curtail his freedom to dispense with a time-table in order to make for greater uniformity in pupil preparation. The teaching is based on Decroly principles and is organized round centres of interest with the child observing and linking his observations with more abstract ideas and translating them into expression work. Between the ages of 6 and 8 (first cycle) the teacher watches for developing interests and activities of the child and organizes the work around them. As the children become more sociable between the ages of 8 and 12, teaching is organized year by year around the four basic needs first enunciated by Decroly: the need for play, rest, work; the need for food; the need for protection against the elements; the need for defence against enemies. This cyclical study is bound up with social training. At the same time, some of the more proved traditional methods of teaching are not despised. In the first two cycles (6 to 8 and 8 to 10) arithmetic and the mother tongue are particularly emphasized. In the last cycle studies become more subject-centred and are gradually expanded and organized in a more systematic way.

Holland. As in Belgium, there is no State monopoly for education in Holland, nor is the Ministry of Education looked upon as the " schoolmaster-in-chief " as in France. There is in consequence a high degree of decentralization which stems from a wish to give as much freedom as possible to all sections of the community. Unity out of diversity is the ideal, it being maintained that a healthy democracy must be based on recognition of and respect for a variety of attitudes and opinions. This reduces the function of the State to ensuring uniformity of standards throughout the school systems, of making for identity of opportunity (as opposed to equality of opportunity), of seeing that all who legally seek to run their own schools may do so, and of footing the bill. In actual practice this means that the State pays all salaries to all teachers on the same uniform scale, and that the municipality meets all the running expenses of all its schools whether publicly or privately maintained.

What are sometimes referred to as the three main pillars of Dutch society are the Catholic Church (accounting for some 40 per cent. of the population and resident mainly in the south), the Dutch Reformed Church, and the Neutrals. Catholics hold the Church to be the only proper educator. Dutch Calvinists, with their extremely democratic organization, argue that parents must be the main if not the sole educators of their children. Neutrals usually refuse to have anything to do with either of the two main religions and are equally averse to falling under State direction, arguing that every parent must be free to choose exactly how his child shall be educated. Thus, there are four types of primary school, three private and one State-controlled. The most recent figures indicate that only about 25 per cent. of primary-age children are in the *Openbaar* (State-controlled) schools. Some 3 per cent. are in Neutral schools, about 44 per cent. in Catholic Schools, and the remainder (roughly 27 per cent.) in Protestant schools.

In January 1950 the period of compulsory education was extended to eight full years making the school leaving age, in effect, 14 plus. It is estimated, however, that 80 per cent of the children voluntarily prolong their schooling beyond the age of 15 and that a large proportion of the remainder follow part-time courses held two or three times weekly. Since 1954, when the full period of compulsory education became free, all schools have been equally subsidized by the Government, but the private schools may still draw financial support from other sources (e.g. Church funds or by charging fees) and thus can give a better education than the *Openbaar* schools. The Neutral schools— usually " prestige " schools—charge the highest fees, attract better staff (because of higher rates of pay) and tend to have much better equipment. A move to counter the disadvantages a child in an *Openbaar* thus runs is sometimes made by the larger municipalities to divide its *Openbaar* schools into categories " A " and " B ", to channel more money into the favoured " A " type school, and to have it pursue an extended curriculum more in keeping with the work done in the private school sectors. The latest coalition socialist government (1973) seeks to do away with all these discrepancies by abolishing both primary and secondary school fees, by making education a joint community responsibility to be financed by taxes, and also to combine not only infant and junior schools but to have all types of secondary education under one roof. How far it will be successful must depend on amicable compromise arrangements amongst the three aforementioned pillars of Dutch society.

The normal age range in the primary school is between 6 and 12, and 60 per cent. of children go through school without missing a single promotion. All but the Catholic schools are co-educational. The pupils are taught the three R's. They learn the Dutch language (and Frisian in appropriate areas), geography, natural history (including the elements of hygiene), singing, drawing, gymnastics (including swimming) and (for girls) needlework. All pupils receive instruction in traffic regulations and the highway code—a very necessary precaution in the " land of the bicycle "! English as a foreign language has now become compulsory in all primary schools from the age of 10, and optional from the age of 6, and plans are afoot to have trained between 1975 and 1980 sufficient specialist teachers of English at this level to cope adequately with the needs of all primary schools.

Outside observers often remark on the traditional and teacher-centred approach in all schools, and particularly at the primary level. Methods of teaching here, they say, are not child-centred enough. Dutch educationists are well aware of the criticism. Their reply is that a true democracy must safeguard the freedom of parents to choose an education for their children in accordance with their principles and beliefs. The role of the educationist must be to advise and guide, but never dictate. Parents consider the main function of the schools to be that of instilling knowledge and the ability to think as well as to prepare boys and girls for their future careers. The idea of a comprehensive type of education finds little favour and the people refuse to hanker after any kind of increased social mobility which might be based on a lowering of standards in the schools. The primary school is now a " basic " school frequented by all children, but it carefully prepares each and every pupil for the appropriate kind of post-primary education for which he seems to be suited. Social differences, it is claimed, are allowed to be neither a handicap nor an advantage. Thus, the present critical moment for Dutch education centres on post-primary provision which has been reorganized by the " Mammoth " School Law (1963). This new law began to be implemented in the autumn of 1968 and will be considered in our next chapter.

Italy. It is often said that the structure of Italian education has not changed in any significant way since the Casati Law was adopted in 1859, or at any rate since the Coppino Act of 1877. And the most usual explanation given is the poverty of the country, lacking as it does sufficient industrial development to support a mainly rural population. Certainly poverty and illiteracy are the two main obstacles still to be overcome. Statistical data for the school year 1952–53 revealed that no fewer than 43 per cent. of children between the ages of 11 and 14 were receiving no schooling of any kind—and this despite the Gonella Plan for 1947 which specifically sets out to combat illiteracy and also created the *scuola populare*, a people's school open to all children over the age of 12 and to all adults wishing to learn to read and write and complete their elementary studies. In 1951 it was estimated that 12.9 per cent. of the population over the age of 6 were illiterate, and some slight satisfaction was drawn from the fact that ten years later this figure had dropped to 8.4 per cent.

Meantime, a ten-year plan for education had been drawn up in 1958 to make education compulsory and free for all for a minimum period of eight years' full schooling. This was followed five years later (1963) by a new school law principally regulating post-primary education but also stressing the importance of a sound, basic primary education for all. The primary school now extends between the ages of 6 and 11 and is divided into two cycles, the first being from 6 to 8 years of age and the second from 8 to 11. Oral and written examinations must be passed at the end of each cycle, and success at the end of the second cycle leads to the award of the *licenza elementare* which qualifies for entry to post-primary education. Along with the study of the usual basic subjects there is emphasis on religious, civic and moral training. Manual training (*lavoro*) is not interpreted in the narrow sense of manual instruction, or handicrafts, or domestic science, but rather as a form of honourable productive activity. Here there is a faint link with Decroly principles. School furniture will be repaired. Girls will not only do domestic science but also learn the economics of balancing the domestic budget, learn to shop, and learn to bath the baby. Town boys in particular will have their gardens in which to cultivate and raise saleable vegetables. It has to be remembered that Italian labour exports itself the world over, and that a stable economy in the present age of automation depends on the workman realizing that his is an honourable calling. It has also realistically to be accepted that there will still be many " drop-outs " from full-time compulsory education—particularly in the poorer south—and that real basic education at the primary level is therefore most important.

England and Wales. One critic has summed up the present approach towards education in England and Wales as being an attempt to secure social equality even though it be at the expense of academic excellence. Today 95 per cent. of all children between the ages of 5 and 11 are in public primary schools. As in France, primary education in England sees old methods interspersed with the new, though the school is now regarded more as a lively community where the teacher is increasingly becoming a guide and a friend rather than an instructor. Unlike France, however, there is no attempt made by the Department of Education and Science to impose a curriculum on State schools. Each Head Teacher (with his staff) devises his own curriculum, plans his own timetable and uses his own methods of instruction subject only to inspectorial guidance and discussion, and even then usually only as requested. Instruction covers the three R's, history, geography, nature study or some general science, craft, art, music and physical education. Government-sponsored experiments have also led to the teaching of French in selected primary schools on the most modern oral methods to children between the ages of 8 and 11. The only ministerial directive concerns religious education which is made compulsory on a non-denominational basis and which is usually given by the class teacher.

The modern approach, whilst in accord with traditional English dependence on slow natural growth and the gradual assimilation of new ideas rather than on sweeping changes, does now recognize a child has his own special and individual needs and that the timetable must be made as flexible as possible to cope with these needs. Heed is paid to Whitehead's statement that the curriculum should be conceived of as " a seamless robe of knowledge ", and the division into separate subjects is increasingly seen as an adult concept not easily acceptable to children. Work nowadays tends to take the form of projects and centres of interests conducted in groups or by individuals. Primary education has tended to begin with an introductory two-year infant stage (from 5 to 7 years of age) usually in the same building as the primary school proper but kept separate from it. During this two-year period the child should have learned to read simple books, to write with fair ease, and to do simple sums. In practice, and for a variety of reasons which include shortage of teachers, large classes, and (in most towns of any size) problems associated with immigrant children, as many as a quarter or a third may not meet these simple requirements before passing on to the second stage—a four-year period in the junior school (from 7 to 11 years of age). Children usually move up, however, on attaining their seventh birthday and remedial classes then become necessary.

Since the publication of the Plowden Report, " Children and their Primary Schools " (1967), many local authorities have already implemented a recommendation therein that the primary school should re-divide itself into a " first " school to about the age of 8 or 9 or 10, and then into a middle school from the age of 8, 9 or 10 to 12, 13 or 14. There is a wide variety of possibilities, all turning on the provision made by a given local authority for post-primary education up to the compulsory school-leaving age of 16 (implemented 1973). In the past it has been common to stream classes in the larger junior schools on an intellectual basis and with special references to the basic skills, but the necessity to do so (although in principle still stoutly defended in some quarters) vanished once the country as a whole (with a few notable exceptions) decided to abolish the notorious eleven-plus examination purporting to decide for what type of post-primary education a child was best suited. Again, and as the creation of various types of " middle " schools indicates, debate now centres on the question as to whether eleven-plus is the right age for transfer to secondary education proper.

It is not possible to discuss here in any detail any of the 197 proposals contained in the Plowden Report, but it is worthwhile noting that in its own way it sought to do for the primary schools of England and Wales much of what was attempted in America by President Johnson's own Federal Bill. How many of the recommendations will be partially or fully implemented remains to be seen over the next decade or so. In any case, whatever is done cannot be considered as an isolated exercise. The new pattern that is emerging of some form of comprehensive education at the secondary level must affect the primary school, and the primary school in turn will condition work done at the lower levels in comprehensve schools.

Conclusion. The discovery that education for to-day must be " total " in the sense that it cannot be separated from the over-all social framework in which the children will have to function as adults has brought somewhat tardy realization that education must constitute one continuous and unbroken progression from the nursery school onwards. It has focused attention on nursery school provision as never before. It has led to debate as to what is the best age to start and finish compulsory schooling. It has killed the old conception of a terminal *elementary* education. It has challenged, and found wanting, all the various procedures whereby children have heretofore been selected at the primary school level for some form of post-primary education. Educationists have moved much further towards the Marxist view that intelligence, in so far as it can be measured, is largely acquired. It is further agreed that children brought up in homes with what is loosely termed " satisfactory emotional adjustment " will tend to go to good schools, to stay longer at school, and to take up that employment which really interests and challenges them—the whole process making them in all respects more intelligent than those to whom (for a variety of reasons) these things do not happen. So is the myth of equality of educational opportunity challenged and more proper emphasis given to securing identity of opportunity. Or, again as the Swedes have put it, not *idem cuique* (the same for everybody) should be the ideal but rather *suum cuique* (to each his own).

It is again to be noted that, except for Japan and Czechoslovakia, Great Britain is the only country which starts primary school as early as five years of age. On the other hand, this is offset by the fact that more and more children in other European countries are flocking to nursery school from the age of 3 on a non-compulsory basis. This again raises the question of the proper function of the nursery school: should it merely try to " communize the maternal functions " (to use the classic Montessori phrase) or should it in some measure prepare the child for more formalized instruction at the primary level? If education is now seen to be a continuous flow, however, how much should nursery school practice influence attitudes at least

in the lower classes of the primary school? How far can the
primary school liberate itself from the requirements of various
forms of secondary education now that the various examination
hurdles set at the close of a primary school course are in process
of being minimized or abolished altogether? What can be said to
constitute a " general education " at the primary school level?
Is streaming in the primary school either necessary or desirable?

Increasing importance is now attached to the primary school as
a " basic " school (a *Grundschule*) to ensure that it really does
provide a sound basic training from which the child may draw
strength and confidence to embark on some form of post-primary
education. At the same time, it is recognized that a well-informed,
inquiring mind is much more necessary to the nation than one
which is passively stocked with information. Hence the pro-
minence generally of techniques derived from the " new "
education and the gradual abandonment of teaching in the mass
in favour of more individual attention. The influence of men
like Decroly has become more widespread throughout Europe
generally. The old-fashioned idea of having a programme to
work to that is theoretically suited to an average group is on the
way out. Television and radio have furthered the trend towards
more imaginative teaching. School orchestras of various kinds
are not unusual. Plays and puppet plays are a commonplace.
And, perhaps most important of all, parents have been brought
to greater self-involvement in the whole process as one important
step towards achieving better emotional adjustment in the home.
Healthy (or rather health-giving) activities are geared to all this.
Modern buildings and playgrounds bring new amenities and
possibilities, not least amongst which must be numbered the
decline of formal teaching in favour of group and team-teaching,
the introduction of science lessons, and (in many cases) of a
modern foreign language.

Yet there is another side to the picture. Classes in primary
schools are still far too large. There is an inadequate supply of
good teachers just where they are most needed. And it has to be
admitted that the " new " education makes greater and more
imaginative demands on the teacher than the old formalized
system of instruction. Can we recruit sufficient teachers of the
right intellectual calibre? And can we train (or educate) them to
function adequately? Colleges of education for teachers are often

subjected to much criticism on this score, the point being frequently raised as to whether freedom in the primary school can go too far in the wrong direction and lead to a lack of real discipline in the use of the basic tool subjects. The general opinion would seem to be that America has provided us with an important example of what not to do. In England and Wales there seems to be a move to check too much of a drift in the American direction.[1] In America since Sputnik (1957) there has been much tightening up. France sublimely goes its own way. Norway, Sweden and Russia in particular all prove that if you pay close attention to the work done in the *Grundschule* you can have a unitary school system and still train an *élite*.

[1] At the moment of writing there is serious concern about the success rate in learning to read and a special commission of inquiry has been set up to report (it is hoped) by 1974.

CHAPTER TEN

Secondary Education

THE breakdown of social barriers that started with the Industrial Revolution and which gained increasing impetus as the nineteenth century drew to its close inevitably threw up all kinds of problems in the field of post-primary and secondary education that left most European countries (as we shall see) bewildered and uncertain about the right solution to seek. In the first place, there came a challenge to the traditional concept of what was meant by the term " secondary " as applied to education. For centuries, it had been assumed that secondary education was education that befitted a gentleman, and that gave some training for the learned professions, and for offices of government, very much according to the pattern established by John Locke in his *Thoughts on Education*. There was a governing élite, and tradition decreed that the basis of the curriculum for the formation of this élite should be the Latin and Greek tongues, ancient history, and some philosophical training usually arising as a by-product from a thorough grounding in the classical languages. Only towards the end of the nineteenth century did a study of foreign languages grudgingly find a place in the curriculum, along with mathematics, and finally the sciences. Even then, however, it was still held (as in not a few public schools in England to-day) that the study of foreign modern languages and the sciences should become easier options for the less able pupil. That traditional outlook still persists almost everywhere in Europe despite the post-war reforms that have taken place.

The second problem arose from the prevailing idea that only those of wealth and a certain social status were fit to govern and to form an intellectual élite. The children of such parents had a pre-emptive right to profit from the kind of education given in what we will call the classical secondary school, and to this end

all classical secondary schools established their preparatory departments through which it became almost imperative for a child to
pass before gaining entrance to the main school at the age of 11 or
12. Thus, two clearly-defined and distinct types of primary education established themselves : the one for the masses of the people
that led nowhere except to some kind of job at between the ages
of 12 and 14; the other which was a careful preparation for an
advanced academic training up to the age of 18 or beyond. So
did what we have already called the dual system of education come
into existence. Until the nineteenth century, however, education
throughout the ages had been for a select few. Now, the masses
had to be and were being educated. An increasing demand for
a still more highly educated person in science, industry and trade
focused attention on the anomalies in this dual system of education,
forced the classical secondary school to open its doors more widely
to include more and more scholarship children from among the
working classes and to give constantly increasing importance in
its curriculum to modern subjects like foreign languages, history
and geography, and led to the creation of new types of schools to
rival the old classical secondary school and so call for an entirely
new assessment of what was meant by secondary education.

But all this brought still a third problem. Tradition dies hard,
and as more and more pupils came to profit from an increasingly
liberal but still highly classical kind of secondary education such
an education became a sort of *cachet* and was looked upon as a
necessary preliminary to a wide variety of black-coated jobs. The
former matriculation certificate in England, for example, became
necessary for entry to an insurance firm, to a bank, to a commercial
business house as a clerk, and to minor civil service appointments
such as the post office. An army of black-coated workers arose,
side by side with the intellectual élite, and work of a practical or
technical nature came to be despised by the very people most
notably suited for it and at a time when the demand was increasing
for highly trained technical skill.

Finally, as increasing prosperity due to technological advances
in industry and higher standards of living made it possible to raise
the compulsory school leaving age still higher, so again did the
question of what kind of post-primary education to offer become
acute, and so did the cry of equality of educational opportunity
for all make itself heard. It needed none the less the serious chal-

lenges to the by then accepted ideals of democracy that came from the totalitarian states, allied to insistent demands for better and better trained workers in science and technology, to make most countries in the immediate post-war period recast their whole way of thinking and re-form their school systems drastically at the post-primary level. It is in particular with such re-formation that we shall be concerned in this chapter, though we shall relegate the whole complicated and vexing question of what kind of technical training is offered to a chapter on its own. In other words, we are by implication defining secondary education to-day as that kind of post-primary education which is not directly concerned with man and machines but rather with a kind of broad, modern and humanistic culture that it is hoped will enable man to release to the full his potentialities and so direct him towards the kind of employment for which he realizes himself he is most especially suited.

As the American approach to education has been one which requires education for the masses first and education for the most talented second, so have the Americans anticipated practice everywhere in Europe both in recognizing the need for a kind of secondary education suitable for those not going on to institutes of higher education and in developing a wide range of courses supplementary and alternative to those offered by the traditional classical curriculum. All this has, of course, been made possible by the phenomenal increase in the wealth of the U.S.A. which has both kept adolescents off the labour market and made more money available for the building of more and more high schools. We must not forget also, however, the strong egalitarian feelings of the American people which have caused them to move more freely and naturally towards the idea of equality of educational opportunity. Thus America once again becomes a starting-point for this particular survey of practice and changes in education at the post-primary secondary level.

U.S.A. We have already noted that the break between primary and secondary education comes either at the age of 14, when normally there is a four-year high school course to be followed, or at the age of 12, after which three years are spent in a junior high school to be followed by a further three years in the senior high school. This latter plan (popularly known as the 6 – 3 – 3 system) has gained favour because of the opportunities it offers for the better guidance and counselling of pupils and for providing exploratory courses to discover a pupil's abilities and interests. It is this aspect of the work in the junior high school which has caught the attention particularly in Western Europe and caused countries which had no clearly defined middle school system in operation to implement one when they carried out their post-war reforms at the secondary level.

Because the American system of education is dominated by the idea of the comprehensive school, all pupils, whether gifted, average or backward, are expected to attend the same school, and this policy—if in practice it is not extended to work in the senior high school—certainly holds as far as the junior high school. In consequence, all high school education is free and text-books are also provided free of cost. There are incidental fees for games and certain clubs, and parents must naturally bear the cost of clothes, transport and maintenance of the pupil. It thus is not unknown for pupils to engage on wage-earning activities either before or after school in order either to obtain pocket money or to contribute in some degree to their support at home. Again, because the schools are considered the parents' schools and because the children are expected to stay ideally for the whole of the high school course, all kinds of vocational subjects have crept into the curriculum, and the academic traditions holding in Europe are strongly criticized as being no longer suited to the needs and abilities of the mass of the pupils who now fill the high schools. A close study over a number of years of the intake of the high schools reveals that there are roughly 20 per cent. suited to academic subjects, 20 per cent. to vocational subjects, and 60 per cent. for whom entirely different curricula must be devised. It is estimated in the Middle West that of those born on farms only one in ten will stay in farming. The remainder will seek jobs in urban communities. High Schools in the Middle West in particular, therefore, are gradually introducing a change-over from various agricultural options to some others more adapted to the needs of the majority of these youngsters. High Schools everywhere, however, have to cope with the problem that not only does 30 per cent. of an intake never complete the course but also with the fact that of those who do finish High School just under half will go directly to work. Similarly, of those who do proceed to college from High School, fully 50 per cent. will never complete the college course.

The curriculum of any given high school is therefore not easy to describe. As time goes on, and as social demands change, new subjects are incorporated displacing those that are outmoded. The fundamental " core " subjects taught in both junior and senior high school are : English, history, mathematics and science. In addition, a number of " elective " subjects are studied, these being chosen by the pupil after consultation with his teacher counsellor, who, because of the wide range of abilities that exists amongst the pupils he has to help, fulfils a very important role in the high school system. A pupil, after counselling, may elect to do a subject for one or two terms, and then drop it in favour of something else.

The senior high school, designed to complete secondary education, must make provision for a more or less complete training in the fields of study chosen as a result of the work in the junior high school. Differentiated curricula are provided by means of which each pupil will be able to pursue, once his decision is reached, work systematically planned with reference to his needs as an individual and as a member of society. The main lines of work found in the senior high school are : college preparatory, business and commercial, industrial arts, agriculture, home economics (domestic science, etc.), and special subjects such as music and art. Differentiation can also exist within these special curricula. The college preparatory programme, for example, can subdivide for entrance into liberal arts colleges, schools of engineering, schools of medicine and dentistry; a commercial course can provide for salesmen, secretary typists, buyers and business managers; the agriculture course can have grain-growing, dairying, fruit-growing and livestock-raising subdivisions. How far the ramifications extend depends on the size and resources of the school, and the Americans favour large comprehensive schools in order to be able to provide as many " elections " as possible. Certain large cities will have special-type high schools, as for example a commercial high school or a technical high school.

Those pupils who graduate from high school on the college preparatory programme can then normally pass to what is termed the junior college which supplies two years of training beyond the standard high school course. The junior college may be the first two years of a fully organized university, or it may be a separate institution. Such a course represents either the preliminary training to the reading for a university degree proper, or the pre-professional requirements of schools of medicine, dentistry, etc., or the requisite two-year course to qualify in pharmacy.

One marked feature of the American high school is the emphasis placed on extra-curricular and out-of-school activities, these being regarded as increasingly important in the development of character and in teaching the young adolescent the correct use of his leisure time. Games and athletics loom large in such programmes, of course, but they form in reality only one small part of the whole. There are schools at which something is going on every night, and on Saturdays as well, organized by the pupils on an often extremely elaborate scale. The fact that most of the drive behind these activities comes from the pupils themselves is evidence that they are genuinely interested. The initiative is left to them, but teachers naturally supervise generally and proffer advice and help as required. As is to be expected there is a wide variety of activities ranging from pupil government of the school and student councils to movie clubs, school bands, rodeos (in the far West), broadcasting stations, running their own cafeteria, organizing their own bus services, down to the more humdrum European idea of out-of-school activities such as dramatic societies, dance clubs, language clubs, debating societies, producing the school magazine, and so on.

On paper, it is all very fine indeed, but in actual practice discerning Americans find much to criticize. The idea of a comprehensive school running into hundreds of pupils of both sexes is all very well, but the close personal contact between teacher and taught that can hold in a European school of smaller size is lost. The school becomes a depersonalized machine, and the teachers automata for enabling children to make their grades and amass the necessary credits required for the graduation ceremony. All these extra-curricular activities which make the school the pupils' school day and night mean that increasingly the home and home influences recede into the background. Again, is the gradual crowding out of academic subjects in favour of an increasingly widening range of vocational subjects going too far? Does not each country need as large an academic élite as it can muster? Has not the American's inherited belief that all men are created equal led to the conception that all school children have the same potentialities, and is not America confusing equality of opportunity with identity of opportunity?

Many people began to think along these lines after the launching of Sputnik in 1957, and the strident strictures of Admiral Rickover pin-pointed it all. The best pupils were nowhere near being fully stretched. They were being allowed too much freedom in their choice of options. They were not being pushed hard enough from an early age. The quality of teacher performance left much to be desired. In its public school sector America had signally failed in combining the ideals of a universal education and those of scholastic excellence. In proportion as it was discovered that the majority of children had neither the gift nor the desire for an academic education, so was the curriculum downgraded to meet the needs of the lowest levels of competence. An intellectual conformity with the average common mental denominator had thus set in, and bright and potentially able students were firmly harnessed to the mediocre. Their development was impeded and their gifts lost to the nation. Admiral Rickover also illustrated how much better and richer was European and Russian performance, and also revealed how much better work was being done, of a more rigorous academic nature and comparable with that in Europe, in the best of the High Schools in the *private* sector of American secondary education. It was also noted that the intake into the private sector of secondary education had been steadily on the increase since the end of World War II.[1]

Obviously these criticisms had to be met, and the former President of Harvard University, Dr. James B. Conant, was charged to consider the question: *Can a school at one and the same time provide a good general education for all pupils as future citizens of a democracy, provide elective programmes for the majority to develop useful skills, and educate adequately those with a talent for handling advanced academic subjects—particularly foreign languages and advanced mathematics?* Dr. Conant came to the conclusion that no radical alteration to the basic pattern of American education was necessary, but he did admit that too often the demands made on the time of High School students in out-of-school hours was too great; that the academically gifted student did not work hard enough and that his programme of academic studies was neither of sufficient range nor sufficiently challenging; that there were too many small High Schools which could not be economically viable and whose

---

[1] Consult for example: *Education and Freedom* (New York, 1959), *Education for All Children* (Washington, 1962) and *Swiss Schools and Ours* (Washington, 1962).

offerings therefore (particularly for non-academic elective programmes) left much to be desired.[1]

His first major recommendation therefore was for a drastic reduction in the number of such small schools through district reorganization and an increase in the size of existing schools to give America about 9,000 High Schools in place of 21,000. This recommendation met with immediate response if only for the fact that for the last two decades Americans had been worried by problems arising from the development of " neighbourhood " schools—schools which acquire standing and prestige originally because of the social position of parents in a particular catchment area (e.g. a High School serving a district chiefly inhabited by university teachers or other highly trained professional men and women) and then attract to themselves, in all kinds of devious ways, children of ambitious parents who should normally be attending school in a different area. Such " neighbourhood " schools almost always offer high-powered academic teaching exclusively on a liberal arts programme, and by their very nature disadvantage High Schools in socially inferior catchment areas.[2] The present tendency is to build what are called " education parks " catering for as many as 10,000 pupils and thus killing " neighbourhood " demarcation lines. It is also leading to the hiving off of the Junior High from the Senior High School, often with two separate and equally large buildings either on the same neutral campus or in some cases (dependent on the nature of the neighbourhood problem) strategically placed at different points in the school district to achieve the same neutrality.

In 1967 Dr. Conant published *The Comprehensive High School* to report on how far his recommendations had taken effect. He was reasonably well satisfied though admitting there was still room for improvement. The study of one modern foreign language for at least four years was well under way. Ability grouping particularly at the Senior High School level in various subjects— setting not streaming—was becoming more usual. A sharper edge was being given to guidance and counselling. It was being shown that the academically gifted could cope with English,

---

[1] J. B. Conant: *The American High School Today* (New York, 1959).

[2] It is not unknown for parents deliberately to change their place of residence in order to secure " good " High School education for their children and then to move out of the area again when their children's education is finished. The problem of " neighbourhood " schools is already being felt among comprehensive schools in Greater London and in some of the larger cities in England and Wales.

mathematics, science, a foreign language, social studies, physical education, and art or music in any one year. Some schools were beginning to use a " track " system offering differing levels of instruction in a given subject to suit individual needs. And, particularly in the big cities, " advanced placement " courses are run for the future university student of ability to cover work normally done in the Freshman year and so cut down the length of time actually spent at the university in acquiring a first degree.

All this, of course, as we have noticed earlier, was running alongside the passing of the various education acts between 1958 and 1965. It is obviously too early yet for a full and proper appraisal to be made. There are still many difficulties to be surmounted, not least amongst which must count both problems associated with vexingly large and growing conurbations and also those of the rural areas (particularly the Middle West) which throw up the remarkable statistic that nearly half of America's secondary schools still have fewer than 500 pupils. What we can note with some interest is that as a result of all this re-thinking the traditional three-year Junior High School is coming under attack as being too imitative of the Senior High both in curriculum and activities, and for allowing immature children to choose electives unwisely. The familiar 6 – 3 – 3 division into elementary, Junior High and Senior High is being replaced particularly in New York City by a 4 – 4 – 4 plan and elsewhere by a 5 – 4 – 3 plan both of which replace the Junior High by an Intermediate school.

U.S.S.R. Since the eight-year school in Russia is considered basic for all we have already mentioned generally what goes on there. Specialist teachers take over only in the last five years and at the end of that time a pupil will sit a fairly simple passing-out examination, though this presumably must disappear as schooling becomes compulsory for all to the age of seventeen. In any case, cumulative records on the pupils have always been the prime consideration, and these are carefully assessed in deciding to what form of post-basic education he shall be directed. The majority will go on to complete their secondary education for a further two years in the ninth and tenth grades and will then sit an important maturity examination (the *attestat*) which is necessary for admission to a preferred course in higher education. High achievement at this examination will not only provide the student with a good scholarship but—most important of all—will exempt him from a two-year work period which is compulsory for roughly 80 per cent. of all school leavers before proceeding further with their studies. Students unfortunate enough not to get exemption may, of course, begin their studies on a part-time basis (by attendance at evening centres, correspondence courses, broadcast courses) during this working period.

About 15 per cent. of children completing the eight-year school will be absorbed into a *tekhnikum*, or specialized secondary school, which will combine technical or vocational education with continued general education for a further three or four years. Many primary school teachers are still trained in such establishments, but numbers must diminish as the Pedagogical Institutes fully assume their comprehensive role. The majority of the students there are trained either for jobs of a lower grade civil service nature or as skilled professional workers and middle-level specialists in commerce and industry. As to the remaining 10 per cent., these will either attend a lower level vocational school for some two years or go straight to work, completing their education as fitting by day release, by correspondence courses, or by attendance at evening classes.

Scandinavia. We have seen how in NORWAY a comprehensive school compulsory for all between the ages of 7 and 16 has been gradually introduced, legalisation coming with a formal School Act of 1969 and full implementation being achieved in 1971. The most academically able pupils, who have been carefully sorted out and given more rigorous academic training particularly in the last year (the ninth grade), will now pass to the traditional *gymnasium* to follow a three-year course in preparation for the *Examen Artium*, success in which will gain them admission to the university or some other form of higher education. Serious attempts are now being made to widen entry to the *gymnasium* which (except in the capital city, Oslo, where the entry level is as high as 50 per cent. of 16-year-olds) caters only for some 20 per cent. of school leavers. The majority of the *gymnas* are separate institutions, though in some rural areas they run perforce alongside the *ungdomsskole* and staff may be teaching in both schools provided they are university trained. Alongside the traditional *gymnasium* there is also a commercial *gymnasium* offering a course of three or four years' duration and which gives entry to higher institutions of learning other than the university.

The traditional *gymnasium* is nowadays not dissimilar in function from the traditional sixth form in an English grammar school, but it offers five distinct lines of specialization. Almost 96 per cent. of the pupils, however, follow either the *Engelsk-linje* (specializing in modern languages with English as the main subject) or the *Real-linje* (specializing in physics and mathematics). The remaining specialisms are classical languages (*Latin-linje*), Norwegian history and language (*Norronlinje*), and biology and chemistry (*Naturfaglinje*). Not all schools will necessarily offer all options, and there can, of course, be experimental variations even if the curricula is closely controlled by the Ministry and by clearly defined requirements for success at the *Examen Artium* which consists of both a written and an oral test. Pupils must pass in all subjects studied to be successful at this examination.

Teachers for the primary sections of the nine-year school will move at the completion of compulsory schooling to a four-year teacher training college where they can be later joined by others for two years who have completed the *gymnasium* course. A voluntary tenth year is available for pupils who are deliberating as to what form of technical or vocational education possibly to embark upon, whilst others, having already decided, will pass directly either to work or to one of the commercial, trade, technical, and agricultural and fishery schools which we shall discuss in the next chapter.

We have so far considered education in SWEDEN for the first six years of the compulsory nine-year school and noted the choice of options possible in the sixth year. It is to be stressed that the fundamental principle is that of free choice on the part of pupil and parents in contrast with the selective system earlier operated (as elsewhere in Europe). Guidance and counselling, however, now become increasingly important. As the optional choices are finalized for moving to the seventh grade in the upper school so is the child allowed some initiation into the world of work by having a " look-see " at various occupations to which (in theory at the time) he might feel attracted. The seventh grade insists on a compulsory core curriculum of 30 periods a week, reduced to 28 in the eighth grade when the options now begin to be grouped into nine possible offerings for detailed study in grade nine. In the eighth grade also the child may now spend up to three periods a week gaining practical experience at different places of employment to gain insight into his final possible choice of occupation, and on his return to school his impressions are fully discussed with the teacher responsible for this activity and with other pupils in the class.[1] Differentiation also starts in the seventh grade over the teaching of modern languages (French and German), one course being more theoretical (academic) than the other. In the eighth grade two courses are likewise offered in mathematics and English is no longer compulsory, a pupil who did not begin studying German or French, in the seventh grade now being able to rectify the omission.

Once the pupil arrives in grade nine he is assigned to one of nine streams. These are 9g (the *gymnasium* stream), 9h (humanities stream), 9t (technical stream), 9m (mercantile stream), 9s (social-economics stream), 9tp (technical-practical stream), 9ha (commercial stream, 9ht(domestic science) and 9pr (general practical stream). Since July 1971 a new-type *Gymnasium* has come into existence which aims at combining the former traditional *Gymnasium* with the Continuation and Vocational schools to provide post-school courses of 2, 3 or 4 years, and which comprehensively offers 27 " lines " of study that can be roughly divided into three groupings: Arts/Social, Economic, Technological. It is all very complicated and subject still to experimentation, but reference to the diagram printed on page 282 should make it clearer. It should finally be noted that entrance to the university still depends on passing through the pure academic *gymnasium* streams and successfully passing the *studentexamen* held at about the age of nineteen. On the other hand, the Swedes could proudly boast in 1973 that the structure of Swedish education had reached the point of non-differentiated *upper* secondary education; that over 80 per cent of the present generation were receiving eleven to twelve years schooling; and that this figure should have reached 100 per cent. by the end of the decade. It is now estimated that some 30–35 per cent. of pupils will be following a typical gymnasium programme, some 23–35 per cent. will be in the vocational schools, and some 20–25 per cent. in continuation schools.

In DENMARK we have seen how " mild differentiation " between courses is allowed to occur in the sixth and seventh

---

[1] It is more recently proposed that this became two full weeks in grade nine for all pupils (1970–71).

grades. As from grade eight pupils split into the " A " line or the " B " line, the former being expected to continue their studies at a lower academic level for at least a further two years whilst the latter embark on a three-year programme to sit for the *realeksamen*, success at which guarantees entry to a number of worthwhile middle-range jobs. Pupils who have gone to line " A " and later show promise can be transferred to line " B " but they usually lose a year in the process. Success at the *real eksamen* can be of help in gaining a place at the *gymnasium*, and about one-third of the students there have passed this test. The remaining two-thirds will have sat a special entrance examination in Danish and mathematics at the age of 16 and will thus leave the *realskole* for the *gymnasium* after only two years there. Possession of the *realeksamen* will also gain admission to a teacher-training college.

In the *realskole* the basic subjects are Danish, English, German, mathematics and the physical sciences. Latin may be introduced as an option in the second and third years, and French in the third year. In the third year it is also possible to set up a technical stream with extra mathematics and physics (to the exclusion of French) and such pupils will sit for a special technical *realeksamen*. The weaker " A " line pupil will have the accent placed on securing a general education which, whilst not aiming at providing specific training for a given trade, will add a range of optional subjects with a view to possible future occupation. A pupil staying the full three years in the " A " line may present himself to follow a further two-year course leading to the award of a diploma which will (at about age 19) gain him admission to teacher-training and to various other forms of higher education other than the university.

Entry to the university is, of course, via the traditional *gymnasium* which offers a three-year course of an academic nature with six possible " lines " available. These options are: Modern Languages, Classical Languages, Modern Languages with Social Studies, Mathematics/Physics, Science, Science with Social Studies. The common-core curriculum of the *gymnasium* consists of Danish, English, French (or Russian), History, Geography and Mathematics. The final *studentereksamen* is pretty searching. On the other hand, since 1971 pupils have been given advance notice of questions to be set and may present themselves for the examination with notes and reference books they feel can be of use to them. An able mind as opposed to a well-stocked memory is what is sought.

In addition, it is to be noted that the Danes have paid particular attention to the organization of education in villages and remote districts where it is not feasible to run a multilateral school such as we have described. There is a special village school which has classes covering the whole range of compulsory education from 7 to 14. There is no leaving examination, and whilst most pupils will continue their education on a full-time or part-time basis at youth schools or vocational and technical schools, many regularly pass to the *gymnasium*. Further, if the parents demand it and if there are at least fifteen children between the ages of 14 to 18, then the local authority must establish afternoon or evening classes for pupils to prepare for the *realeksamen*, or combine suitably with other local authorities towards the same end.

Germany. Just as Germany (or more accurately Prussia) was the first modern State to create a comprehensive national system of education and to recognize the importance of education amid the changing economic and social conditions heralded by the Industrial Revolution, so has Western Germany in this present post-war period been farsighted enough to introduce into the re-formed school system sufficient elasticity to allow children who have been misdirected into the wrong school, or who develop late, to change in time. Similarly, the preparation of an intellectual élite to hold all the really responsible posts has in no way been neglected, though elasticity in seeding out the élite has been encouraged. This again, however, is no new departure, for as early as 1901 the classical *gymnasium* saw the birth of its rivals in the *realgymnasium* (which taught Latin but not Greek) and the *Oberrealschule* (which taught neither Latin nor Greek), both of which were empowered to prepare their pupils for the *Abitur* (school leaving examination) and so for entry to the *Hochschulen* (higher institutes of learning—including the universities). To-day the *Realgymnasium*, which emphasizes the teaching of Latin and one foreign language (usually English) together with more instruction in mathematics and the natural sciences than the classical *gymnasium*, is easily the most popular school. Next comes the *Oberrealschule* with two modern languages (English and French) and emphasis on the sciences and mathematics.

Only relatively few children, of course, pass from the *Grundschule* to one or other of the *gymnasien* to follow an intensive academic course lasting eight or nine years where the *Grundschule* has been a four-year school, six or seven years where the *Grundschule* has been of six years' duration as in Hamburg. Much thought has been given, and continues to be given, as to how best the *gymnasium* can fulfil its task of educating the future leading personalities of the intellectual life of the country and yet continue to act as the people's school that will meet the requirements of every type of talent and promote intelligence in every way. It is to-day felt that whilst the *gymnasium* must aim at a substantial widening of the intellectual horizons of its pupils, and at the creation of a mind capable of discriminating judgment, it must also give as full and complete an introduction as possible to the various categories of scientific and scholastic thought prevailing, and that in consequence the traditions of devotion to high academic endeavour must constantly be maintained. The entrance examination to the *gymnasium* is therefore a searching one, and a number of *Länder* have gone so far as to require intending pupils to spend a trial fortnight in the school under direct observation.

An attempt to be just to all children deserving some kind of academic education is being made by using the *Mittelschulen* increasingly to take those pupils who show promise and are yet not amongst the cream recruited to the *gymnasium*. *Mittelschulen* were first established in 1894, and the course they offered was of six years' duration, its avowed aim being that of giving " general education, the aims and objectives of which go beyond those of the elementary schools." To-day, they recruit their children in the main from amongst those who wish to be skilled craftsmen, minor civil servants, employees in trade, industry or commerce. One, and usually two foreign languages figure on the curriculum, and the schools are already performing (and could increasingly perform) the useful service of educating along Western European democratic lines that amorphous " middle-man " upon whose actions, in any form of democracy, so much ultimately depends. According to the time spent in the *Grundschule* the course now lasts four to six years, and it is possible in a few *Länder* for the pupil who betrays outstanding promise as a late developer to transfer to the *gymnasium*. Generally speaking, however, the *Mittelschule* has a character of its own, and its curriculum is not

designed to link up with the *gymnasium*. Pupils having satisfactorily completed the course gain their school leaving certificate
and then either take up some business employment or follow some
further period of full-time or part-time vocational or technical
training.

A still further type of secondary education is offered in the
Aufbauschule which gives children from the country who have not
had a secondary school within easy reach the opportunity to start
out on a secondary school career after completion of six years of
primary education. This, of course, is often a boarding school. It
runs a seven-year course along the lines of the *Realgymnasium*,
with English as the first foreign language, and Latin. In Bavaria,
however, this type of school has become so popular and so much in
demand that since 1950 *Aufbauschulen* have been instituted
representing all types of *gymnasium*, and adding one additional
type with the emphasis on art and music. It should be noted in
passing that art and music are increasingly figuring on the
curricula of *gymnasien* throughout the whole of Germany.

One factor determining also the kind of secondary education
offered in Germany is that—unlike all the other countries we have
so far discussed—Germany looks upon co-education as a practice
of expediency rather than one based upon principle. Small rural
schools of necessity instruct boys and girls together, and secondary
schools for boys will admit girls if no girls' school of a similar type
exists in the vicinity. On the whole, however, there is determined
separation of the sexes. In point of fact, it was not until 1872 that
Prussia made secondary education for girls a possibility, and it
is from these early beginnings that the present *Frauenoberschule*
originated. It is a three-year course based on a ten-years' school
for girls (lyceum) and it combines education along academic,
scientific and artistic lines with a study of the domestic sciences.
The school leaving certificate, however, is not recognized for
university entrance, though graduates from such a school may
enter a teachers' training college. In consequence, the *Frauenoberschule* is steadily failing to attract girls, who obviously prefer in
these days of equality of the sexes to attend in their own right their
own *gymnasien*.

A relatively recent creation is the economics high school which
runs a three-year course leading to university-level schools of business administration and also to studies in the economics depart-

ment of universities. Pupils are admitted to this economics high school either on satisfactory completion of the middle school course, or from the *gymnasium* at the age of 16 plus.

No one can deny that the organization of education at the secondary level throughout Germany is thorough, enterprising and forward-looking. It is highly specialized and it seeks constantly to provide an appropriate élite at all levels of public endeavour: academic, commercial and technical. It still holds fast to a belief in dual streaming, though it strives conscientiously to give every child of promise a chance. To this end, most *Länder* have made *all* education free, and those *Länder* which make a charge at the secondary level do not allow the very nominal fees usually asked to deter the poorest child from attending school. Of course, the majority of children do not have the necessary intellectual capacity to profit from any of the kinds of secondary education we have been discussing. These children go on to the *Oberstufe* on completion of their primary school training. This is an advanced elementary school which takes the child at either 10 or 12 years of age and keeps him in full-time attendance for a further two or four years. A few *Länder* have added still an extra year, making this period of further elementary education last until 15 plus. There then follows compulsory full- or part-time attendance at vocational or technical schools until the age of 18. We shall discuss this in greater detail in our next chapter.

We need, however, to note impending changes arising from the Structural Plan of 1970 (of which we have earlier spoken) and from a decision taken in 1969 to set up some forty integrated comprehensive schools. The Structural Plan would have a four-year *Grundschule* followed by an orientation stage of one year (possibly to be extended to two years by agreement of all the *Länder* in 1972) and then followed by a lower secondary stage from 12 to 15/16 years of age. A first school-leaving certificate (*Abitur I*) could then be obtained after ten full years' of schooling at about age 16. The upper secondary stage (ages 16 to 19) would have pupils now specializing according to their proven interests and (important departure) would amalgamate both technical-professional courses and the traditional *gymnasium* course. Successful competion of this course would lead to the award of *Abitur II* granting admission either to the university, to a technical university, or to teacher-training.

The forty integrated comprehensive schools are obviously to be regarded as models for future developments along lines of the Structural Plan, and different organizational types can co-exist even within one city or *Land*. The general organizational basis is that of the Swedish system of a nucleus of subjects studied without differentiation, and the remaining subjects taught in groups differentiated according to ability after an initial period of non-differentiation. In the German comprehensive school the " nucleus " is confined to social studies, music, art, sport, and to a limited extent German. Berlin has no fewer than four such comprehensive schools and they are all organized into (a) the nucleus subjects, (b) ability subjects (maths, natural sciences and a compulsory foreign language), (c) compulsory electives which include a second and/or third modern language, economics, social science, technical, practical and commercial courses, and (d) advanced courses (optional electives). The differentiated groups are at four levels: advanced, expanded, basic, contact. The optional electives provided on the advanced courses are for those pupils who are not otherwise fully stretched or provided for at the advanced level of instruction—e.g. a pupil wishing to specialize in Classics and ancient history, or to enter the medical or legal professions, or some highly specialized branch of technology.

Holland. The Dutch have had to be equally enterprising and thorough as the Germans in arranging a secondary system of education that will enable them to compete at a high industrial and commercial level with other countries, and in practice the solution they have found to their own particular problems is not dissimilar from that of the Germans. Like the Germans, they have through their continued elementary and advanced elementary school courses perpetuated a kind of dual system of education, but they have also produced a secondary system that is bewilderingly diverse in the types of education it has to offer. Admission to these schools usually takes place after the pupil has passed an entrance examination set by the teachers in the appropriate schools, and on the production of a satisfactory report from the head teacher of the last school the child attended. The average age for admission is 13. Fees are payable, based on the parent's income, but no one of ability is denied secondary education through poverty.

By far the oldest (the *Gymnasium Erasmianum* of Rotterdam was probably founded in 1328) and most traditional type of secondary school is the *gymnasium*, which has a six-year course of studies based on the classics. Dutch, French, German and English are also compulsory (as in all secondary schools). After the fourth year of study (this since 1876) a pupil may opt to go on the science side, but the study of Latin and Greek must still continue. On the satisfactory completion of this gruelling course a pupil is awarded his diploma (by his own teachers) which gives him right of entry to a university or some other place of higher education.

A much more flexible type of secondary school, and one which has been willing to show adaptability to changing circumstances and to experiment more freely, is the *Hogere Burgerschool*, first established as long ago as 1867 to cope with the then growing commercial and economic enterprise of the nineteenth century. The school course generally comprises five years of study, the main subjects being : mathematics, physics, chemistry, geology, botany, zoology, cosmography, geography, economics and statistics, history and commercial subjects (with the four modern languages already mentioned). There are two distinct types of school, the one having a scientific basis, the other a literary-economic basis. The programme of the former is taken up largely with the exact and natural sciences, that of the latter has in view, above all, the preparation of its pupils for a commercial career, though naturally pupils are prepared for jobs in all walks of life as well as for university entrance.

The *lyzeum* is interesting in that it has no legal basis proper to itself, being a combination of the *gymnasium* and the *Hogere Burgerschool*. The object in view when establishing this school was to defer the choice between the *gymnasium* and the *Hogere Burgerschool* for at least two years. Thus, for at least two years, the same curriculum (without Latin or Greek) is followed by all pupils. There then follows either a four-year specialized study of the classics, or of mathematics and science, or of social subjects. The *lyzeum* is proving increasingly popular in these post-war years and is cautiously experimenting to meet constantly changing and modern demands.

Other forms of purely secondary education deserving of note in the light of post-war economic developments are the *lyzeum* for girls only, comprising usually five years of study of the usual secondary school subjects with the emphasis on domestic and economic science; day commercial schools offering three to four years of study, and with the emphasis on political economy, commercial law, political institutions, the history of commodities, the organization and the technique of commerce—along with a study of the French, English, German and Dutch languages; evening commercial schools with three-, four-, or five-year courses, taking young people between the ages of 14 and 20 who have already had some experience in the commercial and business fields. All these schools award State-recognized diplomas to successful students, and these diplomas are a guarantee to employers of the ability and competence of the holder.

However, the implementation of the " Mammoth " School Law, which insists that every pupil must *in so far as is possible* be allowed access to the type of school which best fits his capacities and interests, has now changed this somewhat traditional pattern. After completing primary education all Dutch children now face a *brugklas* (a transitional class, or bridge year) to enable teachers and pupils, in consultation with parents, to decide to which of three types of school they are most suited. A common-core curriculum is (as far as possible) provided in the *brugklas* so that, in theory at least, all children may change to a different type of school from the one in which the *brugklas* is placed. However, there are variations in the *gymnasia* and the lower technical schools in particular which in reality prevent complete possibility of transfer. The basis of division between types of post-primary schools is founded on the recognition of three different functions: (a) pre-university or preparatory scientific education, (b) continued general education, (c) vocational education, the last two categories being divided into lower, middle and higher provisions.

Thus, in practice children are sorted out for streaming at the age of 13, and will, during the bridge year, be considered in two distinct groups: (a) *Gymnasium*, *Lyceum*, *Atheneum*, all of which offer a six-year course on grammar school lines: HAVO schools providing a five-year course in general education and for entry into higher vocational education, and which are comparable with the former *Hogere Burgerschool* except that they do not lead to university entrance; MAVO schools to take the place of the former Advanced Elementary School and offering courses lasting three or four years (the four-year course normally granting entry to higher vocational education, the three-year course to middle vocational education); (b) LAVO schools offering technical, commercial, domestic, agricultural courses, together with general education (one-third of the time) for two to three years. It is estimated that between 40 and 50 per cent of children will be in such schools. Their bridge year is different in that only one foreign language (English) is taught instead of two (English and usually German) in other bridge classes, and a further disadvantage arises from the fact that two-thirds of the time in LAVO institutions is devoted to vocational subjects.

Pupils in the *gymnasium* are separated into two sections for the last two years of their course. The Alpha Section places the emphasis on Greek and Latin and the Beta Section, whilst including Latin and Greek, emphasizes science studies. Similarly in the *Atheneum* there is specialization, but for the last three years of the course. The Alpha Section stresses economic and social studies and languages, the Beta Section mathematics and science. This specialization period constitutes pre-university training and replaces the former function of the *Hogere Burgerschool* in that respect. Schools combining the functions of a *Gymnasium* and an *Atheneum* are known by the title of *Lyceum*. It should also be noted that possession of a LAVO leaving certificate will give admission to a MAVO school as well as to secondary technical and vocational schools. A MAVO certificate entitles the holder to enter the fourth year of a HAVO school and certain types of technical and vocational training at a higher level.

It all adds up, of course, to an insistence on the doctrine of *suum cuique* rather than *idem cuique*, to a refusal (so far) to accept the full comprehensive principle, and to an attempt to heed the firm demands of parents and the three broad sectional interests of the community—the three pillars of Dutch society. Experimentation is taking place, though. Some school authorities are arguing for a three-year bridge period to postpone early choice and excessive specialization. The " Mammoth " School Law does allow for comprehensive type schools to be established. Some already exist and are either of a vertical nature (schools following after one another as far as their educational level is concerned) or a horizontal nature (schools of different types at the same level). Others have been based on the Swedish experience. One final point of interest about the new School Law is that it makes it obligatory to set aside four fifty-minute periods in each week as study lessons to teach children how to learn.

Switzerland. The Swiss are faced with similar problems to those of the Germans and the Dutch, and they also have felt the necessity for prolonging education beyond the *Grundschule* proper to at least nine full years of schooling for those children who are not to follow some course of secondary education, and to prepare them more adequately for entry to a society which is becoming increasingly specialized. Thus, project methods, practical work and "learning by doing" are much to the fore in their continued elementary schools.

Pupils who show any ability to profit from some form of secondary education, however, are encouraged to attend a kind of intermediate school (variously called the *Realschule*, or the *Handelschule*, or the *Progymnasium*, or the district school) where the education is entirely free of cost. Like the German *Mittelschulen*, these schools aim at giving a sound general education, but they also do prepare pupils to enter the higher forms of the secondary grammar school. The courses are usually of two or three years' duration and stress the teaching of mathematics, science and modern languages (for a German-speaking pupil, for example, French and English—or Italian—are compulsory). Most pupils, on completion of this school course, enter on some form of apprenticeship or continue their studies at commercial and technical institutions.

The secondary grammar school has a function similar to that of the German *Gymnasium*, but is rather confusingly referred to as the *Mittelschule*. All pupils are expected to be capable of taking the State school leaving examination which gives entry to the universities and higher institutes, and there is therefore a searching test for entry to such a school, intellectual ability and not the parents' social position being the sole criterion. This academic secondary education is not left entirely to the cantons, though they have much freedom in running and organizing their schools as they will. Ultimately, however, because the State lays down exactly what shall be tested at the State-leaving examination, and what standards shall be attained, the schools must conform closely to a "type" curriculum.

The duration of the school course varies from *canton to canton*, and is usually from six to eight years. Fees are payable in this

Mittelschule, but again they tend often to be nominal and no child of ability is denied an academic education through poverty. There are three distinct types of school, as in Germany, preparing for university entrance : the *gymnasium*, concentrating on Latin and Greek; the *realgymnasium*, concentrating on Latin and two modern languages; the *Oberrealschule*, without Latin but concentrating on mathematics and the natural sciences.

Yet even cosy Switzerland has succumbed of recent years in some measure to current trends in reform at the secondary level of education. It is impossible to cover in detail variations from *canton* to *canton*, but if we take the French-speaking *Canton de Vaud* as an example and study the diagrams on p. 283 showing changes which have taken place over a twenty-year span we shall have a fair picture of what is actually going on. Put briefly, there has been growing concern that 1967 statistics revealed only 6 to 8 per cent. of pupils entering a *gymnasium* continuing to the equivalent of the English Upper Sixth and only 4–5 per cent. entering the universities. The first step was to improve the process of selection by standardizing examinations for entry to secondary education, by trying to assess a pupil's ability rather than his knowledge through various aptitude tests, and by instituting a two-year orientation phase to be the same for all pupils, with compulsory German but no Latin (this despite strong traditionalist pressures). It is to be noted, however, that this orientation (or guidance) stage has been limited to only those pupils selected in advance for secondary education (see diagram 2 on p. 283) and the move is now to extend it to all post-primary pupils (see diagram 3 on the same page). A further variation holds in Geneva where the orientation cycle has three different tracks: Latin-Scientific for children who hope to go on to higher education; a general course for those who will enter commercial, technical or vocational schools; a practical course for the less-gifted who will undertake unskilled manual work of various kinds. There is no entrance examination to secondary education and pupils (according to proved ability) may switch from one track to another.

Belgium. The Belgian system makes a real attempt to cover every possibility and to see to it that none shall be deprived of that kind of secondary education they most justly merit. We shall leave the manifold provisions made for technical education to the next chapter, and here concentrate on the two types of purely secondary education offered. As a child completes his primary school course the parents are invited to state what they now want for their child and they are guided as skilfully as possible to make the right choice in view of school performance and general school reports on the child's proved aptitude so far. The options in the field of pure secondary education are either the *école moyenne* (middle school), which is either mixed or run separately for boys or girls, and the *athénée* (for boys only) or the *lycée* (for girls only). Secondary schools run by religious orders are usually called *collèges*.

If, on the satisfactory completion of his primary school course, a child enters the *école moyenne*, he now follows a course of study over a period of three years which is so skilfully planned that it offers both a Greek and Latin, and a general section, exactly parallel with the work done in the three lowest forms of the *athénée* or *lycée*, as well as what is termed a pre-professional section in which girls have domestic and homecraft courses (as well as the usual commercial and secretarial work), and boys do general crafts and agricultural and industrial training, with technical streams in wood and metal work. A further skilful arrangement of the time-tables makes it possible *within* the *école moyenne* for a child to change at almost any time during his three years of study from one to the other of the three sections if it is found desirable for him to do so. Thus, the final and irrevocable choice of specialized study is postponed until the age of 15, when the work of the *école moyenne* ceases. It is also at the age of 15 that children are increasingly seeking and profiting by guidance given by one of the psycho-medical centres that are becoming an important distinctive feature (there are thirteen large centres operating at present) of the Belgian educational system.[1]

A variety of possibilities are open to pupils who satisfactorily complete their studies in the *école moyenne*. Some may enter an *école normale primaire* to train as primary school teachers. Others will transfer to a technical school, there joining up with those

---

[1] There is no space to tell in full the fascinating story of the working of these psycho-medical centres, nor of the gradual evolution of techniques of vocational and child guidance. Let it be noted that Belgium, along with America, was a pioneer in this kind of work, the first centre being established as long ago as 1909, in Brussels. There is nothing in England even vaguely comparable with the best that now exists in Belgium.

pupils who, instead of going to an *école moyenne*, either went
direct to the technical school where the first three years of study
of the cultural subjects are again parallel to the first three years in
the *athénée* or *école moyenne*, or came to the technical school at
14 plus after two years extended primary school work. Others
will pass to the three upper and specialist forms of the *athénée* or
lycée. It should be noted in this connexion that not a few *écoles
moyennes* have been empowered to offer a full six-year course to
university entrance standard, and thus rank as *athénées* or *lycées* in
all but name. These circumstances usually hold when no
athénée or *lycée* is conveniently placed to cater for the pure academic streams from the *école moyenne*.

The three lowest forms of the *athénée* (*lycée*) have a programme
parallel to that of the *école moyenne*, and, in the basic cultural
subjects (i.e. not Latin and Greek), not dissimilar from that in the
12 to 15 year range of the technical school. Naturally—as in the
French *lycée*—Latin and Greek are the core subjects (if not the
only important ones) in an *athénée* which seeks to give a sound,
modern academic discipline and expects from its pupils a constantly high standard of work and achievement. From the fourth
year onwards specialization begins, and five possibilities are open
to the pupil to meet as far as possible both desire and aptitude.

The traditional Greek-Latin section still draws to it some of the
ablest pupils in the school, and normally only those who started
their secondary school career in the lowest forms of the *athénée*
(*lycée*) will opt for this. The remaining four sections are : Latin-
mathematics, Latin-science, pure science and economic-com-
mercial studies. All these later modifications came about in 1948.
All pupils will have courses in at least one modern language
(English or German) and all have now to learn the opposing
mother-tongue—French or Dutch. On the completion of a full
six-year course a pupil presents himself for a passing-out examination that is controlled by a special jury to ensure uniformly high
standards throughout the country, and this leaving certificate con-
fers on him the right, should he so wish, to enter a university or
higher institute of learning.

The only significant recent change in Belgium is an attempt to
reorganize the secondary schools as schools open to all pupils
between the ages of 12 and 18. To this end all secondary schools
are to be divided into three cycles, each of two years' duration.

The first cycle will constitute a period of observation, the second a period of orientation, the third a period of specialization. At the moment of writing a number of schools are changing over to the new approach whilst others carry along as before. It is obviously too early yet to make a full and detailed appraisal of the situation.

France. The four most important influences in the development of education in France have been the Catholic Church, the Revolution, Napoleon, and the development of industry in a country that, like Germany, has been primarily (and mostly still remains) agrarian in outlook. The destruction of the Church control of education by the Revolution and the introduction of Napoleon's highly centralized system of educational administration that none the less eventually recognized the Church and the Church's influence led to the nineteenth-century struggle between Church and State. The final outcome has been the recognition of a separate Church system of education, parallel to the secular State system, and with State subsidies eventually granted to Church-maintained educational institutions. The Church runs its schools as it will, but as it must prepare its pupils for the State *baccalauréat*, it has to conform very closely in respect of curricula. None the less, the strong Republican element in France is repeatedly alarmed at the high proportion of children seeking to be educated in Catholic schools, some 40 per cent.[1] Again, the predominant influence in French secondary education being that of the Jesuits, the classical ideal in education has repeatedly shown remarkable resilience in resisting the encroachment of more modern subjects, and, whilst a variety of solutions have been, and are still being tried, the classical hold is still strong and Frenchmen as a nation remain peculiarly conservative whenever any proposed reform seems to attack the general principles of *une culture générale* and *préparation d'un élite*. In other words, the dual system of education as the best possible means of maintaining the acknowledged historical superiority of French culture over that of her neighbours maintains itself in spite of the many attempts made throughout the twentieth century to secure equality of educational opportunity for all.

It was in 1926 when Herriot arranged that certain higher elementary schools (*écoles primaires supérieures*) and technical

---

[1] The same holds true for Belgium, though the number of children in " free " Catholic schools is much higher—easily 50 per cent.

schools should be attached to neighbouring *lycées* under the same teachers for common " core " subjects such as French, modern languages, history, geography and science. In 1927, as a further incentive, fees were abolished in the three lowest forms of the *lycées* where this arrangement held. And in 1930, fees were abolished in all secondary schools, starting with the *sixième* (the lowest form in the school). In 1937 the minister Jean Zay started his famous series of orientation classes in an attempt to discover what kind of education best suited each individual pupil and then to secure for him that education. The experiment came to an untimely and inconclusive end with the outbreak of war.

During the dark days of occupation much thought was given to the whole question of reform on a basis of effectively killing the dual system, and after the liberation a commission was set up under the presidency of the distinguished physicist, Paul Langevin, radically to examine the structure of the whole educational system and to make proposals for reform. The Langevin Plan that resulted can briefly be summarized as follows : a common school for all, compulsory to the age of 18; primary school education to cease at the age of 11 plus; the years 11 to 15 to be devoted to obtaining a *culture générale*, the first two years of this four-year course being an observation period, the last two years being years in which the pupil should opt to try out those branches of instruction for which he seemed most fitted; the years 15 to 18 to be devoted to specialized instruction in those subjects finally chosen by the pupil; finally, those pupils wishing to pass on to some form of higher education would do so after a trial period to make certain that they were fitted for study at a really advanced level.

It was a bold and sweeping plan which (for reasons which will be obvious to the reader) no Frenchman in practice could fully accept though he could not seriously quarrel with the main principles that gave it its inspirational drive : equality of educational opportunity for all; extended development of technical and scientific studies; the harmonization of individual capacity with social requirements; the idea of education as being for the whole man (*l'élève est l'artisan de sa propre culture*); the increasing importance to be attached to the individual, with the idea of the superiority of the child to the adult as the fundamental point of departure, thus leading to a child-centred approach. The real trouble has been that the plan made for an over-exaggerated and

impetuous application of these principles that took no consideration of the prevailing culture pattern, that tried to force the pace
of change and was in consequence in danger of getting out of step
with the national character and the national outlook.

None the less, " new " classes were started in October, 1945, in
the *sixième* of the *lycée*, on an experimental basis, some 200 schools
(this beyond all expectations at the time) volunteering for the
experiment. The exuberance of the early pioneers caught on and
led to the rapid expansion of *Sixièmes Nouvelles* and—in conformity with the suggestions of the Langevin Plan—to the extension of the scheme to the *cinquième, quatrième* and *troisième*, the
latter class being roughly the equivalent of the pre-certificate form
in an English grammar school. But here a halt has been called.
The middle-aged *professeur agrégé* had always been opposed to
the scheme, even if he half-heartedly attempted to conform, and
his words of warning to the effect that intelligence and clear,
precise, and logical reasoning, based on a sound humanistic
culture, were the pride and strength—the very essence—of the
French nation as a nation bore fruit. It has now been decreed that
all *classes nouvelles* shall be closed down with the exception of
those running in four " pilot " *lycées* (Sèvres, Montgeron,
Toulouse, Marseilles) which are intended to act as a spearhead
towards any further projected reforms.

The experiment, however, has been both popular and successful,
and a total of about 800 *classes nouvelles*, with about 200,000
pupils in them, have proved themselves over a number of years
important focal points for experimentation and new developments. What is perhaps most important is that the insistence in
these *classes nouvelles* on activity methods, on correlation of subjects, on child study, on a prominent place being given to handicrafts, music and games, has resulted generally in a considerable
leavening of the over-intellectual and bookish approach that tradition has dictated shall be the lot of the pupil in the *lycée* or *collège*
from the moment he crossed its portals even at the tender age of
9 or 10. Greater freedom of choice in the subjects studied has also
resulted and greater emphasis has been placed on the child, as an
individual, to discover a method of his own that does not conform
to a framework arbitrarily laid down by the teacher.

The latest school plan, which was formulated in 1964 and
began to be operative in 1968, comes closest to the Langevin

Plan in conception, but it has proved so demanding in its requirements for new school buildings that even to-day (1973) there are parts of France in which it is not yet fully operative and where the pattern (in consequence) must for the time being more closely follow that of the 1959 reforms (see diagram 4 on p. 278). In 1968, for example, 39 per cent. of the provision for post-primary education was housed in new purpose-built *Collèges d'Enseignement Secondaire* (C.E.S.); by the autumn of 1973 this figure had risen to only 63 per cent.

As a child reaches the last year of his primary school his case is carefully considered by an appropriate committee and he is drafted, on the recommendation of this committee, to one of three types of *sixième* in a four-year middle school (C.E.S.) where he will be constantly under observation and where it will be possible for him to move at any time from stream to stream. For the first two years of the course (ages 11–13) there is a common core curriculum. The first type of *sixième* is of the traditional *lycée* type and admits children considered to have already shown some aptitude for following a purely academic course. Some 39 per cent. of the present intake to a C.E.S. is to be found here. The second type is the modern *sixième*, has about 36 per cent. of the intake, and has clearly built-in possibilities for possible later transfer to the purely academic courses. The third type, absorbing the remainder, is taught by general class teachers (as opposed to university graduates), is considered " remedial " and in consequence does not in practice follow the common core curriculum. Its bent is strongly practical and it will include those who will attend terminal classes until the compulsory leaving age of 16 (established by De Gaulle in 1959).

On reaching the age of 15 children must then decide (under guidance) whether they are to take a "long" or a "short" period of further training. Parents may challenge the guidance and opt for a different kind of further education, but in this case the pupil must sit an examination to prove (or otherwise) his ability to carry on as his parents desire. This examination is final. " Long " education implies that the pupil will stay at least a further three years (for in France a year can always be repeated at least once) to sit one of the various *baccalauréat* examinations which grant admission to university training. For the first year of this three-year cycle (*classe de seconde*) pupils are divided into three groups:

Humanities, which is predominantly literary and includes philosophy, classical or modern languages, and various options which may lead to later specialization in economics and the social sciences; Maths/Science which is predominantly scientific together with options on the literary side; Technical/Scientific leading to various branches of applied science and technology. In the second year of study no less than seven different options are possible.

If a child goes on the traditional Classical side he may specialize in Greek, Latin and one modern language (Classical A); he may add some science to this (Classical A¹); he may do Latin with two modern languages (Classical B); he may do Latin, Science and one modern language (Classical C). If a child opts for the modern side he may choose between science and two modern languages (Modern M) or science, biology and one modern language (Modern M¹). A child opting for technical studies may also prepare for the *brevet d'agent technique* and achieve technician level in either industry or commerce. There are two choices before him : either science, a modern language and fundamental industrial techniques (Technical T) or economics and two modern languages (Technical T¹). Obviously the Classical side is attracting the best brains (as heretofore) and Classical A¹ and Classical C are the most difficult. The modern side is not so highly esteemed, whilst technical studies leading to the *baccalauréat* are considered very difficult.

At the end of the second year of study the pupil is moved up to the terminal class (to prepare directly for the *baccalauréat*) on the recommendation of a school council presided over by the headmaster. In this final year the options reduce themselves to five in number : philosophy section, a mathematics section, an experimental sciences section, a technical and mathematics section, and an economics and human sciences section. It is to be noted, however, that philosophy is a " must " in all options, great stress being laid on the educated Frenchman's ability to think and reason clearly and cogently. The philosophy option, which caters primarily for those who will read " arts " subjects at the university, is none the less careful to insist on almost one third of the time being spent on science subjects. The mathematics option tends to attract the best pupils in both mathematics and science but similarly insists on a third of the time being devoted to " arts " subjects. The experimental sciences option is taken by the perhaps not so gifted scientist, and roughly one third of the time is again spent on " arts " subjects. The technical and mathematics option demands almost half the time to be spent on technical and workshop practice and also includes at least six hours per week literary studies. The economics and human sciences option splits the time roughly between " arts " and science subjects.

All subjects are examined, but there is from 1966 only one *baccalauréat* to be sat, and not two (or two separate parts, as it really was). On the other hand, those who fail in June may re-sit later. The oral examination has had to be abandoned in a large measure (except for border-line cases) because of the growing number of candidates. Finally, those students who fail to get an aggregate 50 per cent. in the *baccalauréat* examination, but who reach at least 40 per cent., will be given a Certificate of Secondary Studies.

But now it is time to consider those pupils who are guided to take the " short " as opposed to the long period of further training. There is a short general course lasting two years which can comprise some practical training with a vocational bias. The successful candidate receives a *brevet d'enseignement général* (with his speciality noted). There is also a short technical course lasting two or three years leading either to the award of a *certificat d'aptitude professionnelle* or to the *brevet d'agent technique*. It is intended that these two short courses be housed in the same building in what will be called *collèges de second cycle* and they will replace the secondary technical schools (formerly *centres d'apprentissage*).

To say the least of it, the system in its present state of flux and change is bewildering, and some few years will have to elapse before we can clearly assess the value and importance of these changes. It will be most interesting to see what type of pupil is attracted to the various possibilities—and from what social background he comes and whether the long form of *lycée*-type education will still remain the prerogative of the bourgeoisie. What is certain is that in making these latest moves the French have been insistent all along the line of never sacrificing quality because of the need to cater for an ever-expanding secondary school population. They are aiming at quality and richness as opposed to quantity and uniformity. What is also intriguing is the thought that it has required the personal influence and prestige of De Gaulle to get all these measures pushed through with lightning speed. In the space of barely seven years the pattern of French secondary education has changed beyond all recognition. How wryly amused Paul Langevin would have been at the thought that where he failed to get his plan adopted De Gaulle should be so near success!

Italy. Here, the outstanding achievement of the new school law of 1963 (which became operative in 1966) has been the creation of the new *scuola media* which makes Italy one of the few countries which can boast of a single type middle school which sees the entire school age population through to the end of the compulsory schooling period and allows the pupil to postpone his choice of stream until the age of 14. With the creation of the *scuola media* in its present form the elementary school leaving examination (taken at 11 plus) was abolished, and entry into the middle school depends on the final report on the pupil from his primary school. The timetable comprises both compulsory and optional subjects. The former consist of religious instruction, Italian, history, one modern language (either French or English), mathematics, geography, elementary science, citizenship, gymnastics art, music and technical drawing. Music and technical drawing, become optional after the first year. In the second year the study of Italian is extended to include some basic knowledge of Latin, and in the third year Latin becomes an optional subject —it being noted that only those pupils who have studied Latin (and passed satisfactorily at the leaving examination) will be permitted to enter the prestigious *liceo classico*. Generally speaking, the optional subjects available in the third and final year are provided to reflect the now growingly evident capabilities and aspirations of the pupils. For pupils who on transfer from the primary school find the going difficult, there are not only special remedial classes but also extra lessons grouped into courses known as the *doposcuola* and which are given in the afternoons, the normal school day ending at 1 p.m. Similarly, there is additional work also available in the afternoons (to a maximum of ten periods per week) for additional optional subjects for all.

The expressed aims of the *scuola media* may be summed up as (a) offering a general education without any premature differentiation between the academic and vocational sides; (b) guiding the pupil, on the basis of a core curriculum and of a set of optional subjects which are believed to be educationally valuable, towards the most sensible choice for the future; (c) adapting itself both to the mental level of its various pupils and to present demands of social and economic life; (d) firmly committing itself to new methods of teaching and learning as suggested by the latest educational research. The problem of training teachers to use these new methods is, of course, of crucial importance. Recent classroom observation (1973) suggests that the methods employed are still those of a teacher-pupil dialogue with the teacher the dominant partner, though it must be admitted that a respect for learning along formal lines went hand-in-glove with warm, friendly and spontaneous teacher-pupil relations.

For those who pass the middle school examination at about age 14, various alternatives are open dependent to a large measure on attainment but also upon social position and ambition. Whilst more than half of those completing the middle school chose to continue their education in some form or another in 1969, it is anticipated that about 1975 this number will have considerably increased (see diagram 9 on page 281). The real intellectual *élite* will enter the *liceo classico* which offers an introductory course of two years followed by three years preparation for the maturity examination which gives right of entry to a university. The curriculum comprises: Italian language and literature, Latin, Greek, history, geography, mathematics, natural sciences, one foreign language, philosophy and the history of art. The *liceo scientifico* was created in 1923 for the education of students aspiring to university studies in medicine and science. Originally a four-year course, it was extended to five years after 1945. In its curriculum the study of Greek is replaced by double the time spent on a foreign language, and the syllabuses for mathematics and the natural sciences are considerably widened. Possession of its maturity award admits to all faculties in the university except for Letters and Law. The *Istituto Tecnico* offers a variety of courses over five years and possession of its diploma grants entry to the relevant university faculty or its equivalent in tertiary education. Finally at this level (also granting university admission) is a four-year course of an academic character in fine arts (*Liceo Artistico*). The *Istituto Magistrale* also ranks at the *liceo* level and offers a 4/5 years' training course for intending teachers in the primary schools. Highly successful students may then go on to a university to read for a degree and so qualify to teach either in the *scuola media* or a *liceo*.

England and Wales. Here, as a result of the passing of the Butler Act in 1944, secondary provision has been mainly of three types to which entry has been gained by a process of selection based on tests taken between 10 and 11 years of age. The most academic have been drafted to the grammar (or high) schools, the next most able to secondary technical schools, the remainder to the secondary modern school which has fought hard to upgrade itself —sometimes at the expense of the non-academic child it was created in the main to serve. Grammar schools have taken the General Certificate of Education at 16 plus (or even earlier) and an advanced level at 18 plus to gain entry to universities and colleges of education. Secondary modern schools have insisted they had pupils (usually late-developers) who were academically just as good as many grammar school pupils and asserted their right to enter these pupils for the same examinations. Secondary technical schools have always been in a position to do this, particularly in technical and commercial specialisms. Obviously new curricula had soon to be devised, and obviously new types of examinations were called for, one result being the creation in 1965 of the Certificate of Secondary Education to be taken by all secondary pupils according to ability but being at an admittedly lower level than the General Certificate. The situation is still considered most unsatisfactory and the whole question of secondary qualifying examinations is under full review.

Side by side with the examination confusion, however, has run increasing dissatisfaction with eleven plus selection procedures and the tripartite division of all children at this early age. Many local authorities soon began experimenting with the creation of a comprehensive school system (by 1970 there were no fewer than 1,145 such schools) and several distinct patterns of "going comprehensive" emerged. Inevitably the matter became a political issue. The Socialist Minister for Education in 1965 urged comprehensive development on several approved lines on all local authorities and required them to show the progress they had made. The Conservative Minister in 1970 advised local authorities that they were fully free to decide on the kind of school organization they preferred. The most usual pattern for a comprehensive school is that which covers the whole age range from 11 to 18; some authorities, however, have chosen to have comprehensive education from 11 to 16 followed by sixth-form specialist colleges; others have two-tier systems (like the Leicestershire Plan of 1957) with an all-in comprehensive school from 11 to 14 (high school) followed by alternative schooling either to the school-leaving age of 16 (instituted in 1972–73) or leading to advanced studies to the age of 18 in an upper school; still others opt for a " first " school between the ages of 5 and 9, a " middle " school from 9 to 13, and an upper school from 13 to 18. Extreme positions have been reached where, politically, comprehensive schooling becomes a " must " to the extent of arbitrarily grouping together buildings formally housing schools with separate and distinct functions and having a kind of helter-skelter run of classes (and teachers) from building to building—to say the least uneconomic on time even if we ignore the frustrations which must ensue.

From all of this, though, there is one important lesson to be learned. Political involvement in education is inescapable. To that we must all agree. If political involvement however, so necessary and so often salutary for the greater good of all, should degenerate into political machination, then trouble lies ahead. The various political parties in England and Wales have allowed just that to happen. A new, clean and hard look needs taking at the whole scene. It needs to be remembered that comprehensive schooling is still very much in an apprenticeship and trying-out stage. The Department of Education and Science needs above all to remind itself of the well-worn Latin tag: " *Quis custodiet ipsos custodes* ".

Conclusion. Perhaps the most striking common factor emerging from all these various systems of secondary education is that, no matter what the system and no mattter how centralized or decentralized the machinery of control, there is a determined attempt made everywhere to educate all children on a common " core " curriculum up to about the age of 14, and so postpone as late as possible the final choice of vocation and further studies in view of that choice.

Thus the middle school assumes an increasing importance as being the obvious place in which that common " core " curriculum shall hold. In almost every country the middle school (or its equivalent) shows flexibility and takes into consideration the needs of local economy. It offers, generally speaking, the same subjects that are found in the academic grammar school, but it manages to cut away from a too academic approach at too early an age and gives a sound, broad, cultural and yet practical education. Many observers of continental practice have in my view been too prone to assume that the work done in these middle schools (and particularly in the *cours complémentaires* in France) is roughly parallel to what is achieved in the secondary modern school in England. Nothing could be farther from the truth, at least as far as my experience goes in visiting schools not only in capital but also in small provincial towns. The middle school is not despised by parents abroad but admired. It is admired because it leads somewhere and is given its own individual *cachet*. It strives to keep the child to at least 15 plus and all the time it stretches him intellectually to his fullest capacity. If there is any criticism to be made it is the one that it can drive the intellectually weak child too hard. Let us not, however, exaggerate this. There is a perpetual outcry against *surmenage scolaire* on the Continent, but no one does much about this grievance (real or imagined) but talk.

Finally, we should note that in almost every country in Western Europe, except England, the parent is always carefully consulted as to the type of secondary education he would like for his child and his wishes are as scrupulously respected as possible. The parent's responsibility for his child's secondary education is not entirely abrogated, and this is constantly before him since, though fees have been abolished almost everywhere, he has to supply textbooks and stationery for the use of his child.

CHAPTER ELEVEN

Technical and Further Education

THE growth and development of industrial enterprises throughout the nineteenth century brought in a new phase in human existence which not only altered the character and structure of society but also, as we have seen, made it imperative to organize a system of education that should not only educate the few (the élite) but also the huge mass of the people. At first, not unnaturally, it was thought that simple instruction in the three R's would prove more than sufficient. When a pupil had a fair grasp of this rudimentary and essential knowledge, then according to the job he performed and the amount of technical skill required for adequate performance of that job, so would he pass on to specialized technical training provided for him by some outside and often voluntary body and so gradually improve his wage-earning capacity and his value as an operative to the firm he worked for. Thus, in England, the first attempts made at technical and vocational education were not sponsored by the Board of Education but by the Board of Trade, and in France the Ministry of Agriculture made itself responsible for improving the technical knowledge and resource of the agricultural worker.

It seemed a happy and successful arrangement at the time to both England and France, who, first in the field in industrial pursuits, had then no rivals to challenge them. By 1870, however, Germany had had to make a determined effort through sheer necessity to capture some of the markets and was already outstripping France in the industrial field; and as early as the Paris Exhibition of 1856 it was brought home most painfully to the English that they were facing increasingly strong competition from other countries whose craftsmen were receiving a most thorough and forward-looking training. By the turn of the century Germany had reformed its secondary educational system to include the more modern and technical subjects and under the influence of Kerschensteiner was transforming its continuation school to provide the really high-grade labour that industry was demanding. Smaller countries like Holland, Belgium, Switzerland and Scandinavia, mainly because of the democratic organization of education they enjoyed, were able to grasp more acutely the pressing needs of the time and to make for speedy implementation of reforms. And poverty-stricken Italy, whose main export was its willing man-power, was quick to train that man-power competently for the times and to ensure a constantly increasing demand for its craftsmen and technicians.

In the field of technical and vocational education, therefore, the true starting-point for our study is not the traditionally powerful and rich countries, but rather the " little " democracies, Italy, Germany, and so through to France, Russia and America.

Scandinavia. The Scandinavian countries generally have been least affected by the disastrous consequences of the Industrial Revolution, partly because their economy is even now mainly agrarian, partly because they were already wedded to the idea of a democratic form of education and to the general idea of a comprehensive school system. We have already had occasion to note how the primary teachers in these countries have constantly taken a keen interest in the political life of the country, and it is no exaggeration to claim that the teacher-training colleges and the folk high schools have become the training ground for the political leaders of the people, and in particular of the peasant classes.

Much has already been written about the folk high schools. It will be sufficient here to note that they owed their inception to a desire to bring about a spiritual renaissance in the country, and to Bishop Grundtvig's belief that since farmers and artisans were being called upon to take an increasingly active part in legislation, then they should be educated for this purpose in special schools for adults. It should also be remembered that though the folk high schools were never intended to give instruction in vocational studies, the real strength of the farmers' co-operative movements is held by Danes in particular to be due to the influence of these schools over succeeding generations. Again, as we shall see later, it cannot seriously be maintained to-day that these schools do not include vocational studies as part of their curriculum.

Norway, for example, regularly uses the folk high school to give courses parallel to the work done in the continuation schools and to prepare pupils for entry to specialized technical institutions. At the same time, it is being increasingly realized that the worker in industry or on the farm to-day needs a broad background of general culture, and both the continuation school and the youth schools are firmly opposing too early and too narrow a specialization. Their aim, in brief, is to try and develop the best possible life both for the individual and for the group, and to this end the work in these schools is constantly supplemented by study groups, correspondence courses, women's leagues, farmers' organizations, young people's organizations and home-makers' study circles. In an age of approaching automation it is necessary more than ever before to maintain the traditionally high standards of craftsmanship and pride in one's calling as a craftsman.

The Danish folk high school remains much closer to the original conception of Bishop Grundtvig, and the average age of students attending is continually rising, making the school pronouncedly one of genuine adult education. The Swedish schools, on the other hand, have been successful in attracting a much larger cross-section of the community than those of either Norway or Denmark, but their emphasis is on study groups and on such specific topics as sports, labour problems, religious and temperance questions, and on social, scientific and practical subjects. They also set examinations and award students differing grades on results obtained.

Pure vocational and technical education is provided at all levels in all three Scandinavian countries from the last years of the general school course up to and including the university. The constant aim is to enable the unskilled worker as well as the competent craftsman to acquire as much additional training as his aptitude and ambition fit him for, and it is the proud and justified boast that the pupil who does not seek an academic education is in no way prejudiced or belittled. Technical training (excluding commercial training) is always tied up with work experience and some form of apprenticeship, and much of it is administered jointly by the State and the representative trades and industries concerned. There is at all times a close relationship with industry to ensure that curricula is adapted to technical change and progress. In Norway half the board of control of a technical school must consist of representatives (managers and workers) of industry, and in Denmark many technical schools are still owned by technical societies, though subject to State supervision and in receipt of State grants.

Norway lumps all kinds of vocational and technical training together under the heading of trade schools and then differentiates them under headings such as schools for handicrafts and industry (technical schools), commercial schools, agricultural schools, seamen's schools, schools for domestic industry and handicrafts (men and women), and domestic science schools. Each school usually is divided into a lower and a higher school, and the programmes in all these schools range from evening part-time to full-time courses of up to four years' duration. In effect, there are classes which provide instruction before apprenticeship (workshop classes), classes for apprentices (apprenticeship classes), and classes after apprenticeship for those who wish to push on to a really high standard of achievement. At the summit there is the Norwegian Technical University of Trondheim, founded in 1910, which divides into seven departments : architecture, building, mining, general department (including technical physics), electro-technical and chemistry, machinery and shipbuilding. The arrangements in Sweden and Denmark are not so dissimilar as to warrant separate treatment. Some of the classes in the various schools are free, but in others students must pay a nominal sum for tuition.

Holland. The Dutch also have had early to recognize the importance of flexibility and adaptability in catering for a type of technical education to match the country's changing industrial and commercial concerns, but unlike Scandinavia, Holland is (along with Belgium) one of the most densely populated countries in the world. It is singularly lacking in coal and mineral resources, but its position at the mouth of three great rivers and its adjacency to the great continental powers have not allowed the Dutch to progress serenely and unhindered in their democratic way of life. The Dutch have had to take a great interest in commerce and the carrying trade, and this—together with intensive farming and agriculture—provides the most important source of the country's income. In the manufacturing industry, Holland is noted for its shipbuilding, distilling, the making of cigars, chocolate, margarine, and also of late for electrical apparatus (particularly radio valves and accessories). Delft is famous for its pottery and Amsterdam for its diamond cutting. Most of these are high-grade industries requiring a minimum of raw material and a maximum of skilled labour. Thus, technical education of a really high quality must loom large in the educational programmes, and, whilst it is felt necessary to move children from the age of 12 plus towards some definite specialization of a technical nature, it is also nowadays emphasized that a broad cultural background is equally necessary if really enlightened workers in industry are to be recruited. Similarly, it is necessary to make the universities and the higher research institutes more readily accessible to the product of the technical schools.

There are in Holland four clearly defined offerings in technical and commercial education, and all have been affected by the passing of the " Mammoth " School Law. At the lowest level is the L.T.S. which is attended by roughly 30 per cent. of boys and by somewhat fewer girls. Originally catering for pupils in the lowest to middle ability ranges, it gave a two-year course end on to the basic six-year primary education. The course has now been extended to three or even four years, and since they have now in effect become LAVO schools general subjects have been given more time, it being hoped thereby to " kill " the traditional somewhat narrow basic specialisms and make a bridge for promising pupils to attend higher technical institutions. Special classes are now provided to help such pupils attain their objective. And, of course, evening courses abound for young workers already in industry, often apprentices.

The M.T.S. (a post-1945 development) is a middle technical school accepting students in the 16–20 year range. Pupils are accepted from the LAVO (or the L.T.S.) but qualification through a bridge-year is demanded. Students can equally be accepted from the MAVO sector of secondary education, or even from the HAVO sector, these latter gaining certain course exemptions. On completion of their course they will be expected to occupy low management positions in industry or commerce or to run smaller businesses for themselves. There is a preliminary year of more theoretical work for pupils coming from LAVO, and the basic two-year course is followed by one year of supervised practice in industry before the final certificate is granted.

At the third level comes the higher technical school (H.T.S.) offering a four-year course to students either with appropriate earlier qualifications or experience or who have satisfactorily completed four or five years of a general secondary school course. This means that some 40 per cent. of the intake will come from the M.T.S. and the remainder from HAVO. The first two years consist of formal study in the college. The third year consists of practice in industry. The final year is a specialized period based on experiences gained in the third year " in the field ". Most of these schools have a building section, an hydraulic engineering and road-building section, an engineering section and an electro-technical section. Certain schools have sections for naval engineering and for chemical engineering. There are two secondary textile schools, one mining technical school, and one for leather and the footwear industry. There are also evening schools for pupils who follow a trade during the day. Graduates from the higher technical school come to hold important posts in charge of certain technical sections in large industrial concerns, or in part charge of small concerns, and they are also much sought after abroad.

Parallel with such technical provision are the arts and crafts schools which teach drawing, painting, modelling, the applied arts, advertising, and also interior decoration which is very popular with girls. There are also training schools for navigation and ships' engineers, schools for sea-fishing, and schools for inland navigation.

Much attention is also paid to what is called domestic economy training for girls. There are roughly three sections of training. The girls who pass from an elementary school enter the preparatory elementary classes where they follow day courses for a period of two years and are taught the elements of domestic science. If they wish to continue their studies they may choose a special course which will serve as training for a position as a mother's help, children's nurse or dressmaker. There are then advanced elementary classes for pupils who have the certificate of an advanced elementary school or its equivalent. Courses are here given in general domestic training, training for a nursery governess, tailoress, cutter, housekeeper, domestic head of an institution. Finally, these courses are followed by classes of a secondary standard. There are also short duration courses in domestic management usually given in the evening. Obviously, in a farming country like Holland, it is highly important that the farmer's wife be suitably trained to do the many technical tasks her husband will expect of her. Agricultural domestic economy, as a special branch, is therefore much to the fore. Since the war many girls have also entered industry, and special courses—including apprenticeship schemes—have also been arranged for them.

Schools for agriculture, horticulture and dairying naturally have an organization and a high standard of work and achievement parallel to that in the technical schools proper. Entrance to secondary agricultural schools is determined by an entrance examination of about the standard a pupil will have reached after three years in a secondary school. Entrance to the dairy schools is also by examination and the minimum age for entry is 19. Courses last for two or two-and-a-half years. There are also certain winter day schools for agriculture and horticulture, the duration of tuition being two winter periods of six months each.

Summit technical and vocational training is given in four schools of university standard: the School of Engineering at Delft, the School of Agriculture at Wageningen, and the Schools of Economics at Rotterdam and at Tilburg (Roman Catholic). The courses last in these institutes for five or six years. Entry is usually at the age of 18 or 19, and whilst anyone who has registered may attend the courses, only those who are certified as having reached an agreed preliminary standard of secondary technical or commercial education may sit the examinations. This peculiarity holds, incidentally, in the universities proper also.

Visitors to Holland are often surprised to find that the country also boasts no fewer than seven folk high schools, drawing their inspiration from Bishop Grundtvig but developing along their own individual lines that make them resemble more than anything the English residential college. Their importance to Holland lies in the fact that they are able in a most effective way to surmount the political and sectarian divisions into which the country is split and to become a focal point where people of all religious and political beliefs can meet and examine each other's point of view. The first two schools were founded well before the last war, and one founded during the depression of the 1930's to do something for the unemployed has now set the tone for the rest to follow : some form of practical work must be attempted by all students during each morning session. The standard course is of a fortnight's duration and is usually social in character. Longer courses are held from time to time to give students of technical or domestic

subjects the liberal as opposed to the vocational part of their training. And in the summer there are courses of three to four days'
duration on subjects like music, puppetry, drama, etc. There are
also opportunities on all courses for some form of creative activity.

Students attend from all over Holland and are required to pay
one-third of the cost, the rest being made up by State grants and
private contributions, often from employers. Many students are
willingly released on full pay by their employers who often pay in
addition the full cost of tuition.

Belgium. Like the Dutch, the Belgians have had to provide
themselves with both technical and commercial training to suit
every possible need and changing circumstance, and over the post-
war years in particular an intricate ladder has been evolved
whereby the promising and ambitious boy or girl from even the
humblest home or the remotest district may, in a variety of ways
from primary school and *quatrième degré*, from *école moyenne*
and *athénée*, be given a thorough part-time or full-time training
extending over the years from the simplest of technical or commercial courses up to work of a graduate or post-graduate level.

Technical education in Belgium began first of all through the
initiative of private organizations and then through that of the
State, the provinces and the municipalities. At the present time
there are State schools under direct State management and recognized schools which are subsidized and controlled by the State.
Curricula and certificates in both types of school are identical in
value and grant access to private employment as well as to public
offices. Like the Dutch, the Belgians early sensed the necessity for
adaptability to changing conditions, and a central administration
for technical education co-ordinates the initiative of industrialists
and of the schools in order to elaborate the best training methods.
This central body is assisted by a higher council of technical education composed of representatives of industry (managers and trade
union leaders) and of the administrative and inspectorate divisions
of the Ministry of Education. This council is assisted by *Conseils
de Perfectionnement* composed of managers and workers whose
task is to see that curricula and methods in each technical school
are in actual practice constantly being adapted to technical progress. These " competence boards " (as we may call them) also
arrange " refresher " courses for former pupils of a given technical
institute. Finally, in industry itself, various organizations of

managers study problems raised in the training of future technicians and arrange discussion groups in an attempt to see implemented their suggestions. The training of teachers is given particular attention at all these levels.

Children who have completed six years of the primary school at about the age of 12 may be admitted to full-time technical education. Such children start in what is termed the lower secondary grade and as far as cultural subjects are concerned follow a programme of work not dissimilar to that in the first three years of the *école moyenne*. Two kinds of institution have, however, to be distinguished : the vocational school in which the child will learn a trade and above all develop manual skills in order that when he starts working he is at his level professionally competent; the technical school where the training is based on a theoretical education plus considerable time in the laboratories and workshops. Pupils who wish to seek employment directly from the vocational school have a four-year course leading to a diploma examination. Pupils in the technical school acquire a technician's diploma after three years of study.

The higher secondary grade of technical education lasts two or three years, and is again divided into vocational and technical sections. It recruits its pupils from the *école moyenne* as well as from the lower secondary grades. Diplomas are again awarded at the end of the course and an attempt is made to get each pupil firmly placed and established in a post before he is called up for military service.

Lastly, there are courses in advanced technical education open either to pupils who have completed the full technical school course successfully or who hold the school leaving certificate from a secondary school proper. At this level there are commercial schools, schools for technicians, architectural schools, schools of agriculture and horticulture, and schools for arts and crafts, as well as a colonial university for training administrators for positions in the former Belgian Congo. This latter establishment is open only to young men from the academic type of secondary school. Courses in these establishments vary in duration from three to five years, and many of them have a standing comparable with that of the university proper. Amongst these should be mentioned : the School of Mining and Engineering at Mons, the Agricultural and Forestry Institutes at Gembloux and Ghent, the Military Academy at Brussels and a veterinary college near Brussels. In addition there are a higher textile institute at Verviers for the study of clothes and fabrics, and three *universités du travail* at Charleroi, Mons and Ghent. These latter institutions can best be described as comprehensive technical institutions in that they take pupils from the age of 12 as full-time day students and carry them up to the highest levels as well as run complicated part-time and evening school courses.

Like its full-time counterpart, part-time education includes a vocational and a technical section which are in turn divided into grades. Certain courses lead to the same titles and qualifications as the full-time courses. The curriculum is then extended over a larger number of years : six instead of three, usually. In part-time training there are also courses intended to fill in gaps left in earlier training that are taken by students seeking promotion. There is also what is termed " short-term technical education." Schools in this category are intended to meet an urgent and temporary need of man-power or to promote an enterprise undertaken by industrialists on an experimental basis.

Outstanding characteristics of the Belgian system of technical and commercial education are : the deep and personal interest taken in all aspects of the work by industrialists and trade unions to the point of often large and valuable gifts of both machinery and money; the lack of an apprenticeship system (except in certain trades such as butchers, bakers, hairdressers, tailoresses (and tailors), plumbers, decorators—i.e. mainly businesses that are run as one-man businesses or family concerns) and of any system of day release; the healthy rivalry existing from province to province in an attempt to secure the best possible training that can exist; close collaboration at all times between the various interested parties which, whilst safeguarding the academic and disinterested character of technical education, maintains a close connexion between technical education and the economic life of the country; the bias given towards the specialities of the region where the schools are located; the luxurious boarding accommodation provided for both boys and girls in the larger schools in the provincial centres, usually subsidized and therefore well within the reach of all who come from a distance and need to live away from home to pursue their studies; the provision of adequate grants-in-aid for needy students, though many schools pride themselves on making all tuition either free or negligible in cost.

Switzerland. There is in Switzerland the same close co-ordination between the educational syllabus and technical requirements as in Belgium or Holland; there is the same necessity for producing technicians in a variety of different fields and for securing a maximum of highly skilled labour; there has to be the same emphasis on extensive technical education both in the schools and on a part-time basis; there is insistence on providing a broad basic general education and achieving thereby parity of esteem between secondary technical training and ordinary secondary school teaching; great importance is placed upon fundamental studies in mathematics and science in training the technologist, and there is universal postponement of specialization to as late a stage in the student's career as possible.

The diversity of arrangements that exist from *canton* to *canton* in Switzerland make it impossible to be other than extremely general in a survey short as this has to be. A pupil who has completed the period of compulsory school attendance has already received the barest elements of technical training, and most of these pupils will pass to some form of apprenticeship that will last for at least one year. During apprenticeship, attendance at a " professional " school is compulsory on one or two half-days per week, the school being obliged to train every apprentice who has a contract of apprenticeship with an employer. It should be noted that psycho-medical centres of the type we have already discussed in considering Belgium are becoming increasingly used, and all children who show capacity for profiting from technical school training are enabled to attend, no matter how poor their parents may be.

In discussing secondary education in Switzerland we have noted the part the intermediate school plays in giving the pupil a sound general education, and it should now be stressed that the more progressive of these schools prepare pupils, particularly in isolated districts, for agricultural and trade jobs. Similarly, all pupils who satisfactorily complete this school course pass either to some form of apprenticeship or to technical and commercial schools for about a further period of three years to the age of 19. In all the technical schools there is careful adjustment of the school programme to regional needs.

Another institution, the *technicum*, only admits young people who have served a three or four years' apprenticeship in industry. The course in the *technicum* also lasts three years, and because of the period of apprenticeship and the obligation for military service the average age of entry is 20 to 21 years. There is an entrance examination designed to make sure that candidates have retained sufficient knowledge of their basic *Grundschule* and subsequent education in order to be able to cope adequately with the work. The great success of the *technicum* is due to the fact that students come quite voluntarily because they are determined to improve their prospects. Instruction usually starts in the basic subjects— mathematics pure and applied, physics, chemistry, and then proceeds to more technical aspects. In addition, every student must take a language and literature course, and some instruction in works organization, in accountancy and book-keeping.

At the summit comes the *école polytechnique fédérale* which again emphasizes a broad general training and postpones specialization until after the first two years of study, or later, and which brings students into regional contact with industry through workshop visits so that they may eventually choose between a number of different occupations before committing themselves to too narrow a specialization. This *école polytechnique*, situated in Zürich, is the only federal institution in existence, all other universities being administered by the respective *cantons*. Students are admitted no earlier than 18 on a basis of the secondary school leaving examination proper, or on recommendation of satisfactory achievement from the advanced technical schools. The duration of the course is about four years. The school itself comprises twelve departments : architecture, civil engineering, mechanical and electrical engineering, chemistry, pharmacy, forestry, agriculture, rural engineering and surveying, mathematical and physical sciences, military science, and a department of general education.

Italy. As we have already instanced, technical and vocational education in Italy have enjoyed comparably favourable treatment at the hands of the various Italian governments. The Casati Law of 1859 provided already for a six-year technical school to follow on the elementary school, divided into lower and higher divisions, each of three years' duration. Theoretical though the teaching in such schools may have been, they proved their worth in securing many foreign jobs for Italians and they provided a sound basis on which to build in the 1890's when a new burst of interest in technical studies captured the attention not only of Italy but of the whole of Europe. Thus, apart from the years of the Fascist regime, policy as regards technical instruction was far in advance of policy for other forms of secondary education. Newer types of technical schools were introduced in the 1930's, but Mussolini made it quite clear that training for trade and crafts was peculiarly the province of the people rather than that of an academic élite. It has been left to post-war governments and the proposals contained in the Gonella reform programme to try to iron out this discrepancy.

Possession of the leaving certificate from the *scuola media* is now necessary for entry to all forms of industrial, commercial or agricultural training, though pupils who do not possess this may (on the results of a special examination) gain entry to the *istituto professionale*. This school offers courses varying from two to four years dependent on the qualification desired and seeks in particular to meet the needs of local industrial or commercial concerns. There are, however, five broad specialisms: industry and skilled trades (e.g. art for workers in ceramics and for interior decorators); commerce and agriculture; the catering and tourist trade; seamanship in its various forms. There is in addition a parallel school for girls with offerings in domestic science, home management, hygiene and commercial studies. A good diploma at the end of the course has both professional and academic value since it will allow the holder to proceed to the terminal classes in the *instituto tecnico* in his chosen field. Experimentation in extending courses to five years in the *istituto professionale* to give a more integrated form of training leading to the award of a " mature " diploma has been going on for some time in an attempt to get outstanding pupils into some form of tertiary education at the university level or into higher grades of management, etc. It should finally be noted that, whilst day-release is not common in Italy, industry does look kindly on the work both done here and at the *istituto tecnico* and provision is made in both establishments for part-time courses which can exact a weekly stint of up to twenty hours of study.

Of the *istituto tecnico* we have already briefly spoken. These institutes are highly specialized, and in addition to the usual commercial and economic subjects offer courses in agriculture, land-surveying, nautical training, domestic science (for girls) and in industrial specialisms such as mining, metallurgy, mechanical engineering, electro-technical engineering, building, textiles, industrial chemistry and optical instrument work. The study of

Italian, of history, and of an appropriate foreign language is always compulsory in addition to the specialized professional training. Successful completion of the *istituto tecnico* course entitles the graduate to a diploma in his speciality, and this in turn secures him entrance to the appropriate university department or equivalent institute of higher learning, except that for university schools of engineering, science and agronomy a supplementary examination is also required, mainly in cultural subjects, to ensure that the undergraduate has the same basic cultural background as the pupil passing out from the *licei*.

We have already had occasion to mention the government's preoccupation with the problem of illiteracy, and a determined drive is also being made in the fields of adult and popular education. Through the ordinary State school system adults are being increasingly encouraged to attend suitable classes held for them, and in certain areas where the right type of school is non-existent special vocational and technical schools for adults have also been established. Popular education is left mainly to trade unions, to co-operative movements, and to labour and agricultural organizations. Large industrial firms, in addition to providing technical instruction of the kind we have already mentioned, increasingly occupy themselves with the social, moral and physical well-being of their employees.

Germany. Once Germany had made the switch from an agrarian to an industrial economy she tackled her problems in a typically resolute and thorough way, and vocational schools, known in Germany for more than a century before, spread rapidly after 1870. Similarly, by her Constitution of 1919, Germany was the first country to make attendance at a vocational school compulsory for all young workers and apprentices. It is to be noted that the apprenticeship system is fairly widespread throughout Germany, though certain of the full-time vocational schools aim at replacing apprenticeship either partially or entirely. Opinions are divided throughout the country on the real value attaching to an apprenticeship system, and to-day many would hold that the right kind of vocational school that is realistically geared to and constantly in touch with industry (as in Belgium) can do much more than the apprenticeship system can normally achieve to produce an intelligent, responsive and responsible worker in industry.

In Germany, then, education cannot cease once a boy or girl has

completed the compulsory period of schooling, but must continue
in one form or another, part-time or full-time, up to the age of 18.
If a boy elects to go to work at 14 or 15 years of age he will be
required to continue his studies in the part-time vocational school
a further three or four years as a minimum. He will be required to
attend for between six to twelve periods of instruction per week
either on one or two days of every week. The kind of instruction
given will seek to enrich and supplement the practical apprenticeship training which he is undergoing in the kind of job he has
undertaken. As one *Land* directive puts it : " The vocational
schools have the task of promoting professional training, of en-
larging and deepening general knowledge, and of educating
students to being morally valuable members of society, filled with
love for their professional activities and conscious of their responsibilities as citizens of a democratic state." The influence of
Kerschensteiner is most obvious. All the *Länder* are in agreement
that there are still too few part-time vocational schools, and not
nearly enough of the right kind, and it is their deep and immediate
concern both to increase their numbers and to improve the quality
of the work done.

The full-time school is usually comprehensive and offers courses
varying in duration from one to three or four years. It is, of course,
possible for an apprentice of promise to pass from the part-time
school to the full-time technical school as it is possible for a grammar school pupil or a pupil from the middle school to do the same.
Normally, for entrance to the full-time school evidence of satisfactory completion of primary or middle school studies is required.
Such schools are frequented by twice as many girls as boys, this
being largely accounted for by the fact that it is here that thorough
training in commercial subjects, stenography, secretarial work and
domestic subjects and skills is given. The full-time school may be
maintained by the local community, by a vocational organization,
or by private persons.

The advanced technical school only admits pupils who have
sufficient practical experience in a vocation, which means in practice that applicants for admission must either have completed a
full term of apprenticeship or run an equivalent course in the full-
time ordinary technical school. Courses last up to four years and
a successful student receives a specialized diploma which, if it bears
an over-all " Good " mark, entitles him to continue his studies at

the university level in one of the schools of higher education, where he will be studying at the same level as the pupil entering from the *gymnasium* after passing his *abitur*. It should be noted in passing that in Germany all higher institutes of learning (including universities) are classified under the generic title of *Hochschulen* and that Germany was well to the fore in establishing technological universities.

France. As in all other forms of educational endeavour, the Frenchman shows himself peculiarly complicated and individualistic over his approach to the problems he has to face in technical and vocational education. It must be remembered that France's economy is even to-day primarily agrarian and that the acknowledged stabilizing force in all matters is the French peasantry. Again, the major industries of France are centred on the coalfields in the North and in consequence industrialization has not had the over-all effect we might expect in a country the size of France. There is no tremendously developed and highly organized factory system, but rather groupings of small industrial concerns, and family businesses—still run as such—are much in evidence. French individualism revolts against depersonalization through a vast machine-like organization, and the peasant origins of manual workers are clearly reflected in their whole approach.

Historically speaking, technical education goes back to 1794 when the Convention created the *Conservatoire des Arts et Métiers*. The *Ecoles Nationales d'Arts et Métiers* trace their origin to the end of the eighteenth century, and the *Ecole Centrale des Arts et Manufactures* owes its origin to private enterprise in 1829. The first professional training schools were established in 1881 and 1882, but it was not until 1892 that vocational sections were introduced into the *école primaire supérieure* (now the *collège moderne*). Industrial concerns were then greatly interested, because their whole future was in jeopardy in world markets, and this preliminary technical training was placed for a time under the control of the Ministry of Commerce and Industry with its own budget, personnel, administration, etc. No really important advance in technical training was possible, however, until the Loi Astier of 1919 gave it its charter and laid down that young employees in certain industries must attend part-time schools during working hours up to the age of 18. Since 1945 the administration of technical education has been placed under the supervision of the rector and Academy inspectors, aided by technical advisers. Vocational guidance centres have been associated in particular with technical instruction and each *département* is under an obligation to provide one. Finally, a serious attempt to make technical subjects " respectable " in the eyes of the academically minded Frenchman comes through the establishment of the seven-year courses offered in the *collège technique* and through the creation of technical and commercial *baccalauréats*.

Before the 1959 reforms a pupil not passing from the primary school to some form of secondary education joined what were termed *classes de pré-apprentissage* between the ages of 12 and 14. From there he could enter the *centre d'apprentissage*. The first such centres were opened in 1939 as an emergency measure geared to national defence. They were extended during the German occupation to cope with problems of unemployment amongst youth and came under the control of technical education proper at the liberation of France in 1945. Since 1945 three separate training colleges for men, and two for women, have been opened in order to ensure to the *centres d'apprentissage* a steady stream of properly qualified and right-minded teachers. Entry to such training colleges is, as usual, on a competitive basis, and the course of pedagogical instruction given there lasts one full academic year. Intending teachers vary on entry between the ages of 23 and 45, and they have had considerable experience in their specialized fields of commerce or industry before taking up training.

The apprenticeship centres are neither schools nor factories, but a cross between the two, and are designed with the utilitarian aim of giving rapid training to young semi-skilled workers. Parents were at first chary of sending their children there, but the close contact maintained with them during their child's training and the obvious interest shown in each child have gradually won them over to the new venture. Today, parents have been taking such an interest in the courses offered and the opportunities open to their children that they have even suggested for themselves what they consider desirable reforms, and, though they often think in terms of utilitarian than of general culture, they have insisted on the importance of a serious study of the French language at least throughout the whole duration of a course offered. The most healthy sign about the apprenticeship centres has been the amount of freedom they have enjoyed at a local level to experiment and develop.

Thus, one happy feature about the 1959 reforms is that the slight changes concerning the apprenticeship centres (now *collèges d'enseignement techniques*) meets with the full approval of parents and, indeed, takes note of their general wishes for their children. The training of what we may term the middle grades for industry and commerce is carried out in a variety of ways : through technical sections in the *lycée*, through highly specialized trade schools, through municipal colleges, and, of course, through the *collège technique*. Admission to the *collège technique* is on the basis of an entrance examination (only competitive if there happen to be fewer places than there are applicants). The minimum age for entry is 13. The course usually lasts four years, and fairly advanced theoretical instruction is given along with a course in general education and practical work. Time spent in the workshop or office varies between a minimum of twelve hours per week in the first year and a maximum of nineteen hours per week in the last year of the course. One foreign language is usually included on the programme of general education, and the more progressive *collèges techniques* are encouraging their pupils to travel abroad, not necessarily to speak the language they are learning, but to study at first hand in the factories of other countries what is being achieved, and how, and why—comparative technical studies, in fact ! On satisfactory completion of his course the pupil is awarded his *brevet d'enseignement industriel/commercial/hôtelier/social*. Many *collèges techniques* have a special section in which the more brilliant pupils may prepare either for the *technical baccalauréat* or for the competitive examination for entry to still higher grade schools. Naturally, pupils may also take the easier *Certificat d'Aptitude Professionnel* (usually awarded in the former *centres d'apprentissage*) from the *collège technique*.[1]

It is repeatedly emphasized that the teacher in the *collège technique* has a part to play equally as important as and no different from that played by his opposite number in the *lycée* or *collège moderne,* and the same general requirements as to training and recruitment are therefore expected of him. None the less, there is a special *Ecole Normale Supérieure de l'Enseignement Technique*, first opened in 1912. It has six different sections : industrial

---

[1] See appropriate section in Chapter Ten for changes now taking place.

sciences (boys); applied sciences and domestic science (girls); industrial design (boys); drawing and applied arts (boys and girls); commercial studies (boys and girls); and a faculty of letters and modern language studies (boys and girls).

The higher grade schools offering courses at a university level are too numerous and too diversified to be treated adequately in anything but close detail. One particular group, the *Ecoles Nationales d'Ingénieurs Arts et Métiers*, for entry to which pupils are regularly prepared in the *collège technique* as well as from the *lycée* and *collège moderne*, has enjoyed a very high reputation for more than a century. There are six associated schools situated in Aix-en-Provence, Châlons-sur-Marne, Cluny, Angers, Lille and Paris. Industrial and commercial concerns have also made provision for technical instruction on a private basis at both the middle and higher levels, and there are naturally similar Catholic private establishments.

Not unnaturally, agricultural education has also been given careful attention during the post-war period, and the Ministry of Agriculture makes itself responsible for (a) post-school training in agriculture and household management for boys and girls under 17 whose parents are engaged in agriculture and who themselves are not following any other course of studies; (b) specialized regional schools giving practical training; and (c) higher institutions of university rank which include the *Institut National Agronomique*. In other words, the division into three categories is similar to that in technical and commercial instruction with the exception that at the primary level the agricultural schools are winter schools.

In a country like France which prizes the kind of formal instruction given in the primary schools there is no real desire nor felt need for any kind of formalized adult education programme, and most work done in this direction becomes the responsibility of private groups: trade unions run their labour colleges, for example, as in most other countries, and organize popular lectures and guide leisure-time activities; in the country districts especially the primary school teacher can be a vital force in arranging within his school all kinds of activities; there is a French League for Education which works in close liaison with the Ministry of Education but which receives no subsidies; and in some towns the government has provided centres for popular education and left voluntary bodies to do the rest. It is important to mention, however, the *Conservatoire National des Arts et Métiers*, which gives higher education in the applied sciences entirely free of charge to workers in industry who are prepared to attend evening and Saturday and Sunday classes. Every year, more than 15,000 workers attend its courses. Properly speaking, of course, it is a voluntary and part-time technical school; it has its own private research programmes for inquiring into industrial problems; and its teaching staff is extremely highly qualified and experienced.

U.S.S.R. In contradistinction to the French, the Russians have not been afraid to neglect as and where necessary cultural education until they had their programmes of technical instruction well under way. It was in 1952 that they declared their intention to put into practice throughout the ten-year school a system of " universal polytechnical instruction." Though polytechnical instruction is no new feature in the Soviet school system it is now re-defined for us as instruction which " gives pupils knowledge of the general principles of production, equips them with a series of practical skills, and links instruction with socially productive labour." In effect it means that all subjects are to be given a well-defined technological bias and that there is to be an ever closer link between theory and practice. It is also well to remember that all schools in Russia can be said to have had something of a technical and utilitarian bias since the days of Peter the Great.

The whole course of technical education in Russia must be seen against the background of the Soviet problems of industrialization. The U.S.S.R. is not alone in her realization that survival in the twentieth-century world is materially dependent on scientific conquest, but her task has been far greater than that of any other country in Western Europe. The evolution from an agrarian to an industrial economy has had to be forced into the short period of less than a quarter of a century. If the effect of this change on the Soviet way of life has been unprecedented, the repercussions on the whole educational system have been none the less far-reaching. They have led educationists in the U.S.S.R. to place a greater emphasis on technical education than in any other country in the world, and this emphasis has been coupled with the aim of removing all sense of social distinction between the manual and the intellectual worker. By technical education is meant specific training for industry and commerce, or training in order to give greater skill and knowledge to those already engaged in industry. The aim, whether for the youth or the adult, is twofold : to equip the student with the knowledge of a technical nature required to make him work more efficiently and at a higher level, and to give him knowledge of life in a highly industrialized setting so that he may the better play his part as a citizen of the U.S.S.R.

The whole character of technical education was, prior to the German attack of 1940, in a state of ordered transition. The age at which vocational training was beginning was being gradually raised. A movement was being made towards later specialization, dependent on the increasing demands of industry and the growth of the ten-year school and corresponding falling away of the seven-year type of general education. The aim was that all children should have a general education up to the age of 18. The menace from Germany, however, disrupted all these plans, and a famous State Edict of October 2nd, 1940, resolved " to empower the Council of Peoples' Commissars of the U.S.S.R. to mobilize 800,000 to 1,000,000 persons of 14 to 15 years of age for training in trade and railway schools, and of 16 to 17 years of age for factory workshop schools." Thus was formed the famous Labour Reserve, and it is on a basis of this Labour Reserve that present practice in technical education at the lowest levels is based.

Boys and girls of between 14 and 15 years of age, who must at least have had four years' schooling, are admitted to two types of vocational school in each of which the course of instruction lasts two years. One type of school trains young railroad workers, the other semi-skilled workers in industry. A third type of vocational school is the apprenticeship school which admits pupils between the ages of 16 and 18 and gives them courses varying in length according to the speciality from six months to one year. On leaving all three schools the pupils are mobilized on a basis of the Labour Reserve for four years obligatory service in State industrial enterprises. It is to be noted that the formation of this Labour Reserve has made a serious inroad on the recruitment of children in agricultural areas for agriculture. By changes initiated late in 1953, more attention is to be paid to the country school, and the children of peasants are no longer to be trained for the Labour Reserve, but are to be educated " to love the agricultural professions, and to be prepared for practical work " in the stockyards, collective farms and experimental stations.

Middle-level specialists are trained in what are termed *techni-cums*. The courses offered vary in length from three to four years, and sometimes as long as five. There is an upper age limit of 30 for entrance. Prospective candidates must have completed the eight-year school and there is an entrance test in Russian language and literature, mathematics, and understanding of the working of the Soviet Constitution. The *technicum* may also be attended by students from the final non-compulsory three years of secondary education who do not intend going either to a university or to another institute of higher learning. They do a shortened version (about half the length) of the course taken by the younger intake. There is obviously a very technical bias, but general subjects are still to be found on the curriculum and include the principles of Marxism-Leninism, Political Economy, Russian literature and a foreign language. One feature of the *technicum* is that there is production practice as distinct from practical work on the school premises. Production begins usually in the third year of study and is carried out in an appropriate works, hospital, business or commercial house. *Technicums* for dentistry (and the legal pro-fession, and drama schools) require the student to have completed eleven full years of schooling before entry. On graduating from a *technicum* the student is required to practise his speciality for a minimum of three years, after which he may pass without any entrance examination. Most *technicums* are residential or partly residential.

Finally, there is a fairly comprehensive system of evening studies for those who have just started work on factory or farm. Again, the aim is to give the boy or girl who started work early the oppor-tunity to complete the full ten-year school course. The courses run from autumn to spring and pupils attend four hours a day for five days a week. Much attention has also been paid to adult education through the creation of primary and secondary schools for adults, the former usually being found only in isolated villages. An attempt is made to have adults and children following the same curriculum. The adults naturally attend school only in the even-ing, attendance usually being four times a week. There is also a well-developed correspondence school system for those who live too remote, both at the primary and secondary level. Industrial and agricultural academies also attempt to seed out workers who show initiative and planning intelligence and give them a five-year full-time course, free of cost, and maintaining where necessary all dependants during that time. Nor must we ignore the palaces of culture and trade union clubs.

U.S.A. America's present-day problem is that of any other country in which the apprenticeship system has not been extensively developed: there is a danger of excessive specialization, particularly in industries where mass production methods are widely used. Again, in a country where children tend to stay at school until the age of 18, so many of the subjects that are classified under technical and vocational education in European countries come easily within the province of the comprehensive high school system, whilst in the larger towns and certain country districts technical and agricultural high schools are no uncommon thing. " Learning by doing " is all the time the keynote of American education.

At his high school a pupil can choose between two groups of studies, the one leading to " academic " university entrance, the other consisting of commercial and industrial subjects. Those who choose the technical group have considerable laboratory and workshop practice. On completing his high school course a pupil may then pass to a variety of institutions—colleges of liberal arts, colleges of mechanical and agricultural engineering, institutes of technology—many of which are often nowadays renamed universities. The course in such institutions usually lasts four years to a first " degree," and whilst practice varies considerably from State to State, those taking industrial and allied subjects will often be found to be alternating three months' study with three months in the factory and workshops. From the point of view of the European onlooker, inured as he is to the classical few subjects that are accepted as suitable disciplines at a university level, the picture is bewildering. Side by side with history, mathematics, geography, as accepted subjects, he will find such specialities as : household decoration, grocery and food distribution, hairdressing, store management, and even exotic side-lines such as the technique of playing jazz instruments! This first degree, of course, is a simple graduation and serious academic workers always push on to complete some piece of research. Thus, at a post-graduate level, there is work being done in the letters and art faculties, and in the faculties of applied science, comparable with the best to be found in Europe.

The universities and colleges also make considerable provision for the needs of the part-time student through evening classes, at some of which vocational training may be obtained. Similarly there is part-time adult evening work, success in which often counts as part requirement towards the later granting of a degree. Correspondence courses at all levels also abound.

Part-time schools have been established for those boys and girls who leave school at about the age of 14. The commonest type of continuation school has time allotments of four to eight hours per week for a period of two or three years, or until the sixteenth or eighteenth birthday is reached. Instruction is given during working hours, and centres either upon the pupil's present vocation or upon one for which he desires training. General education, in which stress is placed upon English and studies in citizenship, takes up part of the time. There is also a *co-operative* school in which the pupil divides his time between shop or store and the school. Usually a plan is worked out, in agreement with the employer, where pairs of workers alternate, one having a week or more in school while the other is at work. Evening schools are also provided by the larger cities which usually enrol adults and give instruction in English to foreign-born persons as well as teach fundamentals to those who have had poor educational advantages.

Conclusion. The one important factor that emerges from this present study, limited though it is, is that vocational education is rapidly growing, is being liberally financed, and is eagerly sought after. Only in the nineteenth century did formal schooling for vocations other than medicine, law and theology become a reality. Now, the proliferation of technical and vocational subjects, and the increasingly higher degrees of specialization required in industry, raise several important problems which are met characteristically by each individual country according to traditional belief and practice.

The first problem is that of the relationship between occupational training and a general education. How much general education should the trainee have, and of what kind? The U.S.S.R. "creates" its technicians as it needs them and is prepared to leave the cultural aspects well behind if need be. England has followed closely the teaching of Kerschensteiner from Germany. France remains vowed to the highest possible all-round standard of attainment at whatever level. America pins its faith to the comprehensive high school. All are agreed, however, in practice, that industry needs primarily the communication skills (reading, writing, speech, number), the social skills (co-operation and ability to get on with others), mental qualities of alertness, interest and clear-thinking, and personal qualities of self-discipline, a sense of responsibility, self-respect and willingness to work and tackle problems. Scandinavia, Holland and Belgium have little trouble in achieving in their own special spheres these prime requirements because the temper of the people has long been geared towards them.

A second problem, in a sense inseparable from the first, is that of determining how soon specialization shall begin. It is increasingly recognized that too early specialization does not necessarily sort out the really skilled workers for specific jobs but rather restricts the resourcefulness and initiative of the worker. The general aim, then, is to postpone specialization until as late as possible. Thus, the *centres d'apprentissage* in France always gave training in one or two allied subjects in addition to the pupil's chosen branch. In all technical schools everywhere there is a reaction against extremes of specialization, and whilst the schools might be geared to deal with regional needs and to build their programmes according to these needs, they do attempt to see that each student has a conspectus of the whole. He must know and appreciate the relevance of the task he has to perform, and its importance, in relation to the whole regional economy. The verdict of modern industry is that the individual shall be given a broad technical education with his training in the highly specific skills reserved until he is best able to appreciate them, which is usually " on the job." Actual workshop practice, therefore, looms large in the final stages of a student's training.

A third problem—and in reality a fundamental social problem —is that of persuading the right kind of person to take up technical work, of making such work " respectable " and attractive to those who have traditionally sought an academic type of education and a white-collar job, no matter how unsuited in reality they were to such jobs. A country like America, with its egalitarian ideals and comprehensive school system, has no major problem in this sense. Nor has Russia as long as it can happily direct labour. Nor has Switzerland which has little else to sell to the world but its technical skill. The Scandinavians have likewise early recognized the dignity and importance of labour. It is the countries traditionally vowed to academic studies and the training of an élite that run into trouble. France seeks its solution characteristically by showing that technical studies can be made as rigorous a discipline as any other branch of study. All are increasingly using vocational guidance centres and through wise consultation of parents making them increasingly acceptable. Similarly, and in conjunction with the decision not to encourage too early specialization, an attempt is made to have a basic curriculum for all children during the first two or three years of post-primary education that enables transfer from one type of school to another easily to be effected.

Lastly, there is the problem arising from the rapidly changing needs of the world of work and of the newer and more complicated techniques to be employed in industrial concerns. In countries where the apprenticeship system is in force the problem is not so great, but it still is a problem. The solution generally sought is that of interesting more and more closely industrialists in the work of the schools. Belgium is the outstanding example of what can be achieved through intelligent and generous industrial concern with technical and vocational training at all levels. There, both historically and politically, the middle classes and the schools have always been intimately concerned with one another's interests. In other countries, like France and Holland, industrial and commercial firms are increasingly financing and maintaining their own training schools and seeking fair but not hampering links with the main educational system. In general practice, however, it is found that there must be a central co-ordinating body and French development to-day suffers to some extent through having too many bodies —the ministries of agriculture, of the interior, of health, of labour, and of defence—with a finger in the educational pie.

" In modern education, just as in modern music," wrote Sir Michael Sadler in 1923, " we have got to accustom our ears to unfamiliar harmonies." [1] It is through just that process that the major European countries are now passing in making the effort called from them by the strident demands of modern technological progress.

[1] *Education and Life,* edited by J. A. Dale. O.U.P., 1924, p. 21.

In Search of an Identity

"The Fatherland is the place to which one's soul is chained."

Voltaire.

I

A S I have argued earlier in this book, no worker in the field of comparative studies in education can afford to neglect the importance of that elusive but undeniable entity which Friedrich Schneider and others (like myself) have termed the " national character ". We have used the expression to typify those forces of cultural continuity which determine the social behaviour of a nation as a whole. Besides acknowledging that the Greek historian Herodotus (*c.* 484–*c.* 425 B.C.) was the first to point out that those persons said to constitute a " nation " behaved in similar ways and had the same institutions and artefacts, we can also take our stand with Edmund Burke (1729–97) who, in his writings on the French Revolution, made abundantly clear that there were already throughout Europe sincerely and deeply held feelings of national identity. Burke observes that members of different societies have strongly differing concepts of the supreme values which make life worth living, and that for the preservation of these values they will repeatedly hazard all other values, and even life itself. Nationality, he stresses (though he does not actually use the word), has nothing to do with geographical location or with the fact that a group of people happen at a given moment in time to live under a common government. Nationality is an expression of continuity, an awareness of an extension of people in time, in numbers, and in space. It is the outcome of common political, legal and religious institutions and traditions. More important still, it is based on long continued uniformity of customs and manners. Any group of people, he argues, who have lived together in such a manner for a long time and have shared a common history will constitute a nationality. And each nationality, by this process of historical evolution, will develop a distinctive character of its own.

Ultimately, then, it is a common experience which determines the character of a nation, and a national society can in consequence be summed up as forming a relatively self-sufficient social system. Man is unique among all other living creatures in being able to create his own environment instead of being forced to submit to the environment in which he finds himself. In this sense, his search for a *personal* identity begins when he sets himself, as no other animal can, to manipulate nature in ways that will satisfy his basic needs. Very early on in this process he discovers that to exist in the way he would exist he needs to collaborate fully with other like-minded individuals and so he gradually develops a *social* identity and increasingly comes to depend for his existence on the existence of society. He likewise finds out (often through bitter experience) that to continue to exist and flourish he must be ready to change social forms as both his personal and social needs and the vicissitudes of time exact. He must be dynamic. He must also realize two things; firstly, that the members of his particular social group must be considered as responsible beings in whom a mass of conflicting impulses have to be harmonized for the greater good; secondly, that a convenient abstraction, the " state ", can best represent this greater harmony. Thus there are gradually evolved normative patterns of behaviour, the socio-biological needs of the given group being integrated through some normative structure of customs, feelings and beliefs, and these are transmitted in clearly defined patterns to the children through the educative system, the children gradually acquiring appropriate habits of thought, feeling and action to *accept* the given modes of that particular social group—*accept* being ideally also understood in the positive sense of implying their ability and willingness to initiate desirable change. It is accepted that the educative process is an instrument of the group will for the cultivation of its separate members' ability to make that will effective. It is held that for each group education must be seen as a social process closely related to the social, political and economic scene and must be based upon the fundamental commitments of the given culture. And each country's educational system is seen as having its present character, not entirely because it has developed in a certain manner, but also because it has had to make the effort (not always fully successful) to correspond with and adjust itself to the social realities of the times. In this sense it can be claimed that the social history of a people allied to the national ideals (the cultural totality of the group) is much more significant in determining the nature of the schools than the acceptance of any particular creed or philosophy. Indeed, only those philosophers are given importance and credence whose thinking is found to be germinal in terms of group aspirations. In France, for example, Voltaire signally failed to win his compatriots over to Lockeian thought. Cartesianism triumphed, the spirit of Montaigne prevailed, and only that which Rousseau himself distilled from Locke proved in some measure acceptable.

2

We should at this point do well to remember that the transition from group-identity to the comforting feeling of national identity (at which point national character traits begin to be manifest) is not always possible of exact definition. We should equally remember that different nations, mainly because of the accidents of history, achieve national consciousness in totally unexpected (and often unpredictable) ways, and that the time scale can vary enormously from nation to nation.[1] It would seem, however, that economic factors first played an important part in fostering feelings of group-identity, to be extended to those of national identity, long before nationalism as such became a political force. Similarly, and certainly as far as Western Europe is concerned, non-political ideas of differences between one nation and another got their first real impetus from a deep-felt urge to write creatively in the vernacular to be read (or listened to) by a native as opposed to a European. So we had in England Chaucer's *Canterbury Tales* (begun in 1386) whilst France gave us its troubadours and the classic thirteenth century *Roman de la Rose*.

By the time of the Renaissance and Reformation the idea of a bourgeois urban civilization based on commercial enterprise had rapidly spread throughout Europe, and the most-favoured of the

[1] Belgium is an outstanding example, achieving its independence in a full surge of national consciousness (latent over centuries) as recently as 1830.

commercial centres were rich enough and sufficiently self-assured, sufficiently knowledgeable also through their trading ventures of the validity of other customs and ways of life, to wish to assert their own individuality, to establish their own uniqueness, seek their own identity.[1] Patronage of the arts and learning followed to add further to and exploit the move towards self-identification. And, as the ideas of the Humanists began to make their impact, so did the growing power of the rising merchant classes in the larger towns lead to the foundation of schools outside the direct control of the Catholic Church, thus initiating the inevitable if slow transfer of education out of the hands of the clergy into those of the ruling laity.[2] In effect, the Humanists preached a doctrine which proved highly acceptable to the growing bourgeois-based society: that man cannot accept authority as such but must be allowed to make his own judgements; that this is particularly true in matters of taste and what is right and wrong; and that the ways in which humans think and feel must shape the structure of human society.

Thus we can argue that group character precedes the development of a national character—that what came first was a kind of in-group feeling inspired by devotion to the common good of the group and nurtured by high ideals of duty and a necessary spirit of sacrifice of some immediate personal gain to the common good. Gradually a state of mind emerges in which local loyalty is enlarged for the well-being of a totality of groups to embrace political loyalty which is felt to be owed to the nation—a necessary abstraction. And nation-states emerge wherever the separate communities together come to value the possession of common political institutions and of shared political traditions in proportion as it is seen that a common government and administration can and will quicken both economic activity and social mobility. Most frequently it is found that a well-developed sentiment of common origin, of common history and of common destiny has been latent waiting to be tapped, and processes of

[1] A study of the life of Montaigne, together with a reading of the Essays, clearly reveals how true this was for the town of Bordeaux, for example.

[2] When Dean Colet re-established Saint Paul's School in 1509 he was well aware that he was educating the future governing classes for service to the State. Loughborough Grammar School (founded 1496 in memory of Sir Thomas Burton, Merchant) is but one example among many in England which fall into this category of " merchant " foundations. All such schools were an indirect expression of a new conception of urban existence allied to " in-group " feeling.

territorial consolidation and social assimilation then usually clinch the matter.

On the other hand, it is to be remembered that communities can of their own volition deliberately generate for themselves the nation-state. The Swiss nation, for example, grew out of necessary alliances between diverse groups in the thirteenth and fourteenth centuries in a desperate search for security against external imperial encroachment. The early Dutch Republic owed its origin to a determination to throw off the Spanish yoke. The United States of America resulted from a deliberate break with Great Britain. The Belgians achieved their independence primarily by opposing the arbitrary way in which they had been " annexed " to Holland; and this annexation led to a peak of frustration which they felt at having been for centuries at the behest of the greater powers though supremely conscious of their own identity. It is interesting to note that such self-generated nation-states are usually federal in form. This is immediately obvious as regards Switzerland and America. The kingdoms of Belgium and the Netherlands, however, reveal this federal structure in the way in which the school systems have been allowed to develop, and Belgium today is of political necessity gradually moving towards some form of federal governmental structure. To sum up, we can say that the nation-state is an expression of faith—a superior loyalty above minor loyalties— and that if that faith goes then the " nation " likewise perishes. Despite the constant clash of minor loyalties, realization of this strengthens identity of purpose and there evolves a kind of genetic aspect of continuity, the " nation " living in its subjects who inherit it as well as continually re-create it.

By the eighteenth century most Western European nations had realized the necessary fusion of politics and culture (which ran parallel to the economic factors) to achieve a certain solidarity of purpose and so establish their own separate identities, and this in its turn led to a stressing of those basic cultural and linguistic concepts and a sense of common historical purpose which had originally made for a feeling of separate identity. The Norwegians gave us the very first national anthem in the 1770's. The inhabitants of the then Austrian Netherlands (Belgium) began reviving the name *Belges* for themselves. Herder in Germany developed his theory of the " Folk-Soul ", claiming that " each nation speaks in the manner it thinks and thinks in the manner it speaks ". From France (which had to wait until the Revolution before it had its national anthem and also the first of the national flags in Europe) Rousseau insisted that each political nation must have its own distinctive character, and if this is lacking must begin by creating it. He equally reminded us that it is not the national character which shapes constitutions and forms of government but the institutions of the nation— particularly those reflecting the relationship between the citizen and the state—which form " the genius, the tastes and the culture of a people ". In 1748 Montesquieu had argued in his *Esprit des Lois* that the educational system of a given nation must reflect that nation's principles of government. Characteristically, Rousseau more extravagantly claimed that:

" Education must develop a national consciousness and so direct the opinions and tastes (of pupils) that they become patriotic by inclination, by passion, and of necessity. When a child opens his eyes he must glimpse the fatherland and unto death have that vision constantly before him. Every true republican imbibed love of the fatherland at his mother's breast—that is, love of law and custom and liberty. This love is the mainspring of his whole experience. . . . The moment he is alone he is nothing; the moment he no longer has a fatherland he himself ceases to exist; and if he is not then dead he is worse than dead."[1].

So, unfortunately, out of strongly held feelings of national identity there developed into the nineteenth century the idea of nationalism militant. Representatives of the Third Estate in France precipitated this when they proclaimed themselves a *National* Assembly and sought to convey the idea that a nation was an entity, one and indivisible, master of its own fate, owing no obedience to any power above or outside it, and free to determine itself as it best thought fit. Theirs was to be a demo-cratic form of nationalism by which all injustice would be rooted out by resort to the consent of the governed. Unwittingly at first, this reforming zeal led them to wish to extend the blessings of their new-found liberty (based of course on the doctrines of eighteenth century Enlightenment) to other nations, firstly by propaganda and then more insidiously by a policy of " annexa-tion ", justification for this being based on the vital necessity for

[1] Quoted from the first paragraph of Rousseau's *Plan d'Education Nationale Pour la Pologne.*

making Liberty safe at home. With the rise of Napoleon ideas of imperial aggrandizement took over. But, ironically, the only result of Napoleon's attempt to impose a universal (French) pattern on Europe was to awaken dormant national feelings everywhere, each threatened nation now beginning to identify its independence with the preservation of its own particular way of life and its own institutions.

Thus, it is in this sense tempting to call the nineteenth century the century of Hope, particularly when we remember that Great Britain fought no major war between 1815 and 1914 and France no such war until 1870—and then quietude until 1914. All countries, however, were having to cope with problems of industrialization and oversea markets and possessions, and they tended to solve these problems on a basis of the assertion of their national aspirations. There may have been no wars, but Europe passed from one diplomatic crisis to another to the extent that it came almost as a relief (after years of uneasy material prosperity) when war finally broke out. And war had most subtly been prepared for—in the classroom, in the growing popular press, through patriotic societies innumerable. The nineteenth century might also be termed the age of liberalism and of dawning radicalism, but it was equally the age of opportunism when feelings of national identity were played upon to induce a blinkered form of patriotism narrowed down to imply uncritical love of the land of one's birth. In all of this the establishment of State-controlled school systems of education everywhere played an important part, it being tacitly acknowledged that such systems must reflect the given *ethos* of each particular nation. We are a long way from what Montesquieu intended, and already on the slippery road (first mapped by Rousseau, as I have earlier explained) towards various forms of Fascist control.

Now, in the aftermath of two disastrous world wars, it is recognized that nationalism in its militant form has been an instrument of change which has insidiously poisoned those intellectual ties which once bound together the Christian world. It is accepted that the concept of nationalism has been the strongest force, not only in shaping state-controlled systems of education, but also in determining the aims, content, character of education, and sometimes even the actual methods of instruction. It is admitted that religious and moral instruction have been geared to the principle that law-abiding morality is an essential element of citizenship. It is seen that wherever technical or vocational education has been emphasized it has been so done to ensure the survival of a given country in economic and military competition with other countries. It is finally grasped that, as to-day's individual stands before the vast impersonality of his own man-made world, he is faced by economic, political and social problems which are so complex as to defy solution either by individuals or by nations acting on their own. Direct governmental and inter-governmental action and interference is needed. It is recognized (as John Stuart Mill had earlier to admit) that social justice cannot be fully achieved without accepting State interference as necessary—and the present intervention of the Federal Government in America in social and educational policies is one obvious example. And, on the international plane, of course, we have seen the emergence of several groupings such as the E.E.C. and E.F.T.A.

We need perhaps as never before to heed Matthew Arnold's warning (*Culture and Anarchy*) that " the one salvation of an epoch of expansion is a harmony of ideas ". I would alter this to read " an epoch of rapid and unprecedented change ". As for the harmony of ideas, then my submission is that the only viable solution must be to re-consider the nature of man in society, to remember how his quest for personal identity led him to group identity and finally to feelings of national identity, to recollect how this has been turned to baser ends, but also to acknowledge that any harmony of ideas possible must turn on recognition and acceptance of basic national feelings and sentiments. Put baldly, this means that to be a *good* European you have first of all to be a *good* Englishman.

Students of comparative education, therefore, must base their studies (if they are to be fruitful) on the potency and workings of national character as reflected in the educational systems of various countries. They must come to recognize and appreciate at their true worth what Señor Madariaga has called " the colour, shape and scent " of the mentalities of different nations and also of the signal contributions to the advancement of the human race made by each separate nation-state. Nor must they neglect to register how much each nation owes to cross-fertilization from others in all fields of human activity. At the same time they must make allowances for the individualistic attitudes of separate nation-states and realize (and be capable of demonstrating) how international attitudes (however ideally desirable) cannot be super-imposed on but must grow out of national aims and approaches. They must finally be capable of demonstrating that, whilst there can never be a *universal* system in education (since education must always be adapted to the accepted culture pattern of a given group), there can be *parallelism* in education intelligently geared towards a *universal* goal. The best immediate example of this is the way in which various European nations have evolved for themselves their own special brand of a " comprehensive " school. A detailed examination of the diagrammatic representations of various educational systems given in Appendix Two will clearly reveal this.

4

And so, in attempting to pull together the thread of the argument, we can perhaps best start with a statement from Professor Peters (*Ethics and Education*) to the effect that " a person is an individual who has a certain assertiveness in his point of view . . . his judgements, appraisals, intentions and decisions which shape events have a characteristic stamp being determined by previous ones that have given rise to permanent and semi-permanent dispositions ". Such dispositions which come to be recognized as relatively common or standardized in a given society we can refer to as constituting the national character. In other words, national characer, which (it should be carefully noted) is a determinant of behaviour rather than a form of behaviour, refers to the modes of the distribution of personality variants in any given society, a modal personality structure being one that appears frequently and which is recognizable as such. How many such recognizable modes there are will vary from society to society, it being also possible to " characterize " a given society on a basis of some half-a-dozen or so such modes, some applying only to a minority of the group, others to a more representative number. It should also be remembered that modal personality structure is related to commonalities in behaviour among the *adult* population of a group, and they, through formal and in-formal systems of education, extend their influence (for good or ill) on the rest. Such adult behaviour results from the imposition on the primary biological drives of derived and learned drives inextricably bound up with the value judgements which man must make in terms of his changing life situation, and which push him to find a solution to besetting problems such as the character of innate human nature, the relationship of man to nature, the relationship of man to man, the relationship of man to both the spiritual and temporal forces in human existence, man in relation to work and leisure.

The complex nature of all this can perhaps best be illustrated in simplified diagrammatic form:

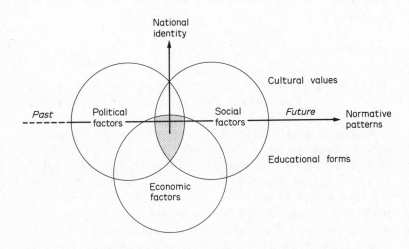

The horizontal line records the passage of time from man's past to his future and is a reminder that in reality all is in a constant state of change and flux. The three interlocking circles represent the three closely-related groups of factors which together, also changing in relative importance and influence, shape feelings of national identity which again are never truly static, however stable they may appear to be. From this combination, and on the reassuring basis of feelings of identity, cultural values and educational forms emerge and these in harmony wth feelings of identity determine the normative patterns of existence of the group to which we have given the name of " national character ".

Thus, as I have argued several times elsewhere, the student of comparative education must be, primarily, a cultural historian noting the way of life of a people and seeking knowledge of their aspirations through their philosophical attitudes, their modes of thought, their religious and political awareness.[1] Trying intelligently to look forward, he needs perceptively to look backwards. He can only properly assess present needs and urges in relationship to past strivings, successes and failures—the present state of reform in education in France being an interesting topical example. He recognizes that educational systems are determined by prevailing culture patterns and that educational reform is the result rather than the cause of changes in social perspectives. It is through close study of educational systems and child-rearing systems, through observation of family and extra-family influences on the child that he will first feel his way into an understanding of the " character " of a particular group. Equally important, however, he must give close attention to what I can best term national images, the national style, and national consciousness. Most of this he will glean from the literary output of the group—and also from the cinema, radio and television—and will gradually build up a picture of the historical, literary and folk characters who are made to embody modes of response to life situations which are approved.

None of this approach, it will be argued, can be termed " scientific " in the sense in which certain students of comparative education would have it. The simple answer to that is that the sustaining principle in man has always been and always will be, not REASON but FAITH. Or, as Pascal once succinctly put it, " the heart has its reasons which reason does not know ". In dealing with the vagaries of man we must be chary of that form of mechanistic interpretation which is (in my view) one unfortunate result of present-day scientific preoccupations which attach priority of value to conceptual thinking and thereby imply that conceptual knowledge is the only true knowledge. Was it not Jung who urged that we need not to know things just intellectually, but to know the substance of things from the inside?

Critics of the concept of national character seem to be baffled that they cannot " scientifically " penetrate the mystery

[1] Or, as Edmund King would say, putting the argument on a strictly practical level: " Comparative Education is concerned with the impact of environmental forms on educational issues."

of custom. They argue that *national character* is a generalization and like all generalizations must suffer from imprecision and vagueness; that it can be used in an impressionistic and subjective way which is not empirically valid; that it can be used to explain away anything. Of course it can! But so can other approaches. And let it also be remembered that such critics, whilst they are content to condemn (or deprecate) the use of the concept of national character, have neither substituted nor applied a more precise working definition themselves. They have, in the main, concentrated on the important predictive aspect of work in the field of comparative studies in education. In proportion as they do only this, however, their work fails to be fully in focus. That the concept of national character is imaginative rather than strictly scientific surely does not detract from its worth, and so long as this is recognized it must remain a valuable and indispensable tool of interpretation.

I can best conclude by taking my stand with Professor Jarrett and with that distinguished German student of comparative education, Friedrich Schneider. In his perceptive and penetrating study of *The Humanities and Humanistic Education* (Addison-Wesley, Massachusetts, 1973) Jarrett argues that the scientific attitude is severely cognitive whilst the humanistic attitude tries to be at once responsive to the sensual, emotional, moral and spiritual as well as the cognitive aspects. "The humanist scholar," he says (p. 85), " has as his aim the dealing with human achievements so as to make them fully and clearly available; to interpret them; and to relate them to each other and to persons, times and places most relevant to them ". Friedrich Schneider is just such a scholar. He argues that the validity of studies in comparative education does *not* depend on their immediate utility value. He deplores the fact that education is being increasingly viewed by some comparatve educationists solely in terms of planning and man-power predictions. For Schneider, educational problems must transcend those of mere training and reach out into the mental and spiritual spheres. He is particularly concerned that the discipline should be applied not only to the solution of " quantitative " problems of educational planning, but equally (and perhaps more importantly) to " qualitative " problems. At a time in the history of man when man's humanity is threatened, the study of comparative education should be seriously concerning itself with " educational ideals, modes of upbringing . . . the political, civic, artistic, and moral education among the various peoples and the description of their typical national character ".[1] In other words, the highest goal of comparative education studies must be to describe, explain and compare educational systems in terms of their cultural totality.

---

[1] *Comparative Education Review*, X, 1 (February, 1966) pp. 16–17.

APPENDIX TWO

Diagrammatic Representations of Education

1. Education in Belgium

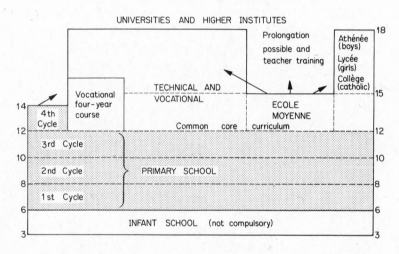

UNIVERSITIES AND HIGHER INSTITUTES

Prolongation possible and teacher training

Athénée (boys) Lycée (girls) Collège (catholic)

Vocational four-year course

TECHNICAL AND VOCATIONAL

4th Cycle

ECOLE MOYENNE

Common core curriculum

3rd Cycle

2nd Cycle   PRIMARY SCHOOL

1st Cycle

INFANT SCHOOL (not compulsory)

2. Education in Denmark

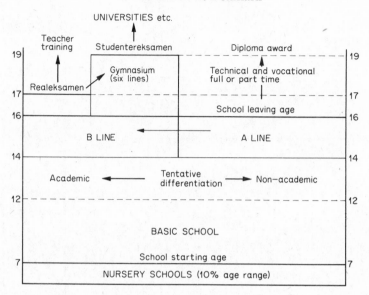

3. Education in England and Wales (present trends)

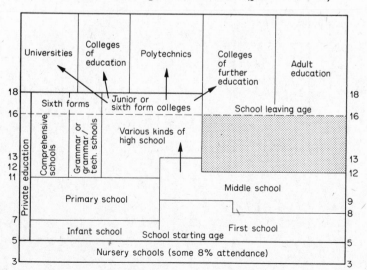

4. Education in France (after 1959)

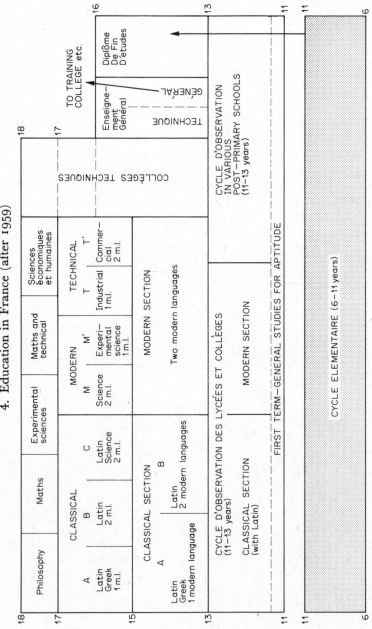

5. Education in France (reorganization)

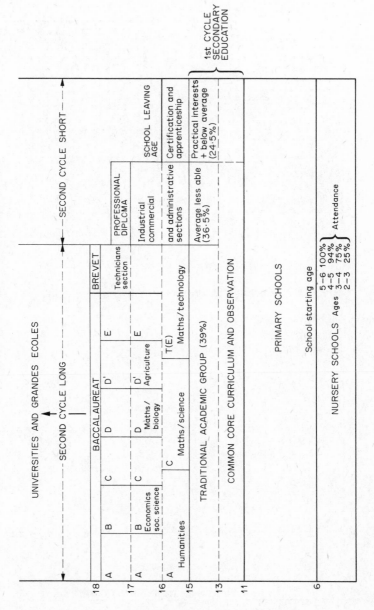

6. Education in West Germany (until recent reforms)

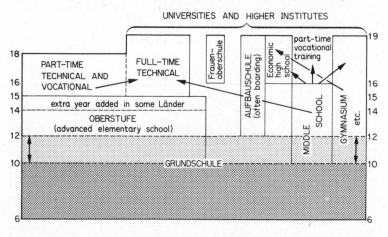

7. Education in West Germany (as developing)

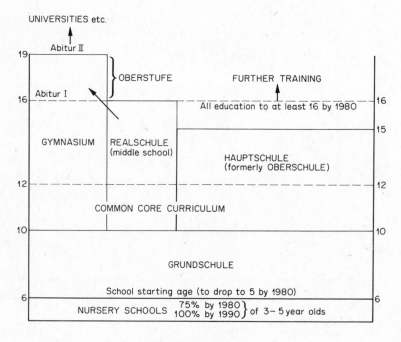

8. Education in Holland

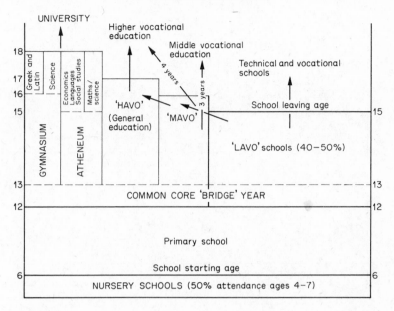

9. Education in Italy

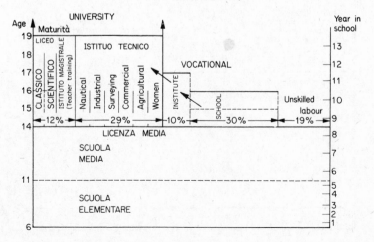

10. Education in Norway

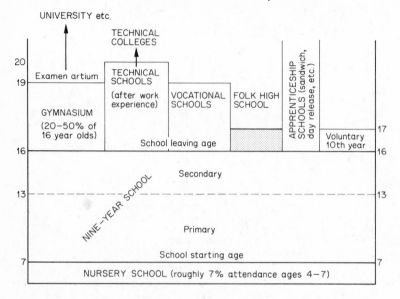

11. Education in Sweden

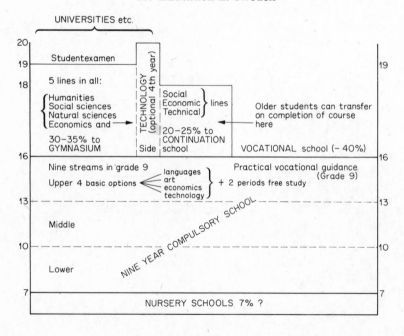

12. Education in Switzerland (VAUD)

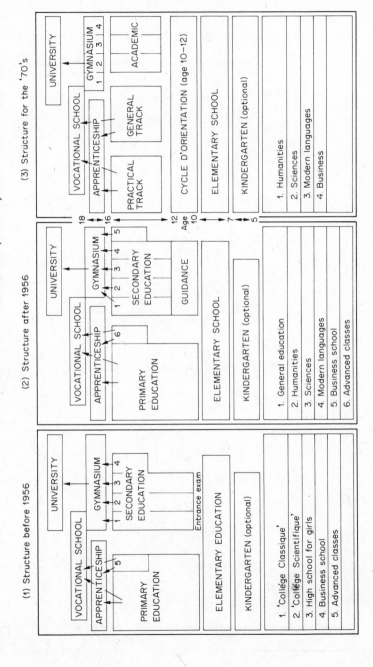

(1) Structure before 1956

(2) Structure after 1956

(3) Structure for the '70's

13. Education in the U.S.A.

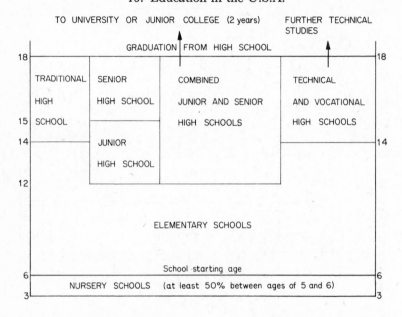

14. Education in the U.S.S.R.

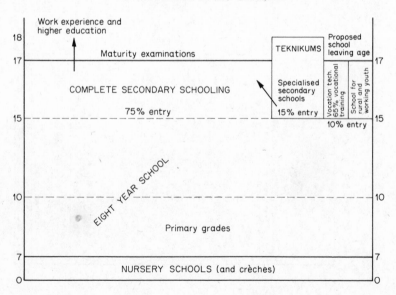

Selected Bibliography

A. GENERAL:
CHÂTEAU, J., *Les Grands Pédagogues*. Paris, 1965.
COMPAYRÉ, G., *The History of Pedagogy*. London, 1900.
HANS, N., *Comparative Education*. London, 1958.
HEARNDEN, A., *Paths to University*. London, 1973.
HOLMES, B., *Problems in Education*. London, 1965.
KING, E. J., *World Perspectives in Education*. London, 1962. *Other Schools and Ours*. (Fourth Edition). London, 1973.
Consult also: *The Year Book of Education*. London, 1948 *et seq*.
    International Yearbook of Education. Unesco.
    All other Unesco publications on education, and particularly the *Problems in Education* series.
    Publications from the *Council for Cultural Cooperation*. Council of Europe.
Periodicals: *Comparative Education*. Oxford.
    Comparative Education Review. New York.
    International Review of Education. Hamburg.

B. BELGIUM:
MALLINSON, V., *Power and Politics in Belgian Education*. London, 1963. *Belgium*. London, 1969.

C. FRANCE:
ALAIN, *Propos sur l'Education*. Paris, 1948.
ANON., *Organization de l'Enseignement en France*. Paris 1959.
DURKHEIM, E., *L'Evolution Pédagogigue en France*. Paris, 1938–41.
FRASER, W. R., *Education and Society in Modern France*. London, 1963. *Reforms and Restraints in Modern French Education*. London, 1971.
HALLS, W. D., *Society, Schools and Progress in France*. Oxford, 1965.

D. GERMANY:
BECKER, H., *German Youth, Bond or Free*. London, 1948.
KERSCHENSTEINER, G., *The Schools and the Nation*. London, 1914. *Education for Citizenship*. London, 1915.
SPANGENBERG/MENDE., *Schule und Hochschule in Deutschland*. Frankfurt, 1973.

E. GREAT BRITAIN:
BARNARD, H. C., *A History of English Education*. London, 1961.
LESTER SMITH, W. O., *Government of Education*. London, 1965.

F. ITALY
BORGHI, L., *Educazione E Autorità Nell' Italia Moderna*. Florence, 1950.
GABELLI, A., *L'Istruzione E L'Educazione in Italia*. Florence, 1950.
School of Barbiana, *Letter to a Teacher*. London, 1970.

G. SCANDINAVIA:
   Anon., *The New School in Sweden.* Swedish Ministry, 1963.
   Dixon, W., *Education in Denmark.* London, 1959.
      Society, Schools and Progress in Scandinavia. Oxford, 1965.
   During, I., *The Swedish School Reform.* Swedish Ministry, 1951.
   Huus, H., *The Education of Children and Youth in Norway.* Pittsburgh, 1960.

H. U.S.A.:
   Conant, J. B., *The American High School Today.* New York, 1959.
   Kandel, I. L., *American Education in the Twentieth Century.* Cambridge
      (Mass.), 1957.
   King, E. J., *Society, Schools and Progress in the U.S.A.* Oxford, 1970.

I. U.S.S.R.
   Grant, N., *Soviet Education.* London, 1972.
      Society, Schools and Progress in Eastern Europe. Oxford, 1969.
   Rosen, S. M., *Education and Modernization in the U.S.S.R.* Reading
      (Mass.), 1971.

Index